SEX AND THE AMERICAN TEENAGER

S E X and the American Teenager

ROBERT COLES
GEOFFREY STOKES

A Rolling Stone Press Book

 HARPER COLOPHON BOOKS

Harper & Row, Publishers

New York, Cambridge, Philadelphia, San Francisco

London, Mexico City, São Paulo, Singapore, Sydney

FIRST EDITION

Designer: Sidney Feinberg

Library of Congress Cataloging in Publication Data

Coles, Robert.
    Sex and the American Teenager.
    "A Rolling Stone Press book."
    Includes index.
    1. Youth—United States—Sexual behavior.   I. Stokes,
Geoffrey, 1940–   II. Title.
HQ27.C65 1985   306.7'088055   84–48147
ISBN 0-06-096002-7 (pbk)

85 86 87 88 89 10 9 8 7 6 5 4 3 2 1

Contents

Introduction

This book is a profile of a generation that could be called "the children of the children of Woodstock." Heirs to the vaunted sexual revolution of the Sixties, they are in some ways conservative in their attitudes and practices (about half the girls want to be virgin brides), in some ways liberal (the fairly substantial group that has combined the experiences feels by a margin of about two and a half to one that both marijuana and uppers improve, rather than detract from, intercourse), and in other ways as confused as any generation that has preceded them (of sexually active teens, about half do not use birth control, and one out of six girls has been pregnant). In other words, though they are themselves remarkably agreed that their parents' attitudes are more restrictive than their own, this is a generation about whom any sweeping, off-the-cuff characterizations are almost certain to be false. They are a diverse group, living through a time of great complexity and confusion, and the multidimensional portrait we've attempted to provide in this book is the least they—and their parents—deserve.

Behind the words on these pages stand 1,067 questionnaires with 358 variables, 50,000 pages of transcribed interviews, several miles of computer printouts, and a formidable array of academic and clinical experience. This seems a substantial research armamentarium to bring to bear on essentially two questions about teenage sex: What do kids do? How do they feel about it? But the nature of our subject is such that something this elaborate is necessary if the reader of any age is to have confidence in what we report.

The book itself is divided into four parts: my colleague Robert

Coles's general discussion of the place of teenage sexuality in society and in the lives of individual teens; my report of our survey findings; selected interview excerpts; and Coles's response—intimately related to the intellectual and moral framework he uses in opening the book—to the particular facts and tendencies revealed in the survey and interviews. Part I, in which Coles draws on his years of studying and counseling adolescents, would be of value on its own, but the final three parts couldn't exist without the survey and its appurtenances. Whatever conclusions Coles and I draw from this information can be only as valid as the data themselves; for that reason, I want to use this introduction to talk about the ways this information was gathered and put together.

Let's begin with the notion of a *survey*, which, in its simplest form, is no more than an enumeration. If a cosmetics firm were thinking of introducing a new line of products especially for people with red hair, it might reasonably want to know how big its potential market was. It could go about getting this information in a couple of ways. If it had limitless time and money, it could send representatives to visit every household in the United States and count the number of redheaded occupants. This is a theoretically possible course (though not without problems: Aunt Jenny, who normally lives in a certain place, might be away on vacation; or again, would all the interviewers agree as to whether this particular strawberry-blond child is really a redhead?), but for economic reasons an unlikely one. It is one thing to ask kids in a classroom whether they'd rather go to the museum or the zoo; quite another to ask it of all the eighth-graders in America. In dealing with large populations—all redheads, all American teenagers—complete enumeration is a virtual impossibility, and the cosmetics firm would probably take a percentage of the population—a *sample*—and project from that.

As soon as a researcher chooses to use the sample method, he or she is taking some risks, for there is almost always a possibility that the sample will yield false or misleading information about the general population. If the cosmetics company decided to insert a questionnaire in certain of its magazine ads, it might turn out that the questions were so worded that redheads were disproportionately likely to fill it out and send it in (and, obviously, the projected results would be bizarrely different if the questions appeared only in *Ebony* or only in the *National Catholic Reporter*). If the company decided simply to eyeball the workers in its factory, it might be misled by the ethnic peculiarities of its particular geographic area, or of its personnel department.

Over the years, social science has found ways to minimize, or at least quantify, these risks, and the company could be told how large the sample would have to be for it to have a 95% or even a 99% chance of being valid. But while the size of the sample is important, its makeup is critical: For a sample to achieve ideal statistical validity, it should be *random*—that is, every single member of the larger population group should have an equal chance of being included in it.

This is not an impossible task; several reliable national polling organizations routinely assemble random samples of populations ranging from registered voters to those who have purchased a skin-care product in the previous twelve months. Once such a panel has been assembled, the validity of the information drawn from it (though not necessarily the inferences) will depend on the response rate (what percentage of the sample actually answered the questions?); the testing instrument and procedures (did people understand the questions? did they have enough time to answer?); and the care with which the data is handled (did all the data get entered correctly on the computer?).

If all these conditions have been properly met, we can say with confidence that the "snapshot" taken by the survey—a portrait of a particular group of people at a particular time—is a statistically valid portrait of a larger universe as well.

All of this is possible to achieve; none of it, as Coles points out in part IV, is easy. But before we go on to this particular survey, we have to look at one final area of possible pitfalls. Suppose the company didn't want to know merely how many possible buyers for its product were out there, but how many of them were actually likely to buy it, and who those likely buyers were. If it asked the proper questions to begin with, it could conceivably use the survey results to choose the marketing and advertising strategies that would have the greatest chance of success. To do this, it would need to *cross-tabulate* the results—match the answers to different questions with each other. Then, if by looking at the characteristics of those redheads who expressed either an interest in or distaste for the product the company found that women were much more likely buyers then men, it would advertise in *Redbook* rather than *Sports Illustrated*. If it found potential buyers concentrated on the East Coast, it could market the product regionally rather than nationally.

This is, by all odds, the most interesting part of survey research, but its usefulness depends not only on the researcher having asked the right questions of the original sample, but on his or her ability to ask the right questions of the assembled data. If, for instance, the company had discovered that midwestern women were the most likely purchasers but had failed to discern that those with above-average family incomes were five times more likely to buy the product than those with low incomes, a marketing strategy aimed at K-Mart and Sears might turn out to be disastrous. Thus, for statistical *inferences* to be valid, researchers must ask the right question (about income, in our example) not once but twice.

That said, we now come to the *Rolling Stone* survey. To begin with, we contracted with a well-known and highly respected national survey organization (which, for reasons I shall explain later, will not allow its name to appear in these pages) to assemble a representative sample. Drawing from families with whom it had already worked (that is to say, from a population *originally* random, but which had distinguished itself in ways that might—though probably not—affect sexual behavior and beliefs by its willingness to participate in surveys), the organization put together a panel of 3,000 households that was statistically representative of the United States population by (1) geography, (2) urban/suburban/rural residency, (3) age, (4) income, (5) religion, (6) race, (7) family size, and (8) age of teenage children.

So far, so good. At this point, however, we ran into the predictable roadblock. Asking questions about sexual behavior—especially the kind of detailed questions that make this survey unique—is different from asking questions about preferences in breakfast cereals. Some percentage of the population is simply not going to be willing to answer. Further, because we were asking these questions of kids, we felt it necessary to get parental permission before even sending questionnaires to the households.

Of the 3,000 households in the original panel, almost 1,500 gave their permission. (This was a simple yes-no option, so nothing can be stated definitely about the households that chose not to respond except that they were fairly evenly distributed across the sample. As Coles suggests, we can guess, but only guess, that the sensitive nature of the subject might have led the more conservative parents to refuse permission. The final sample, then, *may* be disproportionately reflective of children of more liberal parents, but this is by no means a fatal or even serious flaw; as the responses of those who did answer make clear, it is extremely difficult to generalize about what effects parental attitudes have on kids' behavior.) More than two-thirds of these respondents (34.2% of the original 3,000) actually completed and returned the questionnaire.

This is lower than one would wish in an ideal world, but the combination of this subject matter and the respondents' ages almost always leads to relatively low rates of response. *The Hite Report on Male Sexuality*, for instance, achieved only a 6% response rate; and even where the distribution of questionnaires has been rigorously controlled, I know of no response rate higher than 47%. This last was achieved in 1973 by Dr. Robert C. Sorenson, and without at all denigrating the importance of his *Adolescent Sexuality in Contemporary America*, it's fair to state that the amount of detail in the *Rolling Stone* survey is considerably greater (and potentially more controversial) than in any previous study.

In terms of subject matter, Aaron Hass's *Teenage Sexuality* (1979) probably comes closest to ours, but his sample of 641 youngsters includes no 13- and 14-year-olds, and only 10 percent of his respondents came from outside southern California. The stratified *Rolling Stone* sample, representing teens from 49 states, is as good as the state of the art and sampling ethics allow, rivaled only by the samples collected for the National Institute of Child Health by Melvin Zelnick and John F. Kantner of Johns Hopkins University (who have, in all but one case, surveyed only females and have focused primarily on birth control). In the words of the research specialist we retained to critique our procedures, "with the possible exception of the Zelnick and Kantner survey, *Rolling Stone*'s sampling procedure is the most valid and reliable procedure to have been used in this field."

Two final words about the sample, then on to a brief consideration of the questionnaire itself. In those areas where comparison with other, less-detailed surveys was possible—e.g., the percentage of teens who've had sexual intercourse—the *Rolling Stone* sample demonstrates no "liberal" bias whatsoever, which gives additional confidence in the validity of our findings in those areas that other researchers haven't surveyed as deeply. Second, in the original pattern of responses, nonwhites were underrepresented. To make the sample fully representative, we both distributed some 31 additional questionnaires and weighted nonwhite responses according to standard statistical procedures. Because of the way the additional respondents were selected, any white-versus-nonwhite comparisons have to be made with extreme caution. I'll discuss the implications of this a little further on.

The questionnaire, which is reprinted in the Appendix, was of course administered with a guarantee of anonymity. Further, because it was designed to be completed privately at home—thus distinguishing it from school-administered surveys (see Hass, for example), where kids know that they and others are to take some sort of test and are likely to discuss it among themselves—it should be relatively free from the so-called herd effect. Pretesting revealed that the average completion time for the 99 objective questions was about 20 minutes, a length of time most researchers feel is appropriate for teenagers; while a longer or more complex questionnaire might have yielded more data, increased response time can lead to respondent fatigue and less reliable answers. In addition to its objective, multiple-choice section, the questionnaire had room for an open-ended essay response to some suggested topics; about half the respondents contributed a response.

The questionnaire, as distinct from the sample population, was developed and tested by a research team from the Mathtech Corporation of Maryland, and the project was headed by Dr. Douglas Kirby, director of Mathtech's Social Science Group and formerly director of the Sociology Research Center of San Diego State University. Mathtech has completed several sex-education projects for the United States Department of Health (most notably the five-volume *Analysis of U.S. Sex Education Programs and Evaluation Methods*).

Kirby and his team conducted 100 pretest interviews to aid in formulating the questionnaire, composed it together with *Rolling Stone* staff, and put the form through standard—that is to say, relatively elaborate—pretesting to make sure its language was clear and readily comprehensible and that it contained no hints about "right" answers. (It was in fact so clear that the national survey organization we had retained first asked to be released from its contract, then agreed to administer the questionnaire only on the condition that we not mention its name.) Finally, Mathtech supervised and verified the keypunching (an error rate of less than 1%), entered the data on tapes in a university computer center, devised procedures for eliminating self-contradictory responses, and provided both the initial compilations and all the data tables.

These tables are at the heart of our study, and since many of them are printed in Part II of the book, it's important to understand how they work and what they mean. Even apart from a context, numbers can exercise an eerie fascination; the steadily mounting highway death toll broadcast on holiday-weekend radio is mesmerizing, even if one has nothing to measure it against. Given a context, as with baseball batting averages, numbers become totems of excellence. Since sex is at least as interesting as death or baseball, the raw numbers in the *Rolling Stone* survey are appealing in their own right, but the real excitement comes in exploring these numbers to discover significant patterns.

We know, for instance, that two-thirds of our respondents said their sexual behavior was affected either "not at all" or only "a small amount" by their religion, yet it's difficult to measure precisely to what extent we are touched by our religious training. Statistical analysis, matching sexual behavior with religious background, can show us whether the kids' self-perceptions are accurate, or whether, for instance, Catholic adolescents are far less likely than Jewish ones to have had sexual intercourse.

To illustrate the methodology, let's imagine that we surveyed a classroom of kids about their dietary habits. Among the questions we asked was whether they were underweight or overweight, and whether they ate dessert more or less than ten times a week. For the sake of simplicity, let's assume that the class divided half and half on each question: that 50% were overweight and 50% ate dessert more than ten times a week. Our sample is complete—100% of the kids participated—but by themselves, these figures tell us nothing about the *relationship* between dessert-eating and weight. To determine that, we would have to cross-reference the two answers, setting up a table with four boxes.

DESSERTS PER WEEK

	Less than 10	More than 10
Overweight		
Underweight		

We could have, at the extreme ranges of relatedness, two possibilities. The first, showing the strongest relationship, would look like this:

0%	100%
100%	0%

That is to say, 100% of those who eat ten or more desserts a week are overweight, and none of those who eat fewer.

If there were *no* relatedness, the figures would look like this:

50%	50%
50%	50%

And we could say that for this group of kids, the chances of their being over- or underweight were unaffected by the number of desserts they ate each week.

Unfortunately for social scientists, correlations of interesting variables are rarely so unambiguous, and a real-life version of the chart might look something like this:

40%	60%
60%	40%

Looking at it, it would appear that there is *some* relationship between dessert-eating and weight, but the strength of that relationship can only be determined by mathematical testing. This test, called a *chi-square* test, measures whether the particular distribution (here, 60-40), given the size of the sample, could be random. The classic example of this measure is the so-called fair-die question. If you threw a die 60 times and got the following distribution, is the die fair?

Number	Frequency
1	8
2	12
3	13
4	6
5	11
6	10

Given a fair die, in which each number had an absolutely equal chance of coming up, you would *expect* a distribution of 10, 10, 10, etc. The chi-square test determines whether the degree of difference between the expected and actual distributions can be explained by the nature of the random sample (and would thus be expected to even out if you threw the die 6,000 times).

Now suppose, to take an example from our survey, we wanted to see whether place of residence—urban, suburban, rural—affected the likelihood that a teen would have had intercourse. We know how our geographic sample is distributed (52% urban, 26% suburban, 22% rural), and if there were *no* relation between place of residence and virginity, we would expect the distribution of virgins and nonvirgins by region to approximate the population distribution. In the actual example, the distribution is as follows:

	Urban	Suburban	Rural
nonvirgin	58%	22%	20%

Merely looking at these figures, we can see nonvirgins are somewhat more likely to live in urban areas than teens as a whole, somewhat less likely to live in suburban or rural areas. But the chi-square test reveals that in our sample of more than a thousand teens, a variation of this size could very well be random—that place of residence is, in other words, statistically insignificant in relationship to virginity.

In the text, however, we will often be discussing *"statistically significant"* relations. What does this mean? It means that the variation from the expected distribution is greater than chance can explain *and* that if we had sampled every teenager in the country instead of the thousand-plus that we did, the pattern would have *at least* a 95% chance of holding true for all teens. The one exception to this rule—and it is an exception on the side of stringency—involves comparisons between whites and nonwhites. Because of the nonrandom nature of our follow-up survey of nonwhites, I have claimed significance only when the figures show a pattern that has a 99% probability of holding true for all teens.

Finally, in order to make clear the emotional as well as the statistical meaning of our findings, I have drawn extensively on the 100 in-depth interviews conducted either by Mathtech staff or Mathtech-trained *Rolling Stone* researchers. Many of these interviews were carried out before the questionnaire was designed, as a way of learning what questions to ask and what language to use; others were carried out afterward to flesh out the numerical data. While these are not "scientific" in the sense of the survey proper—nor, as Coles suggests, do they plumb the hidden depths that psychiatry or psychology can achieve over a course of therapy that may last for years—they provided a necessary, human gloss to the accumulation of statistics. In citing them, I have of course changed any names, but have otherwise used the transcripts verbatim. On those comparatively few occasions when I've omitted material, I have indicated the omission with brackets ([   ]); ellipses (. . .) indicate either notable hesitations in speech or the trailing off of a sentence. While I suspect that many readers will find some of these teens' conversations as moving as I did, I have used them in Part II primarily as examples of the real-life meaning of the facts our survey revealed and they should be read in that context. I have, however, let them stand on their own in Part III.

In other words, given its somewhat explosive subject matter, this study is as rigorous, conservative, and thorough as ethics and technology allow. No one else has gathered data on so many questions based on such a good sample, and it is the most accurate picture yet developed of sex and teenage Americans. Some may find that picture disheartening or even shocking; others may view it with optimism. But both groups will, I think, recognize it as reliable—and, I hope, as useful in the continuing moral dialogue that searches for a wisdom numbers cannot measure.

—GEOFFREY STOKES
May 1984

I

A Psychological Perspective

ROBERT COLES

This survey, and the comments offered by those who took it, remind us, yet again, how variously young people (and the rest of us, also, needless to say) experience sexuality and respond to what has happened in their hearts and minds. The comments, in particular, are helpful, even revealing. They offer important glimpses of young men and women struggling with the urges of their bodies, with one another as the human beings toward whom those urges are directed—and not least, with the social, cultural, and moral assumptions of the changing late twentieth-century American scene. Here are youths proclaiming their desires, their satisfactions in one another—but also their worries, confusions, fears. Here are youths who know how to enjoy their own bodies, and those of others— or who, indeed, are exceedingly reluctant to take part in such enjoyment. Here are youths who let themselves go happily, fully— or who are exceedingly constrained. Here are youths who respond to nature and its rhythms, its calls, with no regret and much gratification—or who declare themselves plagued by loneliness and guilt as a consequence of their sexuality, whether it be expressed with another or alone. Here are youths who have no interest in judging anyone, themselves included—and those who call upon a given moral or religious tradition with evident assertiveness and conviction.

What all these youths share, of course, is a particular time of life, its possibilities, its frustrations, its occasional impasses. Again and again (first as a pediatrician, then as a child psychiatrist, and finally as a parent myself of three teenagers) I have wondered how to understand young sexuality, so that when I talk to others (patients, friends, my own wife and children) I will have some sense of what I wish to say. As I read this *Rolling Stone* questionnaire, some of my past efforts at such an understanding came to mind, and with them the words once spoken to me by a doctor who also happened to be a poet, William Carlos Williams: "These kids get to be twelve or thirteen and they explode. They'll tell you that—the energy is pushing through them, and some say they don't know where it'll take them, and some say they're going to ride with it, enjoy it, and not worry!" I'm not sure I've heard since then (the year was 1954) a more telling overall description of the different attitudes any number of young men and women take toward a compelling aspect of growing up.

As Dr. Williams indicated, adolescents commonly feel themselves in the presence of an enormous internal energy suddenly exerting itself—a gift, a threat, a mystery, a force to be reckoned with. Out of nowhere, it seems, the body is visited by this transforming presence. A youth of 16 once described what was happening to her and to her twin brother in a manner I have found to be unforgettable and valuable for the rest of us—be we parents or adolescents:

> Every day, just about, something new seems to be happening to this body of mine and I get scared sometimes. I'll wake up in the middle of the night and I can't go back to sleep, and I toss and I turn and I can't stop my mind; it's racing fast, and everything is coming into it, and I think of my two best friends, and how their faces are all broken out, and I worry mine will break out, too, but so far it hasn't, and I think of my sizes, and I can't get it out of my head—the chest size and the stomach size and what I'll be wearing and whether I'll be able to fit into this kind of dress or the latest swimsuit. Well, it goes on and on, and I'm dizzy, even though it's maybe one o'clock in the morning, and there I am, in bed, so how can you be dizzy?
>
> Everything is growing and changing. I can see my mother watching me. I can see everyone watching me. There are times I think I see people watching me when they really couldn't care less! My dad makes a point of not staring, but he catches his look, I guess. I'm going to be "big-chested"; that's how my mother describes herself! I have to figure out how to dress so I feel better— I mean, so I don't feel strange, with my bosom just sticking out at

everyone! I have to decide if I should shave my legs! I will! Damn! I wish a lot of the time I could just go back to being a little girl, without all these problems and these decisions!

My brother isn't doing too good, either! He's got acne, and he can't shave without hurting himself because of those pimples. He doesn't like an electric shaver; he says they don't feel clean to his face. He's a nut about taking showers. Two a day! He's always using deodorant. He's got all that hair under his arms. So do I! We will have our "buddy talks," and a lot of the time we just ask, "When will it end—so we can just have a body that looks the same, from one week to the other?"

We're in this together, my brother and me, and my friends. That's what I think about in the night: how we're all sweating it out—including my parents, and my little sister. It used to be my brother and I ran around naked, or almost naked, but now I don't even look at my own bottom; I just get into a state, wondering and realizing how much has happened to me down there, so fast. And my brother—he's always closing his door, and no one's going to catch him dressing or undressing!

She conveyed with those words, I thought, one of the central psychological themes of adolescence—the burst of self-consciousness that descends upon a particular youth, takes hold, and for a long time won't let go. Even sleep falls prey to the self's insistent deliberations, its obsessive preoccupations: the body's appearance; family shifts of behavior; new attachments or old memories; yearnings that time move back or leap forward; a constant apprehension about what is happening to the skin, to the armpits, to the sexual part of the youth's anatomy. For psychiatrists, as for parents and young people themselves, this increased self-preoccupation (so-called narcissism) is a triggering force of sorts: a stimulus to anxiety; moodiness; apparently quixotic or faddish changes in diet; insomnia; school difficulties; new interest or new attitudes toward others— all sorts of shifts in behavior.

Anyone who wants to understand teenage sexuality has to start here, as the young woman herself indicated: The body's important physical changes prompt the mind to turn inward, to cry about itself, to dance beyond itself, to run through an apparently endless number of reveries, scenarios, situations. And the body, too: It makes its demands, and they are either banished energetically from awareness or contemplated and then given reign. The youth quoted above blushed and stammered and fell into fits of anxious silence as she struggled with her embarrassment and shame: how to tell a doctor that she knew her brother was masturbating, and that she herself was beginning to do so, also. Eventually she found a way to convey what was on her mind—through a note handed to me, her doctor. This is not a rare form of communication for any number of adolescents who, for one reason or another, have sought a doctor's help in understanding what is happening to both their minds and bodies.

I remember as a young doctor being encouraged by a psychoanalytic supervisor to suggest to a young man, painfully shy, that he write me a note if he wished, mentioning some of the difficulties he was facing. I did so. He sent me a letter; I replied with a letter of my own; and eventually he was able to speak about his worries to me, face-to-face. But this young lady needed no such prompting. She told me outright that she had to figure out how to "mention things" to me and had decided to do so by letter. Hence this excerpt from a fairly long, personal, handwritten statement:

> I don't know how to bring up the subject of these feelings I get. I can't even *write* about them! Girls aren't supposed to—they're not supposed to get excited. I know my brother does. I mean, he plays with himself. It's hard to know what to think about this subject. I wake up, and I've had a dream, and I'm all excited because of the dream, I think. So then my body starts moving on me. Do you know what I mean? I'm not sure I do, myself! I'm sorry I can't write better. I mean, express myself. That's the worst part of being a teenager, there's so much going on inside you, but you can't talk to anyone about it, even to your closest friend. I have this one girlfriend, and we used to be able to say anything to each other. But now even she—well, I can't talk to her about a lot of things. Last year she got a crush on my brother, and was I surprised! I never saw her give a second look, and there she was mooning over a picture I have of him, and asking me if I could get a copy for her! I think I was a little jealous, to be truthful! I'm sort of possessive about my brother, and I'm possessive about her, and I got all mixed up. And that's it, I feel all mixed up. I'll be thinking about this boy in school, and I get worked up. Then I just wish I could be open with my closest friend and I picture her giving me a long hug, and then I relax. But usually I'm not relaxed. I saw this movie "Cat on a Hot Tin Roof," and I thought to myself, that's you,

and when will you get off the roof, or when will the roof quiet down. I think I know the answer! When I'm all grown up, and I've met the man I'm going to marry, or I'm going out with someone steady, and I mean steady for a year, not a week!

A psychiatrist spending time with this forthright young woman begins to comprehend her struggles as those not of a "sicko," as she once feared, but of a relatively normal youth, who sometimes felt closer to (and safer with) women than men; who found moments of pleasure in the stimulation by herself of her body— followed by intense shame and even disgust; who kept up her "front," as she put it, by day (in school, and mostly in the company of her friends and parents at home) but by night went through repeated spells of panic, which ultimately, as a matter of fact, brought her to a doctor's office, because *normal* was the last word she was prepared to use to describe herself. As Anna Freud once pointed out to a few of us gathered in her office for a discussion of adolescence, *normal* or *abnormal* are not the clinical words for us to favor when trying to make a judgment about an adolescent. That advice especially holds these days, when social and cultural shifts of attitude with respect to sexuality are obviously substantial.

This survey, for example, indicates a widespread sexual frankness on the part of young women—an obvious contrast with the so-called double standard of earlier times. Even as I've heard my middle-aged patients who are parents compare their memories of being girls growing up with their observations of how their own daughters are maturing, so I hear, today, young women scarcely able to imagine what it once was like for women: "The hypocrisy, and phoniness and pretense—women must have been enraged! I've heard my grandmother talk, and even my mother, but I wonder how they really felt. My mother says no, she wasn't as 'galled' as I think she was. But if that's the case, they were slaves! No one I know (the boys as well as the girls!) could go back to those 'good old days,' when men could do anything and more power to them, so long as they were discreet, and women were supposed to be saintly stay-at-homes."

No doubt the feminist movement has enabled this college woman to assume sexual and cultural and political prerogatives considered beyond the reach or desire of her counterparts of the past. On the other hand, the matter of social class has to be mentioned here, as elsewhere—the personal constraints that some small-town or rural young women still hold dear, as against the strong if not urgent independence demonstrated by many urban, well-to-do young women. Still, as one reads some of the comments of these *Rolling Stone* interviewees, one sees the same worries and guilts and loneliness in women as in men—a reminder that "sexual liberation" is not destined to spare a particular generation of Americans the trials that human relatedness always creates: how to trust others, how to accept and love them, not to mention oneself. When a young college woman (17 years old) tells a doctor that she finds "masturbation preferable" because she finds herself becoming "terribly upset" when she is "away from" her boyfriend "even for a day," and "even guiltier with him because of the sexual demands he makes" than she is when alone and turned on by her own sexual fantasies, a more general statement is being made about this life. "No matter what changes there are in the social climate," Anna Freud once observed, "the young person will continue to be just that—young, and so inexperienced and unsure and afraid, or more afraid than he or she really knows."

As I read the statistics in this study, I began to wonder whether there is actually all that much rock-bottom change in the sexuality of this generation. Those who are sexually experienced still hunger for those old staples of the human scene—the loyalty and commitment of another human being. Promiscuity is regarded with disfavor, even morally condemned. A majority of the young women respondents chose virginity, monogamy, and "love." Moreover, there is a more than occasional earnestness to the male interviewees—a desire to share the pleasures of intimacy with their girlfriends, rather than "hit and run" in the supposed manner of the old "double-standard" tradition. Much has been made about feminism—its achievements and lingering discontents. But men have perhaps changed, too—are in significant numbers more willing to respect the hopes and expectations of their women friends. These young people, boys and girls alike, are notably responsive to one another; are notably judging themselves by the way they are regarded in the eyes of their close friends. When 82% of a given sample of "nonvirgins" declare the sexual satisfaction of their partners of great importance, one may go beyond a certain skepticism that would see today's youth as rendering a sex-manual kind of piety.

I have been listening to young people for a fairly long time, and I acknowledge the above skepticism as, for a long time, my own. But at a certain point one hears enough earnest aspirations and intentions to justify a reconsideration, as in these comments—companions, surely, to the ones made in the course of this survey:

> You just can't be out for yourself in this world. A lot of the time I probably am, I admit it. I'm a guy who wants to win, and when you're trying to be on top, you're not exactly worried about the next guy! But I think I can only be that kind of person so long. Even in school, even in sports, I get disgusted with myself some of the time. I mean, I've been rude to someone, or I don't stop and think of someone else, only myself. That's no good. You have to give your all to school—otherwise you don't get into a good college. But you can help out the guy beside you, too!

> With my girlfriend I try to remind myself that she tries hard to help me out: She's always worrying about me, and suggesting I do this or the next thing. No, she's not bossy! She's just a person who really thinks about someone she's got as a friend. She makes me stop and think about what kind of a person I am. If a person can get you to do that—well, you're in love, the two of you!

> My dad can get down on this generation—mine! He'll sound off; he'll say we're selfish, and we've lost the values, the important values, of the older generation. But ten minutes later he'll be telling me that he's not so proud of some of the things he did when he was my age; and he thinks we show more respect for each other, even if sometimes we don't always respect older people. (He means that we argue, he and I do!) Once he told me that he wasn't brought up to think about women the way guys like me do, and it was vice versa back then. "We were scared of each other; we didn't really have *friends* of the opposite sex" is the way he said it to me.

> Now that's changed! I can talk with girls I'm not dating—I mean, be real friendly with them. There's one girl at school who's the person I feel easiest with there. We're pals, but I've never wanted to make out with her! I think she's had a rough time with her parents. They don't talk to her. They're too wrapped up with their own lives. They tell her what to do, and then they're not around if she has any questions, if she wants to say something to them. She had an abortion and they didn't know until later, and then her father was more worried about who might know than what happened to his daughter!

Those last remarks, surely, are not unrepresentative of what can be heard from today's young people as they struggle not only with the body's urges but with various social and economic strains on family life—strains that have a direct bearing on adolescent sexuality. Parents who are themselves overwhelmed by joblessness or a precarious survival; parents who are just barely getting by, often through second jobs, never mind the effort of both a mother and a father to stay employed; parents who are well-to-do but obsessed with their own lives, with their appearance, their social commitments, their travel plans and business obligations—such men and women are often not able to muster the interest and concern their not-so-young but still not fully grown children usually need, seek, urgently crave.

In recent years many of us have learned to pay rather a lot of attention to babies, to preschool children, as if their entire future will be settled in accordance with the quality of our responsiveness. A glut of books has made us aware of various critical "periods" and "problems" in the life of the child. As for teenagers, what we tend to know about them is their independence, their need to express themselves, to find their own particular habits and preferences, to embark upon a search for their "identities." It's true, of course, that adolescents have always tested certain constraints, social and sexual and even political. But I wonder whether this inclination to stand apart, so to speak, on the part of many parents who have adolescent children is not a serious mistake—a misreading of what adolescents want and require, and maybe in some instances a rationalization to relieve some of us of a responsibility, thereby sparing us time for ourselves. Years of work with adolescents persuade me that they are the last ones in the world to want a freedom, a sense of privacy and autonomy that deprives them of the advice and counsel, the warm support and understanding of their parents, and, for that matter, of others (teachers, doctors) who are older and might have a good deal to say about some of the difficulties that confront a person of 15 or 16 or 17.

The youth quoted above mentioned a particular abortion. This survey reminds us yet again that teenage sexuality can have sad, even disastrous, consequences—that teenage pregnancies are in fact a growing national problem, some say an "epidemic." When thousands and thousands of young women (of high-school age, even junior-high-school age) end up pregnant and then in abortion clinics, all of us wonder what ought to be done beyond the suggestion that contraceptives be made available. As the respondents in this survey indicate, an abortion is not something easily undertaken and quickly forgotten. Many young women go through hell as a consequence of abortion, thoroughly saddened and even tormented by the experience. The issue is moral, and, for a large number of people, religious as well as psychological. As for those much-recommended contraceptives, they may prevent abortion while encouraging in some a promiscuity teenagers themselves begin to regret.

I again call upon a particular informant, because she had a very difficult childhood—harrowing, I'd call it, despite the affluence of her parents—and because I believe her stated yearnings (for intimacy with her parents, for candor and a constant, mutual regard) best describe what parents might hold in mind for themselves as they contemplate adolescence:

I'm only sixteen, but there are days when I'm sure I'm fifty-six, maybe. When I was little, my parents were always away. They left us with maids and nurses, and they'd come back with all these presents from this country or that country. I used to *hate* those presents! I'd never touch them. Then my father would say that I was ungrateful. I *was!* I didn't want anything—only my mother and father. Then I'd fight with a governess, and she'd quit; or I'd make her do something wrong, and she'd get fired. It was hell!

I remember dreaming that I'd be grown up and everything would be better. I'd be a teenager, like my cousin. She seemed so free. She didn't need her parents anymore. She had her own life! Well, now I know: She'd been molested when she was young (by her own uncle!) and she was wild—"out of control," her mother said—by the time she was fourteen. I never really knew about her and her troubles (two abortions by the time she was eighteen and in college). All I knew was that she had a car, and she had all those clothes, and records, and boyfriends. Now I know that she was the loneliest person in the world. She had no one she could talk with—no one older she could trust.

You should always have a friend of your own age, at least one. If you don't, then you're in the worst possible shape. But you need more. My cousin needed more. She needed—I need—what everyone needs: your mother or your father to lean on and talk with. I don't mean those mushy talks you see on the sitcoms. I don't mean the forced talks Ann Landers thinks are so good: Go and talk with your parents, and that will settle everything! The trouble is a lot of us can't talk with our parents. All the good advice in the world won't help us talk with our parents if all our lives have been— well, if we haven't learned to depend on our parents for advice, if we haven't learned to *look up to* our parents while we've been growing up!

I had to go to all these doctors in the last few years. You'd think they would be of help, but each one was scarier than the other! The first one was a psychiatrist, and he was too smooth for me. He was supposed to help me, but it didn't work. I told my mother I could handle things by myself. I went four times.

Then there were the gynecologists. They know "procedures." That's all they talk about: We have a "procedure," and now we're going to do a "procedure," and soon the "procedure" will begin. When I asked one of them what he thinks I should do about sex, he said I should "be careful." He's pretty careful himself: He got a thousand dollars, I think, from my dad. The psychiatrist got a hundred dollars for each three-quarters of an hour.

My father kept on talking about the money I was "costing" him. He pretended to be complaining, but he was really bragging. I could tell: I'd been hearing him talk like that all my life. No wonder I keep trying to find a man who is quiet, and who doesn't want to impress people, and who will listen to others! But then sex gets going, and I lose my control, and so does the guy, and it's as if we're trying to find one thing and we get so excited, we get lost. Then, who do you turn to—if you want to stop and think about where you're headed? Your parents are away, or they're too busy; the minister (at least ours) preaches at you, and I just feel so bad after he gets through listing my sins. The teachers aren't the ones— that sex-education course is a joke, and the guy who gives it is another joke. There's no one!

Young people (all people) need what that young person found so elusive—an adult to respect, a person with whom to share worries and doubts, even an occasional secret. In that regard, as one youth told me, "a parent will do." But not all parents are available or interested; and some have even been told by "experts" to stay away, to respect the adolescent's "need" for distance, his or her own demand for independence. Meanwhile, as this survey shows, young people struggle with all sorts of problems. A significant number (14%) have been raped. Probably a similar percentage have experienced one or another variation of childhood sexual molestation. There are strong sexual urges—and plenty of known instances of pregnancies threatening. Homosexual worries (and fantasies) are not rare. Sexual practices, for the initiated, stir up any number of emotions—shame and guilt, as the respondents testify in their comments, as well as curiosity and pleasure and no rare amount of pride and self-confidence.

Above all, if my ears have heard correctly these past years, there is, along with curiosity and confidence, an abiding sense of perplexity, of self-doubt. These are years of pain and confusion as well as assertive, even truculent proclamations of one's maturity, one's sexual interests and capabilities. Parents belong nearby, eager to listen; willing to acknowledge their own qualms and misgivings; unafraid to state their values; their beliefs; and not least, quick to declare what ought not to be. If these are obvious pieties from yet another American doctor, then all of us know how intensely grateful we can be sometimes for that everyday "banality": a nod, a smile, a voice of reassurance or, yes, earnest reprimand. When the young lady quoted above "really flipped," she told her hospital doctor that "no adult" she knew ever stopped to pay attention to her, to listen to what *she* was saying. "Just a smile and an arm around me at the right moment might have saved me," she exclaimed. The self-assured doctor may insist that her adolescent life was more complex than that, required more than "a smile" and an arm extended—or he may conclude that the real problem was that such a smile, such an arm offered affectionately, seemed beyond her life's reach.

There are youths who at 15 or 16 already know they are in distinct trouble, or are "different" from others. Adolescents struggle with all sorts of sexual urges and connect them to all sorts of fantasies—even as do adults. But young people have a right to have their sexual worries taken quite seriously. I again draw on remarks made by Anna Freud at a clinical conference (1978):

> I would hesitate at any quick diagnosis when examining an adolescent. The young person in question is struggling, as we do, to figure out *his* sexuality, *hers*. The young person is struggling to know the limits—what is permissible, and what is normal or pathological. These limits vary, of course, with a given society, and

history has its say, too. What holds in one period will not do so a
century later! A period of sexual obsession may give way to sexual
repression—calm restored! Homosexual thoughts may break
through, then disappear—and never reappear, or reappear in
greater force, to take ultimate control of the youth's sexual life. We
have to take careful stock. We have to ask the young person to
come back and see us as he sees fit, as she may wish to return.
We have to wait and see. But without question, some adolescents
know they're in trouble, and for them we must be ready to do all
we can do—to clarify and explain, certainly, and to judge whether
treatment is wanted and needed.

Such a tentative or guarded way of looking at the possibilities
or advantages of psychotherapy is a response to the volatility of a
given aspect of existence—wherein change is the norm. However,
young sexuality, we ought all to remind ourselves, is not a special
consequence of our postindustrial society.

What many of us call "teenage sexuality" was, for millions of
ordinary men and women, whether living in towns or in the
countryside, a matter of reaching one's maturity—indeed, responding to its requirements. Put differently, for generations, young men
and young women (of, say, the age of 16 or 18) began "seeing"
each other, became engaged or married. They didn't think of
themselves as "school dropouts" or "impulsive." They were, of
course, adults who happened to be young, and who were working
in one way or another: on farms, as apprentices and artisans, for
guilds, in sweatshops and factories. Here, for instance, is the voice
of a young American mother who thought my wife and I a bit
peculiar because the two of us (I just over 30, and she in her middle
twenties) were just about ready to start having children:

> When I'm your ages, I'll have grown-up children. They'll be
> working with us, taking in the crops, and moving up the coast. I
> started working when I was seven, I think it was, or eight. I was
> through with school by the time I was ten or eleven, maybe. I had
> trouble with school, because we were on the road until late October
> or November, and then with the two crops to pull in here, my
> daddy always would be coming to me and saying he and my
> momma needed my help, and everyone else's, to make the money
> while it was there to be made.
>
> I met Jimmie here in 1955; I remember the month: April. I

remember hearing on a radio in the car "It's April of 1955, and in three days it'll be May, and then for thirty-one days it'll be 5/55." I pinched myself and said I should really try to remember what I'd just heard, so when my kids asked me about when I met their father, I'd be able to say, pronto, almost 5/55, or April of 1955, toward the end of the month. I knew it was love by then; I knew Jimmie and I would stay together. He was the first one I'd given myself to, and I don't think he knew too many before me, though it's different with men and women, because men wander more.

If you work with the crops, and you're a boy growing up, you're going to be traveling down two roads—one to pick the crops, and then there's the road where you'll meet someone who is for you, not just for now, today, but for all the time you're here, and it's only a short time, I tell my kids: We're just passing through, courtesy of Him the Almighty, and so don't get too stuck on this place. But if you find the right person, then you're not alone; and I was lucky (though I sure know my man's faults!) and now we've got our three kids and another to come.

She was barely twenty when she spoke those words. For her, "teenage sexuality" had meant the following:

I met Jimmie one day when he was sitting near the road; he was tired and a little sick to his stomach. We were both picking beans that day, his family and mine. I was sick myself: I'd gotten my period, one of the first times, I remember. My mother had warned me, though: "The blood will come down there, and that means you're a grown woman, and you can have a child anytime, anytime!" She'd repeat herself to make sure we paid her the attention she wanted. She had no schooling at all, my momma, and she can't even write her name, but she doesn't need those people who come here [a campaign then in operation of Planned Parenthood] to tell you with their picture books and stories how to raise the right number of kids, and no more. My momma used to tell us she worked extra hard so she wouldn't get to depend too much on us working—because then she'd want more and more kids to do the work for her.

She told me, with my first period, to watch out when the bleeding stops, and make sure the man who's with me (when I start having men!) buys himself plenty of rubbers and knows how to use them. And she told me how she made sure my daddy didn't spend all his spare change on beer, no sir: Buy the rubbers first, and then go for the beer, and never drink hard liquor, because it makes a total fool out of you so fast you lose all there is in your head, everything you know, and you're like some dog, barking and running around and getting yourself into a heap of big trouble, but not even knowing that it's trouble that you're in. My momma would point at a dog, running in the street, and puking, and she'd say there's no one to teach the dog and protect it from itself, from being a *wild* animal, and the same with us: If you don't watch over yourself, you'll be drunk, bad drunk, and you'll spread your legs open, come anyone, and you'll be in trouble, and the kids will come, and you won't even know who their father is, and you're on your way to dying early.

Well, Jimmie started telling me he felt better, now that I was sitting beside him, and I'd gone and got him some water from that spout, the only spout we had in that whole place. He asked me if we could do picking together; that way, if he got sick or I got sick, we could help each other, and since I'd told him I'd just been sick, but I wouldn't tell him more—well, the more I wouldn't tell him, the more he knew, and he said he had a sister who was older and she'd taught him a lot, and so he knew his way around women! Suddenly I felt I was with someone who was smart, and he wanted to protect me! He got me water, after I'd gotten him water, and then he took my hand and he held it, and I still remember it, he started moving his right hand up my arm, back and forth, and he pressed his knee against mine, and I felt good, and I wished there were no beans out there, and no families picking the beans! And that was the beginning; and a year later we'd gotten together and maybe we weren't married, like you are in a church, but we were in our lives, married; and I was going to have my first kid.

That twenty-year-old, mid-twentieth-century American woman was unquestionably poor, barely literate, and thus quite unlike most of the respondents to the questionnaire featured in this book— and yet, in one or another way, she had been struggling with problems similar to theirs. Like many other women in this world, she had tried to figure out which man was truly trustworthy, and what the consequences of such trust on her part would be. Actually, I recall being well aware of her personal circumstances—the hard life she lived, the early marriage, the early arrival of children—and not being inclined to think of her as a "teenager" at all. She was a young migrant mother to my wife and me, and to the public-health nurses who knew her and her children.

Yet, she had certainly told us of a given sexuality: at 13 and 14, heavy petting, intercourse, pregnancy; and soon enough, a life of harvesting crops, moving from place to place (for six months of the year), taking care of one, two, three children, responding to her husband's sexual requests, and, yes, she would truly acknowledge, making a few of her own:

> I sometimes want to escape from the life we have. There are two ways: to get lost in a movie on TV, or to get my husband going, until for me he's the best lover in the whole world and I can't think of anything but him making love and making love and making love to me, and I wish we could just go on forever, but even when it does seem we're doing it forever, I'll look at the clock afterwards, and it's only an hour or two at the most, and that's about as long as a movie lasts, so I told my daughter (the oldest one) that you can't have any pleasures in this world that last more than a couple of hours, and she's almost six, and she gave me a funny look. It's the same look she had on her face when she came into our room once and she said her tummy hurt real bad, and then she asked me whether daddy was hurting me, and I said no, just the opposite, and the next day she asked if I was going to have a baby, and I said wait a minute, not so fast.
>
> But there are times I don't care, and I don't even like those rubbers—don't want them—and I say to myself, it's worth getting pregnant if I can feel so good I'm in heaven. I have a friend and she hates sex. She obeys the man she's with, but hates it, and she hates every man she's with, and I told her she'll change one day, but she's twenty-two, I think, and she's not changing, and it's too late by now, I think.

Twenty-two and too late—yet another reminder that the notion of "maturity" (not to mention youth, or old age) is not fixed. As for the 20-year-old woman whose words I've been setting down, she possessed lots of "maturity." She worked long and hard, and she tried to take good care of her children. She was, too, an able, knowing, sensitive observer of young sexuality. Not that she would have claimed such a (dubious) distinction for herself; on the contrary, she always regarded herself as impetuous, shortsighted, badly educated, and at times far too quick when it came to speaking her mind. Still, as one thinks about her remarks, one is gradually made to connect them to the big and important matters we all, as human beings, struggle to comprehend. Again and again she reminds her listener, reminds herself, that a sexual life has to do with loneliness and the effort to overcome it; that a sexual life has to do with the struggle to find meaning in what we do, how we live; that a sexual life has to do with pleasure, of course, but pleasure exacted from a life that can be, often enough, boring or demanding or puzzling—and so, ironically, what is meant to provide release and escape ends up enabling endurance: the oasis that nourishes the progress of the journey.

A sexual life is usually an intensely imaginative one. All sorts of personal memories and experiences become worked into our sexual imagery and activity. This young migrant worker provided a sensible and shrewd account of the process:

> When I was a little girl, maybe six, I don't know exactly, my gramma told me that no matter how bad it is, no matter what's hurting me, I can use my head and give myself a real boost that way. Close your eyes, she said, and make up pictures, and make up words, and make up heaven itself, and you in it, and give yourself the best time you can ever want to have, and before you even open your eyes to return to this place, remind yourself that you'll be closing your eyes again soon, real soon.

Sexuality, then, is imagination stirred, symbolism evoked, past experience summoned directly or slyly. Sexuality is each person's great secret. Each of us has our utterly unique "code," as that uneducated young woman kept calling it—the mix of images and voices that "gets things going." Speaking candidly to my wife, she once not only revealed her own sexual imagery but also made us see the various human needs it serves. "I'll be with my man, and no matter what's going on, I have to close my eyes to get us out of this damn place! I don't *actually* close my eyes all the time; what I mean is that I'll picture us on a boat, in my mind, and then it's as if we're really there."

Why a boat? Her answer provides a rich example of how our sexuality knits us together:

> I see people on their boats sometimes when we're traveling. We'll go over a river, and from the bridge you see them, and you say, oh, they're having the time of their lives. They're away from work, and they can't be rung on the phone, and there's no mailbox nearby, and they're free of the land and all the bad, bad troubles

that can come around any corner, and so they have a big feed,
and then give each other "all the pleasure God filled us out to give
each other" is what my momma would say. I believe I had my eye
out for boats long ago! I believe, to hear my momma and to hear
her momma, I was dreaming boats when I was but a baby. The
high point of my life—my life with my husband—is when I'm
tingling all over from being with him, and in my mind, every time,
we're on a boat, and we started being there as soon as we started
having our pleasure.

There is a certain decorous, even stately quality to her language—
not rare in rural black people, who speak in the Bible's cadences.
There is, too, an uncanny blend of realism and vigorous openheart-
edness. What one hears from her is direct sexual testimony: an
avowal of her own sensuality—its lifelong connections to the
movement of water and to the luxury of boats. A teenager's avowal,
too, that a sexual life draws upon a person's whole experience for
its energy.

We have heard much about sexuality as a drive—the powerful
stirring of bodily impulses, which crave and press for expression,
which yearn and seethe and brazenly demand, until (one way or
the other) the body must act. But many young people prefer
fantasy to action—a much safer initiation into sexuality.

I remember well a 15-year-old boy whom I saw for a while
because he had become indifferent, self-absorbed, and surly to his
teachers. He had also been caught smoking pot at school and at
home. One weekday evening at the dining-room table, he had
renounced all his former ambitions.

"I want out," he kept saying to me: out from a private-school
education, meant to take him directly to one or another of the
nation's leading colleges; out from all of the bruising, gung-ho
demands of varsity athletics; indeed, out from a whole way of life,
as he made quite clear:

> I was brought up to be on top—on the top of the honor roll,
> and on the top of every sport I take, and on the top of the social
> world, but not on top of any woman. But I don't want to waste
> half my life being "a good boy." That's what I used to hear my
> parents calling me, "a good boy." Every time I heard that, even
> before I became a teenager, I swear, I'd think of some girl or
> woman taking off her clothes, all of them. It was an automatic

thought, a connection I couldn't stop myself from making if I wanted to, and usually I didn't.

One time I must have smiled: Cheryl Tiegs was undressing herself! My dad asked what was so funny. (I'd just got on the high honor roll, and they were doing a dance, my folks!) I said nothing. He said I was smiling "a big smile," so something must be funny. I said no, just that I was being *happy*. Then my mother said my grades made her happy, too; and my dad said he was as happy as could be. Later, when I was in my room, I remember wishing Cheryl Tiegs was there, so *she* could be happy. But she'd already made me pretty happy, and so I thought I should sit down and write her a fan letter, but I had all this damn math to do, algebra and algebra and algebra, and a composition on the Eskimos. . . .

I think it was Cheryl Tiegs who got me into all this trouble. I mean, I started getting heavy with her. I mean, she started taking over my mind. I mean, I surrendered to her. I stopped holding back, or trying to welsh on the deal I had with her. In the beginning I'd get her all worked up and she'd be ready to do anything—I mean anything I wanted. Then I'd up and leave her. They I'd come back to her, when my mother or father were talking to me. But lately I've been going steady with her! I can't leave her. If I smoke pot, I'm her slave! The girls I know, they don't mean much to me. I fool around with them, but I don't react to them, you know? I'm uptight with them. I told Cheryl the other night: "I think of you when I'm holding one of them, Mary and Marylou and Mary Alice," my three Marys!

When I started "tuning out," the teachers thought I was sick; they kept sending me to the school nurse to have my temperature taken—physically sick. If I'd told them I was carrying on with Cheryl Tiegs in their classes, while supposedly learning my Caesar and my Latin vocabulary, they'd have thought I was—well, delirious. I *was*! I'd even think of Cheryl while jogging; I'd have to stop sometimes because it'd hurt down there! You can't run and have sex—or can you? The same with football: I'd even have flashes; Cheryl coming right at me, not some big hunk of an uptight preppie, knocking everyone down so his "surplus energy" (my dad's words!) won't go and get him into bad trouble! Now, I guess, it's hopeless. I'm not doing very well: I'm getting a flunking grade in "sublimation"!

I learned that word last year in a "social issues" course, and I remember thinking to myself: I'm with Cheryl, and I'm teaching her the word. She wants to know how to spell it. We sit down at a desk—at our dining-room table—and I spell it for her, in big capital letters. She starts pronouncing it. She's trying to be a wise-ass intellectual like I'm supposed to be. She crosses her legs and uncrosses them. I can't even hear what she's saying. I've forgotten the stupid word *sublimation;* it means nothing to me. I ask her what in hell it does mean. She says it means—But she can't go any further. I'm stopping her. I'm kissing her. I'm pulling her away from the table, toward my bedroom. She says no, she prefers the outdoors. She's an outdoors girl! I say, what the hell, why not, and fast as can be, presto, we're in a meadow, a half a mile from our house, and the sky's the limit; I mean, everything goes, and you want to know something—I don't feel "bad" afterward.

I feel a little sad, that's all, and the reason is that I know damn well that I'll never even meet this girl Cheryl Tiegs, and yet I know her better than anyone in the world, and she knows me better than anyone knows me. It's crazy—but I'm not crazy! I just get horny a lot! Now, one of these days, I guess, I'll make Cheryl Tiegs start being a student. I'll make her study with me first, *then* (and only then!) can we have a good time together! Poor Cheryl Tiegs: She'll become a Latin scholar, an expert in how to identify adverbial clauses! Right now I have a number I do with her, and, boy, we both get high; but someday she'll end up knowing about higher numbers.

It's a dead world in that school, lots of perspiration on the forehead, and lots of underarm sweat from push-ups and running and knocking guys down, but the 300 or 400 calories you burn with having sex—that's for later, much later. Like the teacher read—one of T. S. Eliot's poems, I think—I'm ready to say "Resign," "Resign!" But who will accept my resignation without calling in ten doctors, ten ministers, ten teachers, and ten best friends, and each of them comes with a lecture, and the big deal, though they don't use the word, is SUBLIMATION? So it looks like Cheryl and I will both have to buckle down and keep our fun for special moments.

This youth was trying to let me know how energetically playful his sexual fantasies were, how very much *his* they were, and how well they served his rebelliousness. Who is this Cheryl Tiegs, and why her hold on a boy half her age whom she'll likely never meet? Why this strong, bemused, idiosyncratic response to her by a 15-year-old inhabitant of a New England private school? Why is he so much more susceptible to her charms than to those of the young

women he knows, or other women he spots regularly in movies,
on television, in various magazines?

A surge of sexual awareness and feeling finds a visionary home
of sorts, as this reflective youth (now) would begin to realize:

> I saw pictures of her, and, my God, she had everything! It
> wasn't only her fantastic body, it was her face, her smile (I don't
> know how to explain it), her name. She was wholesome as well as
> sexy; and she seemed so comfortable with being sexy—not one of
> those strippers, or call girls or models or *Playboy* bunnies; they're
> all working hard, you know it, and they're probably hating their
> work, like a lot of people do. The sultrier the look, or the more I
> know the person is faking—that's when I get cold as a cucumber.
> Cheryl Tiegs caught me with her big open smile, and then I moved
> down to her boobs, and then her waist, and her legs, and I figured
> she'd cooperate, and not give me a real lousy fight, a bad time.

I asked him to spell that out, and as he did, something more
than a private fantasy was described:

> I have to fight all the time in school: Everyone wants to be on
> the honor roll, the high honor roll. I have to fight in every sport.
> Only "wimps" take recreational sports. You push and you push,
> and you watch to see if you're falling behind—and you're ready
> for something else when it comes to sex! At least I am! At least I
> was!
>
> I don't know what I'll end up being like! I hear my parents talk
> about the "right" person for marriage, for my brother or for me,
> and you'd think they were handing out grades to people in a
> school: She's a C, and she's a B-plus, and she's, oh, she's an A-
> minus and *she*, well, she flunks, absolutely flunks. When they give
> a look that means C-minus or D-plus to a girl, I begin to think she
> looks cute. I begin to notice her figure, and think of putting my
> arm around her, and letting it wander around. But I'm supposed
> to outgrow that kind of talk! I'm supposed to do what I'm told is
> best for—the family, I guess that's it. But what's best for me—well,
> don't ask!
>
> If I could meet Cheryl Tiegs, would she be best for me? Would
> I like her if I met her, and would I like her after loving her? I'll
> never know! But when I first saw her, on some magazine cover, I
> thought she was *friendly*, and she was *nice*, and she wasn't a
> grader, and she wasn't a teacher, and she wasn't someone who's
> going to be a debutante and stand there in a line at the waltz

evenings—just Cheryl Tiegs, a girl who will let you take her away with you, and you'll live happily ever after together! Like a buddy of mine says, "No sweat!"

This youth does not go to a whorehouse; does not ogle a barmaid or a pretty girl walking down the street; but rather stays virtuously "good" at home and school (for a while, at least) until Cheryl Tiegs arrives, full of all sorts of attributes and possibilities. She would flunk parental scrutiny, of course—yet she looks as if she deserves an A: blondish, light-eyed, pink-skinned, with wonderfully clean and straight teeth. Put her in a Bonwit Teller dress, make her *appropriately* inviting, the growing man realizes, and she'd get a seal of approval. Teach her a certain etiquette, a certain language, a certain manner of approach (or withdrawal) and she would become—no stranger anymore.

"I don't want to know about Cheryl Tiegs's life," the young fellow insists. He has in mind another kind of figure; he has in mind fantasy unencumbered by too much factuality. He has in mind an escape with a willing companion who has arrived at the doorstep of his eye, courtesy of a large colored picture in a magazine, and who keeps returning, courtesy of what celluloid run through a machine in a film studio can do. He has in mind many travels with someone who, finally, is his creation: She says what he wants her to say, obliges his physical preferences.

"I never thought of myself as being a producer or a director, a playwright, a scriptwriter," he cleverly observes, "but I guess I become someone like that at certain moments." He is under pressure to "analyze" that phenomenon, because he has been letting such previously hidden or unacknowledged talents run away with him, with the routines of his everyday life. But now he has a notion of what has happened, and he is vastly amused, introspective, a bit wistful:

> Cheryl Tiegs, I think you're getting ready to leave me—or vice versa! We can't be together, she and I, if I make her part of my homework! The more I talk about her, the more I think about her, the less she's my own friend and no one else's! Lately Cheryl has become too much for me—I'm fighting with her against "them," all those teachers, and my parents, and when you fight people, you're bound to join them, even if it's for your victory celebration over them!

He wondered if he was making sense. He wondered if he was using lame or overwrought excuses to rationalize a rejection (of Cheryl Tiegs) in truth motivated by an increasing boredom, itself the inevitable result (so he'd been told for years by friends and those who write about a subject called "sexuality") of any long "relationship," even one conducted at the level of fantasy. Indeed, with his marvelous humor and capacity for a bemused look at himself, he could come up with a direction of thought that prompts chuckles about all sorts of authorities.

> The only thing was *afterward:* Usually she has other things to do, and so do I! I get her to tell me she has to go, and I tell her *I* have to go, and we say a passionate goodbye. She gets excited just as she's saying she's going, and so do I. But, hell, we're both grown-ups, or trying to be. I *do* have homework! She's got a busy career, and all the other men lusting after her, while they take pictures of her and interview her! Fade out! Fade in: *Caesar's Gallic Wars.* Interlude: What kind of a sex life did old Julius Caesar have? While he was fighting those Belgae and Helvitii, and playing tricks on poor Vercingetorix, there must have been a few hours here and there for hanky-panky!
>
> Once I pictured Caesar trying to seduce Cheryl Tiegs. I had her dressed up as a barbarian girl, and he was ready to fold her in his stupid toga, but she said, "No, sir, no, general, you're not my type. I'll take a certain Latin student who only got a C+ reading your war journals; and besides, it doesn't help that you're such an egotist and a tricky one in those journals! No wonder my lover boy only gets a C+ reading you; he's wise to what you lusted for—money and power. Well, you can't have everything—not me, anyway! Go back to your wife! What was her name, anyway?"
>
> Will he give us that on the quiz, the Latin teacher who defends Caesar, no matter how gentle we are in criticizing him—ask us to name Caesar's one and only wife? Will he ask us this: What do you think Julius and his wife liked to do in bed? Hey, we're supposed to know that they didn't have the kind of beds we do. But never any mention about what they did or didn't do in their beds!

In theory, a teenager goes from an autoerotic stage to one of strenuous intellectuality—or an absorbing life of physical work. But abstractions have a way of ridding life of its complexity, irony, ambiguity—the muddy inconsistencies that so often characterize the way things happen in our heads and in our workaday experience. A youth's sexuality can itself have an intellectual aspect, can sometimes become a means of considerable reflection, can prompt social criticism, philosophical or political analysis—as in the relationship between Cheryl Tiegs and the Roman Empire.

I could picture Cheryl telling that guy Caesar to get away from her—to work himself into better shape, and stop getting his kicks out of killing people. They never do tell us in Latin class what kind of people these *consules* and *legati* and *imperatores* were; the whole gang of men who ruled Rome and pushed everyone else, from other countries or tribes, all over the Mediterranean. Yesterday in class I turned to Gloria, a real Latin whiz who sits beside me all the time (I see her lingering before the class, waiting to see where I sit, but pretending she's looking at a book on the teacher's desk, or at that damn map he has, "The Roman World"), and I started kidding with her, and, boy, did she light up, and I thought to myself, Okay, Gloria, here's your big test for the year, and you do so well in *his* [Latin] tests, let's see how you'll do in my one little quiz.

There was a five-second pause, and she was trying to bubble herself up with more stupid chitchat, and I looked right into her eyes, and I said it, the word I thought would win her over: "honey." I waited, and I thought she'd melted. She did—she smiled and her eyes twinkled, but I knew the odds were still slim, because like my dad says, people have their "priorities" and they don't give them up so easily, and Gloria's priorities are to get five straight A's every semester, and she's like Caesar: If anyone gets in her way, she pushes or plots. Anyway, I tried: "Honey [I said it again!], why don't you ask the teacher what Caesar's wife was like, and how Roman men behaved toward their wives, and—"

She stopped me cold. She tried laughing, as if I was just kidding, putting her on, and she was going to let me know she knew I was being a wise guy. When she scanned my face and saw I wasn't signaling her the way she hoped I was, she showed the real Gloria with blazing colors. Face straightens. Smile vanishes. Eyes move toward the front of the room: Is the teacher ready to start the class? I'm a pain-in-the-ass Helvetian spy, trying to undermine her empire! Suddenly I realize: This is *Gloria*, and she's only trying to live up to her name, and I'm just a has-been now to her, or a never-will-be: In the clutch it's an A in Latin and no ripples in class, because teachers' recommendations count a lot for admission to the Seven Sisters or the Ivy League or whatever glory Gloria wants.

I looked at that getup she had on, her knee-length socks and the polished loafers and that plaid skirt and the loose blouse, so loose nothing was outlined—not that there's much to outline—and I saw that neutral polish she puts on her fingernails, and I thought, She's going to kill for Caesar, and I don't want any part of her or Caesar, and I'll stay with Cheryl for life—her warm smile and her wiggly rear and her hair all over. She doesn't even want to conquer *me*. She just wants to enjoy me, and she wants me to enjoy her. Caesar wouldn't know what to do with her! He'd want to fuck her, but he'd be through with her and ready for the next slave in a half an hour, if that long.

And Gloria—she's too busy mapping her own conquests to think Cheryl is anything but a "dope." I've heard her call people "dopes"—and then she talks about how important it is for women to be treated equally. If you're below 120 in an IQ test, you're Gloria's "dope," and she wants segregation: a faster track. She's a female male-chauvinist type, and she told me once she hates models because they demean women. She'd demean the whole human race to get an A, and the teacher is her accomplice. He rules us like a conqueror of Gaul: One wrong remark (that contradicts his love affair with Rome) and we've had it in his book. He gives us lots of essay questions, and there's plenty of room for playing favorites or expressing a grudge when you correct an essay!

Cheryl Tiegs won't ever be a teacher, though I've wondered what she'll do with the rest of her life. You get old fast in her line of work. I'm still loyal, but others will defect. I wish she'd come here and teach Latin differently—get us to stop and think what that empire was really like, for the slaves and the conquered people, not just the few people we read. But Cheryl isn't wasting her time with Latin; she's probably keeping that body of hers limbered up—it's work!—and she's dreaming of some future with somebody, just like I am. I'd write her a letter and promise her a year of travel, to places I've always dreamed of seeing (New Zealand! the Galapagos Islands! Patagonia in Argentina!), but she'd never see the letter, probably. It's just as well: I know her, and she knows me! She says things to me I'd never thought of—she makes me more honest. She's the one who spotted Caesar for what he is, and she was right there, helping me discover what Gloria is.

For all the self-induced ecstasies he experiences, he insists on connecting the one who is indispensable to them to a moral analysis of late twentieth-century America, upper-middle-class New England sector. Even as a young migrant worker tries to make sense of her kind of life, and, doing so, struggles to fathom the nature of sexuality, its opportunities and its constraints, so a product of a well-to-do, well-educated home responds to surges of energy, the press of a well-acknowledged "drive," the demands of an instinct— and also tries to fathom what that sexuality means, what it doesn't mean. And both of those "teenagers" seem to have realized that carnality in human beings, by and large, as Freud made very clear, erupts against something, intrudes upon something, has to contend with something. We are the creatures who use words, who make symbols. We are the creatures who worry about what is right and wrong. We possess a visionary willingness to constrain as well as to express, and, not to be forgotten, we possess a strange and unique ability to gain distance on ourselves, laugh at what we do or bemoan our actions. ("But, hell, we're both grown-ups, or trying to be. I *do* have homework! She's got a busy career. . . .") Such attributes are not so readily overwhelmed by the power of sexuality, considerable though it be.

A young woman whose personal life I'm about to describe once observed to me that "we're the only ones in the world who have one organ, the brain, which talks about itself and everything else all the time." Many of us go through life so entranced with our voices that we forget they are lodged in a particular organ of the body, and that, after a fashion, for a person's brain to study itself, to gain some sense of itself (in the seriousness of study, or the attentiveness of ironic amusement), is to achieve a kind of transcendence. Similarly with our sexuality: It surely exerts a powerful effect on us, especially when we are young and, out of nowhere, it seems, stirrings arrive, and they get connected to mental imagery, and are prompted by what is seen—on the street, on the screen, in the classroom, in magazines and books. But our sexuality has to reckon with what watches and takes the measure of all human drives—a cortex, if you will, a mind that works and tries to exert some authority over the body, including its sexual life.

In a so-called working-class suburb of Boston, the young woman of 16 just mentioned, a junior in high school, strained mightily to contain her passionate feelings toward a young man who "comes

and goes," who "plays the field," and who reminds her of John
Travolta, in appearance, manner, and speech, or lack thereof. Even
as a rich young man mixes his moral and intellectual passions with
his sexual ones—and, indeed, uses the last of those three to supply
a defiant if reclusive energy to the first two—so a young woman
who hasn't nearly his prospects in life watches Travolta, watches
her boyfriend, watches the lead singer of the J. Geils Band, and
finds herself not only stirred but vigorously pushed in a certain
direction.

> I see Jack on his Suzuki and I want to leap on it, sit behind
> him for miles and miles until we find a place beside the road
> where we can stop and make out. He's best with me when he has
> that leather jacket on and his bike is nearby! I often wonder what
> would happen if he had to choose between the bike and me. Hell,
> I *know* what would happen! He can whistle and women come
> running; but the bike is so fussy and difficult, it's beyond belief.
> She's his mistress and she keeps him guessing; women are supposed
> to be independent, and if the men want to be pampered, let them
> go find their old buddies to pamper them, or let them get their
> kicks out of a Honda or a Suzuki! But it doesn't work like that for
> me: I see my mother handing my father the world on a silver
> platter, even though she works (she has to, or we'd go under), and
> I guess I end up copying her.
> I know I'm being a damn fool sometimes, like when I fall in
> love with Travolta. I see a guy in a movie, and I hear a guy
> singing—that doesn't mean I know who he is. He's being someone
> else; for all I know, he's being lots of people. My boyfriend, Jack,
> he's just one person, but he's lost himself in a machine, so he
> doesn't act, like Travolta, or sing, like Peter Wolf; he just sits and
> stares, and he wears sunglasses all the time, even when it's cloudy,
> even when it's dark, and he's lost in his own mind.
> I try to lose myself in my mind. That's when I do my heavy
> thinking. I realize then that I'm someone who's *gone*, absolutely
> *gone*, for a guy; so I tell myself, Hey, relax and enjoy the ride, and
> it *is* a ride, a long, long, motorcycle ride! But then I get to thinking
> more. I'm no longer that girl who's gone for a guy. I'm all mixed
> up.
> I hear girls say sex is trouble; they wish they were little kids,
> or they wish they were older and married happily—anything to
> get over being teenagers, with sex on everyone's mind all over the
> place. Well, I disagree! With me it's not sex, it's the worries I have;

with me it's the head I have on my shoulders, and it's working all the time, even when I'm madly in love with Jack—my head noticing what a grump he is, and how bigheaded he gets with some jerk of a friend so each can be Mr. King of the Road on his bike. If I didn't spot these stupid little things, I'd be happy. I'd be Jack's "lay"; I'd be the girl he uses when he's got enough kicks from his bike and now he wants to give another part of his body some action because his hands hurt turning the wheels and his feet from pushing the brake!

As one listens to her speaking, one senses the attraction that pulls her to a particular man. She speaks with obvious excitement of his sweaty pants and shirts, his "body odor," which she loves. She is willing to say, quite forthrightly, that she loves what she also resents, the power of a machine, which, in her mind as in her boyfriend's, is connected to virility. Meanwhile, of course, she has to live with that machine's hungry dominance over Jack's life, over her own—to the point where an apparently enlarged masculinity becomes, in actual daily life, a much diminished one.

Once she tried to solve this problem in her own way. She maneuvered her boyfriend and herself into a long country ride and she became unusually sensual, hoping to prompt a similar response from Jack. Usually he favored rather quick encounters with her, furtively held at night; now they were alone, under a clear blue sky, the sun warm, the air dry, a meadow uninhabited and inviting in its soft, green expanse. "I joked with him," she remembers. "I pointed to two birds having a time for themselves, and then I spotted two squirrels doing the same thing." As she describes what sounds like a Cole Porter introduction to an afternoon of love, she becomes increasingly somber, and finally mute. It was, she offers laconically, "a disaster." It was, she says months later, having only now brought the subject up, "a bad scene," but she should have known what would happen, because she has been part of that "scene" for years. What scene? Her short reply: "The bike and car world." She adds sardonically: "It's a world where you don't need too many contraceptives!"

In a church a few weeks before making that remark, she'd heard the priest bravely defend the Vatican on contraceptives: not to be used. She had this response:

> I felt like going up to our priest and telling him that I have a

plan. If he would buy every teenager in the parish, every male teenager, a motorbike, or a hot-rod car, then he won't have to give so many sermons on birth control or teenage sex. I'm not meaning to slander all the guys; but I'll tell you, not just Jack but a lot of them are more talk and showy stuff than real action. I think a lot of them are more interested in impressing their buddies than enjoying a nice time alone with their girlfriends. We're window dressing a lot of the time. They've put their hearts and souls into their machines. We become a fast fuck for them. They're someplace else even when they're with us; and when they're not with us— well, they're not with us. But that's not how it is for me and my girlfriends: I'm always thinking of Jack.

I've noticed that it's become *my* problem, though: When I think of him, it's always him on the bike; and when I get excited, thinking of being with him, it's that same old idea I had a half-year ago—to have sex with him on the bike, somehow! My best friend, Jeannie, thinks I'm getting "weird," but why is that so? I think if he could just let it happen, it'd be the greatest thing of his life and mine! He'd go wild, I know he would. And I'd be there with him! I could keep up with him; I know I could. But I don't give us big odds that it'll happen. I think that Suzuki has become a part of his body, and it's in his brain as well as his hips and legs. When he sits down on a chair, it's as if he's sitting down on his bike. When he makes toast, it's as if he's giving his bike gas. When he gets on top of me, his bike comes into my mind, and I can almost hear it roaring down the road while we're making out, and in no time flat the bike is gone, and so is he! So it must be part of his mind. Do you know what I mean? It's part of *my* mind!

Such bittersweet sexuality includes not only passionate involvement but also elements of keen, witty, moral acuity. In other words, this young woman's sexual life is an occasion for reflection:

I know life isn't perfect. My friend Jeannie tells me all about her and her boyfriend, what they're doing. Not all that more than Jack and I are doing! Sometimes I think I'm a hopeless dreamer. I'm just "too romantic," my older sister says. As for my younger sisters, they're not yet ten, either of them, so they're still in a state of blissful ignorance; though when *I* was eight or nine, I was waiting so *hard* to be a teenager. I listened to Billy Joel or the Stones and I thought to myself that somewhere there is *the one*, the guy who will come and be my boyfriend and take me away to—well, *full happiness.* Jeannie says when you set yourself up that way, set your *boyfriend* up that way, you're headed for calamity.

But I've heard Jeannie tell of all the trouble in her house, and how her old man drinks and her old lady shouts all day long and never smiles—and then I've heard her say she wished some "wonderman" would come and sweep her off her feet. I hate to say it, but I do: "Jeannie, that's what I used to dream, when I saw my father hit my mother, and hit her hard, and my mother screamed so hard it made me shake and cry and run out of the house, even in the middle of a freezing January night." And now look: *The guy* has arrived, and he does sweep me off my feet, and we ride away, far away, but that doesn't mean all your troubles are gone. It just means that you're away, all right, but you've still got troubles, or maybe life is always a pain, even when it's not so bad. I still love Jack, and he's a good guy, real good, even if he's not the one I dreamed he'd be. But like everyone says, a dream is a dream!

Whereas one youth celebrates an idle, escapist dreaming, another youth has discovered the intense, ideological energies that a suitably disposed mind can generate through pictures and words, all connected into a story of sorts, and all made doubly exciting: the cortex and the genitals both decidedly turned on. It is perhaps too easy for some of us adults, who have come to eager or reluctant terms with the social and economic system, to dismiss out of hand the diversionary or petulant or idiosyncratic or self-indulgent or utterly wild, even crazy, side of adolescent sexual fantasies—even as the bumbling, stumbling, childish or naïve side of adolescent sexual activity is also emphasized somewhat single-mindedly by us: the innocence and insecurity and inexperience that a show of romanticism or boisterousness or silly coquettishness attempt to conceal. On more occasions than I like to remember, I have found myself calling a given youth's reverie "crazy" or "absurd" or "manipulative" in its intentions (to sidetrack me, the listening physician), when a little later on the youth clarifies a point, almost as a critic does with a difficult passage in a novel or some fairly dense-sounding or dense-appearing lines in a poem—and then I'm suddenly made to realize (through the efforts of the youth, or, yes, through some lingering goodwill in me that is now less threatened) that I've been directly addressed with intelligence and concern by

someone whose feverish head and hotly responsive body deserve
no more condescension or dismissal than many all too cool,
calculating, and not so illuminating pronouncements I've learned
to take ever so seriously.

For example, I find the imaginary Cheryl Tiegs a shrewd judge
at times of the Roman Empire, and also an alert observer of how
that empire (among others) continues to have all too ardent admirers
and followers in dozens and dozens of privileged classrooms. One
can see how valuable the fantasy of the so-called adolescent is in
helping him to develop his ideas about this society:

> I kept telling her we should forget everything but herself and
> me. To hell with this stupid world. But she said, "Where can we
> go and not be right here?" She's right. There aren't any desert
> islands we haven't ruined. We're all over Antarctica. Look at Bikini
> [sic]—what we did to that place, exploding our atomic bombs.
> Even "Gilligan's Island" had to end: They all came home!
>
> Once I was looking at a picture of Cheryl, for the one-billionth
> time, and I realized *she* was *my* island—my safe and secure island,
> where no one else but me goes! I couldn't help but realize that
> there must be a million guys out there doing the same with Cheryl,
> but none of us knows each other, and that's fine! Then I thought
> to myself, If some of these guys who are so damn mean and selfish
> in this world, and who want to kill and want to grab all they can—
> if some of these guys could have Cheryl, then maybe they'd forget
> all their lousy, rotten plans. If Caesar knew Cheryl, maybe Gaul
> could have had a quiet time back then—or quieter than it ended
> up having after those Romans took charge of things.
>
> I'll tell you, I'd be willing to give her up, hand Cheryl over to
> the Caesars of this world, if it would work like that, if there'd be
> some quiet and peace for the rest of us. It would be tough on me,
> but I'd do it. But that's my craziest idea yet!

II

The Social Profile

GEOFFREY STOKES

Robert Coles has suggested, by way of William Carlos Williams, that the adolescent years are a time when everything from sex to social injustice to the temporary inability to find a book in the card catalog of a library seems particularly intense. To the extent that this is true—and both memory and observation tend to confirm it—perhaps we as parents, educators, or simply as concerned observers of our nation's conditions make too much of teenage sex. Perhaps this book does, but I think not. While its intensities—the quotidian visits from "Cheryl Tiegs," the terrors of an unanticipated pregnancy—may be all-consuming to adolescents, the theory and practice of adolescent sexuality is of concern to us all.

Some reasons for this concern are immediately obvious. In a society that remains more or less committed to notions of equality and equity, the much-discussed "epidemic" of teenage pregnancies—together with the increasing feminization of poverty—is a major and legitimate field for public-policy response. This necessary social debate may be waged on fiscal grounds or on moral—or, as in many discussions of abortion, on some confusing amalgam of both—but it can't afford to stray too far from the facts: that is to say, what kids *do,* and what they *believe.* Despite the limitations of survey research, it is an irreplaceable tool in such discussions.

The information in this survey may also be of immediate practical concern to those of us who are, like myself, parents of present or prospective teenagers. As the survey reveals, most adolescents find it hard to talk to us about sex. While it would be misguided to attempt to project any *particular* kid's behavior from a survey, this study unquestionably provides needed, and to some degree "secret," information about the norms of behavior and morality against which American teens are constantly testing themselves. Used properly, this information can perhaps help us respond to a confused or unhappy teen with more sensitivity and intelligence.

In addition, and in the long run perhaps most important, the survey and interviews corroborate Dr. Coles's main point: that the routines and rituals of teenage sexuality and abstinence are the preeminent ground on which kids confirm or discover the ethical and moral standards they will carry with them into adulthood.

1

Sources of Sexual Information: How They Learn

All living creatures, from single-celled plants to the most complex animals, are capable of reproducing themselves, but so far as we know, only humans are capable of *understanding* their sexuality. This understanding isn't necessary for the survival of the species—anthropologists have reported the existence of long-established societies that apparently make no connection between intercourse and reproduction—but it plays a central role in creating and maintaining a social order. It is our understanding of our sexuality that lets us distinguish restraint from taboo, intimacy from exploitation, and allows each of us to rediscover the concept of love.

At first glance, America in this final quarter of the twentieth century seems an almost ideal place for kids to accomplish such necessary human learning. Ours is an open society, informed by post-Freudian concepts about the less obvious aspects of sexuality, and committed to universal education. In addition, a large number of American parents, who are, in theory, the primary sexual educators, are committed to values and morals that they try to teach their children.

So one would think that with all the *conscious* effort to educate, and with all the willy-nilly instruction provided by movies, advertising, television, and the print media, American teenagers would be extremely knowledgeable on the subject. Indeed, perhaps in reaction to the 1960s, one hears frequent complaints that kids are "growing up too soon," being "cheated out of childhood." But it's not true. The *Rolling Stone* survey demonstrates a lack of fundamental sexual knowledge that, when combined with the level of sexual activity, can only be called alarming.

Let's begin with a look at what kids know and don't know, move through the sources of their (mis)information, then briefly consider some of the public-policy options now under heated debate.

The misconceptions about the extent of kids' sexual knowledge are probably based on the fact that our culture exposes them to bits and pieces of information about almost everything. But when our respondents were faced with a relatively simple factual question about human reproduction, almost half (45%) failed to answer it correctly. Asked to check the one best answer to a question about when a woman can get pregnant, kids responded as follows:

- When she has sexual intercourse the first time (18%)
- When she has sexual intercourse before she's 16 years old (1%)
- When she has intercourse several times during a month (23%)
- When she does *not* have intercourse, but the boy climaxes near the opening to her vagina (2%)
- All of the above (55%)

There was *no* statistically significant difference between virgins and nonvirgins in answering this question, a fact that contributes to our understanding of the recent statistics showing that teenage pregnancies in the affluent New York suburban counties of Nassau and Rockland rose by almost 50% during the 1970s. Whether such pregnancies end in abortion, adoption, or unwanted children, the consequences for those young mothers—and for society—are severe.

But given teens' lack of knowledge on the only slightly more esoteric subject of *preventing* conception, such undesired pregnancies seem inevitable. Though the condom is by far the most usual birth-control method used by teenagers, kids who were asked to choose the one best answer about its correct employment responded as follows:

- The condom should be pulled on so there is space at the tip (7%).
- Condoms should not be kept in hot, dry places (2%).
- New condoms should be used each time (12%).
- All of the above (35%).
- Don't know (44%).

The figures look only slightly less disastrous among teens who have actually had intercourse. Fewer than half (48.5%) gave the

TABLE 1 Primary Information Source (by percent; because of rounding, percentages may not always total 100% precisely)

Information On:	School	Parents	Sex Partner	Friends	Books/ Media	Clinic/ Doctor	Sibling
Reproduction	50	23		15	9		2
Birth Control	37	17	1	17	20	4	4
Masturbation	21	12	1	32	30	1	3
Homosexuality	22	14	1	26	35		2
Sexual Techniques	14	9	17	26	32		2

correct answer, and more than a quarter (26%) checked "Don't know."

Though it's hard to draw much comfort from these figures, more than half of all teens did answer the question about conception correctly, and almost half of the kids who presumably most needed to know got the second. Where did they learn what they *did* learn?

Table 1 shows that for just about half of American teenagers, such learning—at least on the least controversial sexual topic, reproduction—occurs in the classroom, and close to a quarter learned from their parents. But because much formal instruction about reproduction is essentially reportage—egg travels here, sperm there; stamens, pistils, birds, bees—it can be relatively value-free. Other subjects—birth control, homosexuality, sexual techniques—are more problematic, and it is precisely in such areas that schools and parents seem to turn responsibility over to the street corner.

Thus, though kids are about three times as likely to learn about reproduction from their school or parents as they are on their own, the ratio is exactly reversed when it comes to sexual techniques. Not surprisingly, the shift is even more marked among kids who have had intercourse (and hence, sexual partners), as shown in table 2.

But even once one recognizes that parents and educators tend

TABLE 2 Primary Information Source for Nonvirgins (by percent)

Information On:	School	Parents	Sex Partner	Friends	Books/ Media	Clinic/ Doctor	Sibling
Reproduction	48	22	1	16	10		2
Sexual Techniques	8	5	41	22	23		

to shy away from controversial subjects, the question of whether they are wise to do so remains difficult. One need only imagine Sister Mary Elephant attempting to teach Cheech and Chong how to perform oral sex to see that the classroom may not be the proper venue for such instruction. Besides, too many schools can't even teach reading.

Most teachers—though there are noble and notable exceptions, like Dr. Mary Calderone—approach sex education halfheartedly, as though, unlike algebra, it were something kids ought to learn at home. As we have seen, however, most of them don't, and even allowing for indirect and oblique communications, almost half the teens (45%) reported that their parents taught them *nothing* about sex.

It appears that parents who did attempt to give guidance almost overwhelmingly brought a positive attitude to the subject; only 3% of the teens reported learning from their parents that sex was "not healthy and normal." Despite the vast majority's teaching, however, most kids do *not* find it easy to talk about sex with their families. Three out of four say it's hard to talk to their fathers, and 57% find their mothers tough going. Only about a third (36%) say they would ask their parents for any desired sexual information, while almost half (47%) would turn to friends, sex partners, or siblings.

Our interviews suggest a number of reasons for the general failure of parent-teen communication on sex. Even with mutual goodwill, for instance, parents may be awkward teachers, as one New York City Catholic boy revealed in recalling his mother's instructions: "When I was about five . . . on TV, they had this cartoon on, and it showed a plane refueling another plane. The other plane had lost a lot of fuel and they had this tube running across, and she said, 'That is how the beginning of sex is.' " It is extremely hard to see how this metaphor could be other than mystifying.

More frequently the interviews suggest that a fundamental, though often unstated, difference in value systems between parent and child leads to a mutual tentativeness that can have dire consequences—such as unwanted pregnancy and abortion in the case of this urban 15-year-old: "I must have been slightly ignorant when it happened, or I would have known I was capable of having a baby. My mom should have pushed it into my head a little more.

She told me that she'd told me to come to her when it was time for me to have sex and she'd get me some birth control, but she must have said it *very* softly."

"Did she ever explain to you about sex?"

"Not really. I remember once I wanted to see how a tampon would go in and she wouldn't show me."

Even allowing for the obvious possibility that this girl was trying retroactively to shift some responsibility onto her mother, a basic and important communication does seem to have been botched. Other parents never even come that close. Despite their training as psychologists, an intelligent ninth-grade girl's parents undermined their good intentions by a crucial, "sophisticated" assumption that their daughter was sexually active: "A couple of months ago, before I'd even *talked* with [my boyfriend] about having sex, my mother used to say she knew that I had slept with him, but I hadn't. . . . It was upsetting to me that she didn't believe me that I hadn't slept with him. It was just upsetting to me, and she always asked me to talk to her and I just never found the need to talk to her. . . . I just don't have problems I can't talk to my friends about."

There is a sense here that parents and kids are between a rock and a hard place. A parent can be blamed either for nosiness or for not being intrusive enough; a kid can either find it hard to pry out even basic information or can feel pestered to death.

One might hope that *because* of their routinization and impersonality, schools, which are more than twice as likely as parents to provide instruction on reproduction and birth control, would be more effective at the job. But one difficulty with the lockstep of curriculum (and with the fear, common both to parents and teachers, of putting ideas into kids' heads) is that even effective instruction may come too late. One North Carolina 15-year-old reported having just learned about condoms as part of a junior-high-school sex-education class. He had, however, already been sexually active for more than two years: "And then I realized, man, I've been taking a lot of chances. Thirteen, fourteen, fifteen . . . Lord's been good to me."

And even when sex education is timely, schools can manage to make this extremely important topic a bore. As an academic subject, sex may appear as remote as Latin or Greek, and insofar as the schoolroom is the single major source for teenagers' information about reproduction, much of what they told us they were taught is dispiriting. One 14-year-old northern California boy, a nonvirgin, described his class as all "these dumb little books, and it would say 'a boy's nut is about the size of a walnut'—stuff like that. And all the boys already know what size their nuts are. The girls would probably know, too. And I don't think they could teach me anything, either. Maybe some little things like how many sperms there are in a drop of come—something like that. But I don't even *want* to know that. It's not going to help *me* any."

A school system like his may appear to be taking its sex-education responsibilities seriously, but the potentially unpleasant consequences of sexual ignorance argue that the curriculum's emphasis on theory is misplaced. In the effort to avoid controversy, schools embrace boredom.

But it could at least be argued that this school was *trying*. Others, even with the excuse of a teachers' strike reported by another California 15-year-old, seem to be somewhere between casual and shameless:

"Did you ever have sex education at school?"

"No."

"Nothing at all?"

"No. This year they require family life, which is probably equal to sex education where, you know, they teach you all about the stuff you'll be doing when you get older and all that. Well, before the strike got settled, they had classes and I was at a drivers' ed/ family life and it was only for two days and I didn't learn anything."

"Part of a drivers' ed class?"

"Yeah. Drivers' ed and family life, like the strike really screwed up everybody's schedule."

"So you did that two days of family life?"

"It wasn't worth—"

"What kind of stuff did they talk about?"

"Let's see. They talked about keeping girls from getting pregnant, like the Pill, and they had this thing—I don't know—there's a string you stick in your vagina, or whatever, for girls. I don't know what it was called."

"A string? To keep people from getting pregnant?"

"Yeah, it was to keep the sperm from going to the egg."

"Probably an IUD?"

"I think it was some kind of abbreviation like that."

"A little thing you put in there?"

"And I think we talked something about VD, but I'm not sure. It was two and a half weeks ago."

The last part of this conversation is interesting in a couple of ways. It at least suggests that a kid who can't remember for more than a couple of weeks anything about a subject as potentially important to him as VD may actively have resisted learning. This resistance may represent a failure of timing reversing the experience of the North Carolina boy—the information might have seemed useless even in this boy's most lurid fantasies—but in any case, the notion of combining sex education with drivers' ed seems like a bad joke. And too many classrooms lacking the excuse of a strike sounded like the one the boy described. Surely any "sex education" like his would drive a curious participant to his or her peers for information.

Among friends, however, information is likely to be both random and—because it may be mixed with boasting, exaggeration, and outright lying—inaccurate. The boy who not unreasonably professed himself uninterested in the similarity between his testicles and a walnut sought more interesting facts from his friends: "You listen to other guys that know and don't let them know that you're listening. Like you're talking and you say, 'I did that,' and they talk about it."

"So you lie to them and say you did it?"

"Yeah, and they're telling you how it happens sometimes, like what they did. Like I didn't know how to give a hickey really until a year ago."

I suppose it's useful to learn how to give hickeys (though I always thought of them as a by-product rather than as the *ding an sich*), but one imagines that a participant in such conversations, aware that he is lying, has to face the possibility that everyone else is lying, too. In which case, misinformation is almost certain to be transmitted. A 13-year-old Catholic girl from the Pacific Northwest, whose sexual experience was limited to kissing, had "learned," for instance, that "if you kissed a boy, you'd get pregnant and a bunch of other stories like that. Even if you held hands, you might get pregnant, or if you touched him, you'd get pregnant, and some people said if you had anything to do with the boy, you'd get pregnant."

Finding these perhaps atavistic cautionary tales implausible, she "decided to get it from my mom and my dad," which in her case seems to have been a sensible response. But even older and presumably more sophisticated teens have been exposed to—and apparently believe—some highly questionable "facts." A 17-year-old high-school senior from eastern Pennsylvania, sexually experienced and regularly using birth-control pills, told us that if she got pregnant, "I'd have an abortion, because of the birth deformities."

"What kind of birth deformities?"

"If it's a girl, the genitals. . . . It may start out to be shaped like a penis from the Pill if you don't wait three months."

"Where did you find this out?"

". . . Family Planning."

"So that if you get pregnant while you're on the pill . . . ?"

"The women's genitals may have the shape of a penis . . . not the whole penis; it will be deformed."

One assumes that this information resulted from the girl's misunderstanding what she had been told, and that though the initial communication might have been faulty, it wasn't aggressively wrong. Kids who operate on their own, however, even if they manage to understand perfectly what they read or hear, can fasten on to some pretty unreliable sources. One California 14-year-old, for instance, got a lot of her basic knowledge from "the 'Forum' section in *Penthouse* about three years ago. I was really into reading those." That section, consisting putatively of letters from readers detailing their most bizarre sexual experiences, may be entertaining to those with a taste for gymnastics, but even leaving sexism and politics aside, the fertile imaginations of Bob Guccione's editors are not ideal inspiration for a 14-year-old of either gender.

In this case, the magazines were her father's, and it seems from our interviews that boys are somewhat more likely than girls to have their sexual imaginations shaped through misogynist demiporn of the *Penthouse/Hustler* mode. A number of girls, however, did cite Judy Blume's novels (especially *Wifey*) as sources of information, and one sexually experienced New York 15-year-old complained about Blume's *Forever:* "In the book, they have sex that lasts two minutes, and the girl would never look at his penis, or when she did she freaked out because it was too ugly to her. I thought, This can't be. . . .''

And so she, like more than a quarter of teenagers, turned to her friends for further information, but of course magazines like *Forum* are likely to have shaped their thinking as well. In a number of instances, it would seem "locker-room talk"—which even when true is an objectification and hence pornographicization of sex—is no longer a male prerogative. A 17-year-old college freshman reports dormitory conversations about "how guys kiss and their foreplay and also . . . someone asked about this guy she had been involved with, and another girl said, 'Is he well hung?' We talk about a guy's penis, how long he lasts, how big it is.''

"Is that important, how big it is?''

"No, not . . . Small ones are generally looked down upon, but average is fine. It doesn't have to be big at all, but we'll talk about it. Like one time, one of my friends, she had given hand jobs to practically all the guys we socialize with, and she would just go on and describe their balls and stuff. They look different from each other in size and stuff. It was really interesting. Also, how hard did a guy get, and is there any problem where the guy doesn't get real hard?''

A 15-year-old Illinois Catholic virgin admitted, "We all kiss and tell. We share experiences. . . . We say, 'Didn't that gross you out?' 'Didn't that bother you?' Like the first time we gave hand jobs, we didn't know that a penis was so massive. That freaked us out. Things like that.''

Such conversations, though the level of detail might unnerve any young man imagining them, seem relatively positive—overfocused on minutiae, perhaps, but exchanging a good deal of gossipy information. Straight-ahead boasting seems more typical among boys, as this conversation with a 17-year-old Boston Hispanic reveals:

"Do your friends know you're a virgin?''

"No.''

"You tell them that you have fucked?''

"Well, I told them I fucked a couple, and that Chita, she had oral sex with me. I told them I had sex with three people. We count them actually.''

"And why do you say this to them?''

TABLE 3   Sources of Correct Information

	School (50%)	Parents (23%)	Partner (0%)	Friends (15%)	Media (9%)	Clinic/ Doctor (0%)	Siblings (2%)
1. At first intercourse	17%	17%		24%	18%		20%
2. Under 16	0%	0%		5%	2%		5%
3. Frequent intercourse	25%	21%		23%	21%		25%
4. Climax near vagina	2%	1%		4%	0%		4%
5. All above	55%	63%		49%	56%		49%

"So I wouldn't be separated from them. I don't want to feel different."

"They all say they've been laid, too?"

"Yes."

The best that can be said of such bragging sessions is that they represent a rather haphazard way of accumulating sexual knowledge. Even when the tales told are true (as they might have been, say, in the girls' dorm), there is surely no guarantee that they contain the right part of the right information at the right time. Looking at the way kids *actually* learn about sex, one could argue that the percentage of correct responses to the factual questions in the *Rolling Stone* survey turns out to have been surprisingly high.

In fact, though this might be somewhat discouraging to professional educators, when we put two parts of the survey together—when we match the answers the kids gave about reproduction with the source of their knowledge on the subject—there is *no* evidence for the superiority of classroom instruction (see table 3).

Though some differences exist among groups (kids who learned about reproduction from their parents or from reading were marginally more likely to answer correctly than kids who learned in school, and kids who learned from friends or siblings were even less so), the associations are extremely weak, and the differences not statistically significant.

This table can't comfort those who advocate greater sex education in the schools, but we should remember that these figures make no distinction between fully committed, professional efforts and an embarrassed gym teacher mumbling to a bored or giggling class.

Still, in a time when school systems all over the country are facing budgetary limits, it's hard to argue that sex education has proven effective. And in addition to the dollar-cutting that threatens most aspects of the school curriculum, sex education is under particular political attack from Moral Majority splinter groups who fear that sexual knowledge leads to sexual activity and argue that "sex education belongs in the home."

Home learning might well be preferable for reasons that have nothing to do with the conservatives' antisex bias, but ample evidence suggests that wherever sex education may belong in the abstract, the actions of most parents put the choice in practical terms between the school and the street corner. Between those two choices, street-corner education is strongly associated with both greater sexual ignorance and sexual activity. Those who learned about reproduction in school were somewhat *less* likely to be sexually experienced than those who learned about it from friends, the media, or siblings.

Though this difference is too small to be statistically significant, there *is* a significant difference when schools become more assertive in their teaching role. Students who have been exposed to a greater degree of in-school sex education (including birth control) are clearly associated with a *lack* of sexual activity. Only a quarter (25%) of those who learned about birth control in school have had intercourse, but a third (37%) of those who learned about it from friends and more than half (51%) who learned from siblings are nonvirgins. Those who learned from their parents—the Moral Majority's preferred mode—differ hardly at all from those who learned at school.

In the face of this, and in the face of the distressingly low level of accurate sexual information held by *all* teenagers regardless of their degree of sexual activity, any public-policy attempts to cut back the level of formal sex education in the schools would represent a triumph of ideology over evidence.

2

Influences and Beliefs:
What They Think About

In addition to techniques and facts, of course, we learn *values* from our society. Such teaching may be direct or indirect, by lecture or by example, but it is so pervasive that sudden, broad-based changes in social value systems are consequently rare. Yet changes do occur over time, and the question of what kids think is right and wrong in the sexual arena—and of how they come to think that way—is important not only for the present but also for what it indicates about the likely shape of future value systems.

To get a quantitative handle on the answers, we asked a series of three related questions. Imagining a hypothetical couple in a number of different relationships to each other (ranging from "strangers" to "planning to get married"), we first asked what kinds of sexual behavior were okay for a girl and for a boy. Finally, we asked the kids what they thought their parents would say was okay for them to do in those same situations. The answers are summarized in tables 4, 5, and 6.

Two facts of major importance jump out from these tables. First is the death of the double standard: Though boys are still accorded slightly more freedom than girls for casual sex (with strangers, friends), the next three lines on their charts are virtually identical. Second is the huge gap between what kids believe is right and what they perceive to be their parents' beliefs. I suspect, from my own experience as a parent, that this gap is understated, for many teenagers would classify themselves as "in love," thereby allowing themselves considerable sexual latitude, while their parents might regard them as merely "going together."

Since, as the tables dramatize, about two-thirds of teens report

TABLE 4

	Percentage of Teens Believing It Is Okay for a *Girl* to				
If the boy and girl are	Make Out	Touch Genitals	Have Oral Sex	Have Sexual Intercourse	None of These
strangers	24	5	3	3	70
friends/dating	66	20	11	10	20
going with each other	67	39	23	23	12
in love	64	45	36	41	10
planning marriage	62	46	40	60	9

TABLE 5

	Percentage of Teens Believing It Is Okay for a *Boy* to				
If the boy and girl are	Make Out	Touch Genitals	Have Oral Sex	Have Sexual Intercourse	None of These
strangers	27	8	4	5	64
friends/dating	66	24	12	13	18
going with each other	67	39	24	25	11
in love	65	45	36	41	8
planning marriage	61	47	39	61	9

TABLE 6

	Percentage of Parents Believing It Is Okay for Children to				
If the boy and girl are	Make Out	Touch Genitals	Have Oral Sex	Have Sexual Intercourse	None of These
strangers	10	1	0	0	81
friends/dating	47	4	2	1	44
going with each other	59	8	4	4	30
in love	60	17	8	11	24
planning marriage	57	26	19	29	20

that their sexual behavior isn't influenced by what their parents think, the question arises: What *does* shape teenage values? The conventional answer is that slippery beast called "peer pressure," and like most truisms, the easy answer has some evidence to support it. As indicated by the very different answers given by virgins and nonvirgins about the number of their friends who've

TABLE 7   Friends Who've Had Intercourse

	None	A Few	About Half	Most	All
Virgins	23%	55%	11%	8%	2%
Nonvirgins	2%	26%	19%	40%	14%

had intercourse (see table 7), most kids do hang out with friends they think act more or less the same way they do. More than three-quarters (78%) of virgins believe that none or only a few of their friends have had intercourse; among nonvirgins, the percentage falls to a quarter (28%).

But "peer pressure" is a less than satisfactory answer, for it begs the question of where peers get *their* beliefs. Moreover, it doesn't deal with a surprising fact indicated by our survey: that most teens regard their peers as conservative in some ways. Fully 44% of all the teens, virgin and nonvirgin, thought their friends would be "shocked" to learn they were having sexual intercourse, and a significant number (15%) of those who'd actually had intercourse felt the same. Asked if a kid their age who had *not* had sexual intercourse was socially backward, a huge majority (95%) said no. This number included 90% of the nonvirgins, so the notion that some group of sexually active kids is forcing others to follow them by calling them "squares" is as ludicrous as the image of the dirty old man hanging around the schoolyard trying to get young innocents "hooked on marijuana."

But ideas do not fall from the sky, and if immediate peer-group behavior isn't the influence it's often believed to be, we might push the question back another notch and see whether the traditional sociological groupings—economic class, regional location, career expectations—are associated with certain values and behavior.

To do this, we can go back to table 4 (what is okay for a girl to do in certain situations), isolate a couple of variables, and match the kids' answers with the information they gave us in other parts of the questionnaire. On the question of whether it is okay for a girl who is going with a boy to have intercourse, there was no significant regional difference among teens, nor—somewhat more surprisingly—was there any association between believing intercourse was okay and family income or each kid's own educational

TABLE 8 Okay for Girl Going Steady to Have Intercourse?

	Prot.	Cath.	Jewish	Other	None
No	79%	80%	80%	75%	63%
Yes	21%	20%	20%	25%	37%

plans. And though the absence of any religious affiliation seemed to be associated with greater tolerance for sexual activity, no single specific sort of religion produced significantly different results from any other (see table 8).

Finally, though on this question blacks seemed somewhat more liberal than whites, the most interesting differences in moral beliefs were between urban teens and their suburban and rural counterparts (see table 9).

But *all* these differences—by race, by presence or absence of religion, and between urban and other teens—vanish when love enters the picture. No matter where teens live, no matter what their race, family income, educational plans, grades, or religion, about 41% of them believe that love makes it permissible for a girl to have sexual intercourse when the couples are going steady. The impact of love is even more dramatic among girls than boys. Only 14% of *all* girls (including 13- and 14-year-olds, about 95% of whom disapprove) think it's okay for a girl going steady to have intercourse; but if the girl is in love, more than 35% approve, including more than half the 17- and 18-year-olds. "All you need is love," sang the Beatles. Almost two decades later, American teens still tend to agree with them.

All of which naturally raises the question "What is love?" Asked simply whether or not they have ever been in love, most teens seem to have no difficulty with the concept: About two-thirds say they have. But our interviews reveal that particularly for older teens—many of whom can look back and say, "I *thought* I was in

TABLE 9 Okay for Girl Going Steady to Have Intercourse?

	Urban	Suburban	Rural
No	72%	83%	82%
Yes	28%	17%	18%

love, but . . ."—the definition of *love* is every bit as slippery as it is for adults. Even some younger kids hedge their bets, like the 14-year-old boy from a Washington suburb who first said he'd been in love, then promptly added, "I don't know if it's exactly in love, but it was something."

Whatever it is, there's no doubt kids believe love carries moral weight. A 17-year-old girl from eastern Pennsylvania provides a good example of a recurring theme found in the interview:

"I think that if you really love somebody, that [sexual intercourse] is okay. Now, you know, I know a lot of people who must go out for the fun of it and have sex, but I don't put them down for that, because they believe what they want to believe, and I have a different set of values, but I have to really love somebody before I can do anything with him."

"What about making out or petting?"

"There's nothing wrong with that."

"If you're going out on a date, no matter if you're in love or not in love?"

"For me, if I'm going out with somebody and we've gone out before, you know, I'd kiss him."

"On the first date, what would you do?"

"Probably just kiss him—a little farther than that, but not too much."

"How long would you wait to go further?"

"If I really like him and we really get along, probably the next few dates would determine it—it depends how he acts. But I wouldn't have sex with him really until I was sure I loved him—and I'd let him know that, too."

"As long as the girl is in love, do you think there should be an age limit, thirteen years, fourteen . . . ?"

"I don't know. That's up to them, but at thirteen to be pregnant, that would be a bummer."

Though a nonvirgin, this girl can by no ordinary use of the term be called "promiscuous." She has had sexual intercourse only with her boyfriend, and they've been going together for almost three years. Yet the "in love" standard is extremely encompassing. Even at the age of 13, more than half of all teens (53% of boys, 52% of girls) say they have been in love, and the percentages finally rise to include 85% of 18-year-old boys and 83% of 17-year-old girls.

Of course not all teens believe in a moral standard even this broad, but among those who don't, some give a nod to it in absentia. A 15-year-old New York City girl, a virgin only because her father called downstairs to her at a crucial moment and interrupted her last night with a summer boyfriend she felt she loved, told us that once she "wanted to have sex with someone I loved. Right now, I don't think it really matters if I have sex with someone I love. I think after I have sex for the first time, I think then it'll matter." Later on in our interview, she added that "if I was to go out and have sex with someone who I didn't love, I wouldn't be a virgin anymore, but I still wouldn't have made love."

This distinction, though it is perhaps a rather tortured effort to justify some future scratching of an itch caused as much by curiosity as anything else, also represents a not unusual effort to establish *some* standard for right and wrong in a world where inherited rules seem unconvincing. Though teens surely behave differently from one another, we found relatively few who weren't attempting to be, by their own lights, "good." Indifference was professed only by a 14-year-old rural Pennsylvania boy who shrugged off a question about premarital sex with "I'd probably say it's wrong, but it's just something you do."

His is a cynical and lonely voice, yet his perception is not without accuracy. We have to remember what the survey showed about teens' conservativism. Teens do want their friends to think well of them, and most do want to be "good." That combination can make the generous standard of love a flag of convenience. In the absence of notions like commitment and responsibility, horniness can look an awful lot like "love."

In any case, the attempt to form standards is different from living up to them, and among teens who've had sexual intercourse, two-thirds do not plan to marry their most recent sexual partner, a third say they did not love him or her, and a quarter say they weren't even girlfriend or boyfriend.

3

Logistics: Where and When and How Much

For most teens, though by no means all, the moral and logistic questions about going all the way arise relatively late in their teenage sexual careers. The usual teenager will go through a round of nonsexual and presexual activities (parties, school dances, group dates, church activities, etc.) before pairing off in a serious way. More than 80% of all kids have been to parties (and about half of those attend one a week or more), and an even larger percentage have gone out in a co-ed group. About a third have never gone out on a date, however, including about 75% of 13-year-old girls and 80% of 13-year-old boys. Since fewer than 8% of teens have never kissed someone of the opposite sex, it's obvious that—particularly among younger kids—sex is what happens in quasi-public situations.

Such experiences, it is safe to say, are not always unalloyed successes. A 14-year-old Jewish boy from a Maryland suburb recalled his first party—and his first kiss—from when he was "late eleven, early twelve": "See, this girl had kissed before, so she started Frenching and she had the worst-tasting mouth and her hands were rubbing up and down my back, so I thought I might as well do it too. I think about it now and I feel like a real jerk, you know, moving up and down on a couch. Dumb. Really stupid."

Most kids don't express their distaste for early kisses in such vehement terms, but all except the very youngest tend to look back on kissing games with disdain. One boy admitted that Truth or Dare "was a good game sometimes," but the big winner—and loser—among such games is Seven Minutes in Heaven. The game involves a player's choosing a partner of the opposite sex (usually by lot, but sometimes just by pointing), after which the couple retires to a private spot for seven minutes. Usually, in the case of chaperoned parties (which includes most parties where kissing games are still being played), the private spot turns out to be a closet, but it is in any case theirs for seven minutes, to do with as they will. Predictably, the game is wonderful if you're attracted to your partner, endurable if you're friends (couples have been known to agree to do nothing), and a full-bore gross-out if you actively do not like the one with whom you are to experience Heaven.

Mercifully, perhaps, the era of kissing games is short-lived; certainly most 14-year-olds consider them hopelessly passé. By the time kids are that age, their parties have taken on roughly the shape they will keep for the next several years: There is almost certainly music, and often dancing; frequently, though by no means universally, dope or drink, and usually some degree of sexual activity. As a 15-year-old New Jersey boy says, "Sometimes no parents are downstairs, and some people'll go into a bedroom. You see everybody making out, you know, but not really in front of you." What this last more than implies is that the process of forming couples, however temporarily, is well at work by the time kissing games are over.

Often, it seems from our interviews, any selecting process that goes on at parties is limited, to the extent that it is bounded by stratifications that exist at the students' schools. "Open houses" are comparatively rare these days and the formal or informal guest list reflects daylight social patterns: heads party with heads, jocks with jocks, preppies with preppies, hitters with hitters. Though there is some overlap and blurring of the lines—the freak who is high scorer on the basketball team, the cheerleader who travels with bikers—most kids seem to welcome the security that comes with sharing a group identity. Among other things, the informal screening processes more or less assure that everyone at the party is "all right," that no one is going to gain or lose a great deal of status by pairing off with anyone else. Thus, while cliques limit freedom in an absolute sense, they expand it practically.

So how do kids choose partners? Though there's a certain amount of lip service paid to "personality," it's clear that looks count. As a 17-year-old black New York City girl put it, "Looks attract you. Like if you see some guy eating potato chips and he's real ugly, and another guy getting punch, you'll probably go get punch instead of potato chips." She adds, however, that "if that guy is an asshole, maybe *then* you'll get potato chips, and if that guy is nice, you might stay all night at the potato-chips place." A North Carolina black, also 17, gave a somewhat more elaborate but similar response when asked what turns him on: "Her face first. I always look at the face, and I think, That's a nice-looking girl, and so on. At our school, a lot of people are mixed with something else, I noticed. Like they have girls that are black with a little Indian in them, you know. Like this one girl, she has a little Chinese in her and she has slanted eyes and she's black. Everybody goes after her, right. I look at the face, then the body. I want a girl with a good face, and then I look at the body and whatnot. Then I see what she acts like, what's her attitude, you know. You got some girls think they can beat *you*, they can tell *you* what to do. I know a few."

It's fair to suspect from this guy's attitude that he might qualify in the New York girl's mind as the asshole at the punch bowl, but both are describing a similar process: In a party situation, you first check out the people who are immediately, physically attractive; questions of personality are finally determinative, but they usually arise only *after* the initial attraction. At a party a funny-looking kid is at the same disadvantage as a funny-looking salesman—there's a lot to overcome, and not much time before the door slams shut. Just as such salesmen are likely to do better if they've had some initial telephone contact with their prospective customer, kids who aren't conventionally handsome or pretty are apt to have relationships develop more gradually.

Thus, a quite pretty and sexually experienced 17-year-old New York girl says of her current boyfriend, "I wasn't really attracted to him physically at first. I'd known him a long time and I'd just thought of him as a friend. But then we started being close as friends, and I was really happy about that, 'cause I think it's really important to have friendly relationships with guys, you know—it can be fulfilling in a different way than a friendly relationship with a girl. So we started being close, friendly-wise. I was mostly attracted to his personality more than physically, but as I grew closer to him ... I know he's not beautiful—I wouldn't turn my head and stare at him if he was someone I didn't know—but I'm very comfortable with his body, and the way he looks and acts, and now I love everything about him. But it was definitely not his looks at first."

"Is that usually the way with you? That you're not necessarily attracted by looks?"

"No, usually the guys I've gone out with before have all been, I thought, very good-looking. The relationships I had when I was younger were on a pretty superficial level anyway, so there wasn't much to know about a guy except for the way he looked, and that was pretty much what they were looking for, too. And you're more likely to be attracted to a guy who's really good-looking, even if he's an asshole, than to someone who's really nice but deformed."

Implied in these last three conversations, and present as a thread through many of our interviews, is that girls are somewhat more tolerant of physical imperfection than boys are (though both sexes seem to grow less rigid in their demands as they grow older). Both boys and girls finally regard good looks as a sort of entrance exam, a threshold any potential partner must cross, but boys tend to set the threshold higher, to be more exclusionary. To some degree, I suspect this contributes to the strikingly different self-images normally attractive girls and boys have of their bodies. Asked what they liked least about themselves, or what worried them about their appearance, an occasional boy expressed a desire for bigger muscles, more height, or a longer penis, but virtually *every* girl was quick to list some (often invisible) imperfection: breasts were either too big or too small; hips, in particular, were "gross," or "flabby"; and perfectly well-formed legs were judged "skinny." Though the double standard may be fading in the area of sexual behavior, it seems still very much present in the ways boys and girls judge their own and others' sexual attractiveness.

Once the judgments have been made (or, in the case of negative self-image, overcome), teens face the considerably more difficult task of communicating what they feel. For some, these preliminary conversations apparently come easily, at least as one southern "Joe Cool" summarizes his method: "I come over there and start talking to her, but if she's with someone else—I'm always the kind of person, if it was your girl, I wouldn't try to impose myself on her as soon as you turned your back or something like that, I've never been that kind—but if she's by herself or just came in or something, I go over and ask if she wants to dance or something like that, or start to whisper in her ear or something."

The number of "or somethings" peppering that description leads one to believe that this boy's approach may not be quite as smooth as he obviously believes it to be, and many kids are frank in expressing how difficult they find such conversations. One girl, a 14-year-old Jewish virgin from an urban private school, summed up her behavior with a guy she was interested in as "very strange."

"How do you let him know you're interested? Do you flirt with him?"

"Yeah, I'd flirt with him."

"How?"

"There's one guy on my block that I like a lot, and we're also like 'Hey! How ya doin'?' You know, just smile a lot. And I would say one of my ways is I stick my finger in a person's rib from behind them—you know how you do that to surprise somebody. I always do that to people. I don't know if that's one of my ways of flirting, though; mainly I kind of get really shy and paranoid about the way I should act in front of a person that I like. It's like, 'Oh, no, he's going to think you're a fool. . . .' "

Another girl, a year older, seems to have found a more direct approach. Seeing a boy she'd previously been attracted to at a rock club one night, she waited for a slow song to come on, then "I went up to him and I asked him to dance. And he loves to dance, so, you know, he didn't say no, and I started grinding with him, and I guess he really enjoyed that."

"What's grinding?"

"It's a very close dance where, like—I can't really describe it. It's like where you have *his* leg, and then *your* leg, and then *his* leg and then *your* leg, and it's just extremely close and I think it's very sexual. And then after that he asked me for my phone number. . . .' "

Though this story has a happy ending, or at least a happy middle, the risks of miscalculating a full frontal assault are real. A 16-year-old Catholic girl from eastern Pennsylvania describes being on the receiving end: "Last weekend I saw a guy at a party that I thought was good-looking, but he was a real asshole. I wouldn't have anything to do with him. If I was alone with him, I'd make sure I'd come up with some excuse to get away. Then he came up, and there's this tradition of 'warm fuzzies.' You put 'em around your neck and you're supposed to kiss the person who gave them to you. He put it around my neck and started Frenching. I tried pulling away, but he had my head in such a lock I couldn't. I almost threw up. That grossed me out."

Faced with the possibility of grossing out the object of their desires, it's surprising more kids don't act like the 14-year-old California Hispanic who told us, "There's a girl I like right now, but I don't think she likes me very much."

"What are you going to do about it?"

"I don't think there's much to do. I can't win her heart by slaying a dragon."

"Do you wish you could?"

"Yeah, it wouldn't be that bad. But it's kind of out of the question. If she really likes somebody else, I don't think it's gonna work."

"Does that make you sad?"

"Yeah."

Yet kids often do manage to overcome shyness, shaky self-esteem, fear, and awkwardness to make the first move, which is at least sometimes reciprocated, since 85% of American teens report they have had a girlfriend or boyfriend, and 45% had one currently. It is in such relationships that teenage sexuality begins to assert itself.

4

Intimacy: How They Express It

To flirt successfully—to find a boyfriend or girlfriend—is, for most teens, to open the door to sexual adventure. This intuitive truth can be seen quite explicitly if we look at the differences between virgins and nonvirgins, as shown in table 10.

Actually, because of rounding, the table slightly understates the case: In more than 99 out of 100 instances, having had a boyfriend or girlfriend is a precondition for having sexual intercourse. Though there clearly *is* such a thing as casual sex, most teenage sexual exploration occurs in couples that are, however temporarily, "established." In chapter 9, we'll take a look at the way couples bond; though the subjects certainly overlap in some ways, this chapter will focus less on the development of emotional intimacy than on the physical intimacies that usually precede intercourse.

Though kissing, as we've seen, is very much a staple of early adolescent boy-girl games, it is also the traditional first step on the ladder of sexual activity (and, of course, it remains a favorite activity even among experienced teens—one 14-year-old girl reports, "I could go on French-kissing with a guy forever, but they always have to go further than that"). Eighty-eight percent of all adolescents have kissed, the overwhelming majority of them (97%) by the time they are 15 years old.

Girls tend to have their first kiss when they are younger than boys (73% of 13-year-old girls have kissed, and only 66% of boys), and though the gap narrows with age, it exists throughout adolescence. For all ages, the percentages for those who have kissed are 87% for boys, 90% for girls.

The pattern for breast play begins to develop in a similar way—

TABLE 10 Ever Had Boyfriend or Girlfriend?

	Nonvirgins	Virgins	Total
Yes	99%	85%	87%
No	1%	15%	13%

20% of 13-year-old boys have touched a girl's breast, while 25% of 13-year-old girls have had their breasts touched. Over the next year, however, the pattern shifts dramatically; 54% of 14-year-old boys have engaged in breast play, but only 31% of the girls.

A couple of reasons can be suggested for this change. The first is that even at relatively early ages, girls tend to go out with older boys, and since girls whose breasts have developed are likely to be more attractive to those older boys, some 13-year-old boys are perforce going out with girls who as yet have no breasts to feel. (This may turn out to result in some further anomalies, as a just-turned-14 California girl who had indulged in breast, but not genital, touching revealed when asked if she thought she was about as sexually active as her closest confidantes: "Well, she's flat up top and she would not let a boy go up her shirt because she'd be embarrassed. So he went down her pants, but he didn't go up, so I don't know.")

A second explanation may simply be the different ways a couple might describe the same event. A boy who after a certain amount of maneuvering managed to get his hand on a girl's breast, only to have her remove it, might say that he had indeed touched a girl's breast; while she, who had quickly removed the offending hand, might feel she'd never allowed her breasts to be touched.

The second explanation seems somewhat more likely, for the gap continues through all ages, with a total of 58% of boys saying they had touched a girl's breast, but slightly less than half (49%) of girls admitting to having had their breasts touched. When the situation is less ambiguous—a question about kissing breasts—the gap shrinks to less than two-tenths of a percentage point; 38.3% of boys have kissed a girl's breast, and 38.1% of girls have had their breasts kissed. When these totals are broken down by age, however, they suggest that among younger teens, boys are more sexually active than girls, and that the active girls are more likely during

TABLE 11   Percentage of Teens Who Have Experienced Vaginal Play

Age	13	14	15	16	17	18	Total
Boys	23	50	46	50	56	61	47
Girls	18	21	37	46	61	60	37

these years to have a greater number of partners.

This suggestion seems borne out by the teens' answers to the relatively unambiguous questions about genital touching. In the first of these, boys were asked, "Have you ever played with a girl's genitals with your hands?" Girls were asked, "Has a boy ever played with your genitals with his hands?" The percentage answering yes, by age, is shown in table 11.

It appears here that teens' behavior—especially girls'—is influenced by their standards of right and wrong. Younger boys are more active than their female classmates, but by the time teenagers get old enough to have had "serious" relationships, to believe themselves "in love," both sexes are equally active. The pattern reappeared when we asked the question not about girls' genitals but boys'. Overall, however, the two types of genital play are not quite equal—43% of all teens have participated in vaginal play, but only 40% in penile. And strikingly, about twice as many teens have had vaginal play with more than one partner than have had penile. At least some boys, like this 14-year-old northern Californian, complained. Talking about his girlfriend, "the first girl I ever finger-fucked and the first girl I ever ate out, I tried to get her to jack me off, but she kinda would and she kinda wouldn't."

"She would touch you, but—"

"But she was scared."

"Was that the first time she'd done it?"

"Yeah."

"Did you tell her what to do?"

"Well, we were just talking and I took her hand, put it down there, and she got the idea."

"Did you have an erection?"

"Yeah. Just kissing her I got an erection. Of course. I didn't get anything hardly because she didn't do anything, and that's usually how you have to do it 'cause the girl usually won't ever start and she'll never do anything."

TABLE 12   Enjoy Cunnilingus

	Not at All	Small Amount	Medium Amount	Large Amount	A Great Deal
Boys	3%	6%	34%	29%	29%
Girls	5%	14%	32%	29%	20%

From across the country, a 14-year-old Washington, D.C., girl confirmed the pattern, though she did not seem at all aggrieved by it. Talking about genital petting, she said, "If you've been going with a guy for six months, it's not unusual."

"Do you usually find that petting below the waist is performed by guys to girls?"

"Yeah."

"Do the girls reciprocate?"

"No."

But as girls get older, expectations change. A 16-year-old Pasadena girl said that she used to play with her boyfriend's penis because "after a while, you begin to feel like you're obligated. Like here I am, I've been going with this guy for a year, he must be getting impatient." And a 16-year-old midwestern girl who also reciprocated found it just got boring after a while. "Like giving him a hand job, I'd start watching TV. He seemed to get more pleasure out of it than I did."

When it comes to oral sex, which for many kids comes *before* intercourse, the percentages—though not necessarily the plea-sures—are almost reversed: 41% of 17- and 18-year-old girls have performed fellatio, but only about a third of the boys have performed cunnilingus. This mismatch becomes especially interesting when we look at the different degrees of enjoyment boys and girls receive from oral sex, as reported in tables 12 and 13. It appears that many of the teenage girls who do give oral sex do so less for their own

TABLE 13   Enjoy Fellatio

	Not at All	Small Amount	Medium Amount	Large Amount	A Great Deal
Boys	0%	6%	21%	33%	39%
Girls	10%	27%	35%	16%	12%

TABLE 14   Enjoy Fellatio a Large Amount or More

	Actual	Perceived by Opposite Sex
Boys	72%	96%
Girls	28%	44%

pleasure than for their partners' and that boys are to some extent aware of this.

Since the enjoyment figures for intercourse are *much* more equal (see chapter 7), one can understand why 41% of teens who've had intercourse have never performed fellatio, but it at first appears mystifying why fully 16% of those who've performed fellatio have *never* had intercourse. Our interviews made the practical if unromantic answer clear: For a number of teens, oral sex is a mode of birth control.

A 17-year-old New York girl, now regularly sleeping with her boyfriend, said that she liked oral sex "definitely both ways," and added, "That's what we used to do before we could start having sex, because we didn't have protection and stuff." And a 14-year-old California boy, who'd had oral sex separately with two girls on a camping trip, said they didn't have intercourse "because they were afraid they'd get pregnant. I asked her and she said no."

"You asked them both?"

"No, just the one in the tent. She said oral sex. I asked her if she wanted to go all the way and she said no, and she goes, 'There's still oral sex.' I didn't know she was going to say that."

This boy, though he responded to her suggestion, seemed slightly taken aback by the *notion* of oral sex. Other kids, including both boys and girls who had found the idea of oral sex exciting, had some initial difficulty with the reality. As another 14-year-old boy described his first attempt at cunnilingus, "We'd been doing stuff for a long time, then I went down to eat her out and it smelled. It stunk."

"Like what?"

"I don't know—kind of like no other smell."

"And you didn't like the smell?"

"No, I didn't like it. So I went up. And then later on, though, I did eat her out and it didn't smell as bad."

"You got used to it?"

"I don't know. It just didn't smell as bad."

And a 17-year-old New York girl who lived with her 36-year-old lover bluntly said, "I don't like it when he comes in my mouth. I did it once and I can't take it. Plus I heard it's very fattening—six hundred calories or something. Not that it makes any difference; I just don't like the way it tastes—it's very salty and it makes me gag."

Though most boys seem to overcome whatever temporary aversion they might have had (a 17-year-old Washington boy said, "I love oral sex. Honestly, I think it tastes good, it really does. I get into it"), many girls felt that their boyfriends were reluctant to perform cunnilingus. Their reactions could be described as confused, hurt, or angered, and all three feelings were often present simultaneously. A 16-year-old politically liberal Californian said, "It's hard for me to deal with it, because, you know, when you *know* that a guy doesn't want to give you head but you're giving him head, you wonder if it's because he doesn't like *your* vagina or what. I mean, you wonder if it's personal, or if that's the way they feel about every girl. So it's real hard."

A 15-year-old New York Catholic girl had been through similar experiences, but her response, which was *absolutely* without any male mirror image, picked up the language advertising agencies have created for vaginal deodorants: "Some of my girlfriends say 'I don't understand, my boyfriend won't give me head and . . .' and I go 'Why?'

" 'Oh, he doesn't like the smell or something.'

"I say, 'You have to tell him that you give it to him and he smells, too.' As long as you keep clean, too. With me, I will not *let* him if I don't feel clean. I like to feel very clean and fresh, and personally I like to take a shower before I make love and after I make love. He likes that, too. He always says to me, 'Oh, you're so fresh I can't believe it, you're the sweetest thing.' So it's very nice."

However, she went on to say, "he likes me to give him oral sex, too, but I don't like to as much because . . . I don't know. . . ."

"What's wrong with it?"

"I don't know. I don't find it—it wouldn't be wrong if it wasn't the excretion. I don't like that, I don't like to taste it. I don't like that at all. I would—I don't think you should just spit it out right in front of him, because that's just so very rude, but . . . I couldn't swallow it. I used to do it more because I did it for him because he likes it so much, but now I say, 'I can't really get into it.' So I tell him I'll do it to him, but I won't do it until he excretes in my mouth. I don't like that. But occasionally I'll do it. It's once in a blue moon now; before it was much more because I did it for him because he liked it so much."

To some extent, then, it appears that teens do not find oral sex an equal-opportunity employer. The question of which partner may find more pleasure varies sharply from couple to couple, but despite their differences, most couples operate on an unstated but clearly felt ethical standard and so reach an accommodation. A 15-year-old who went to an all-girls Catholic school articulated the principle when she was asked what most turned her on: "The ears really get me. Like somebody licking your ear, blowing. I don't know. What else? I like getting head. Those I think are the two best."

"How about giving head?"

"It's not my favorite thing to do."

"But you do it?"

"Yeah. I'm not going to let them give me head and not give them head."

On the basis of our interview data, however, there is one glaring exception to the rule of accommodation: Black boys do not like cunnilingus. Indeed, based on the not untypical comments of a 17-year-old Boston black, they are at best ambivalent about oral sex: "A lot of white people do that. Black people, I don't know. I wouldn't, I'll tell you that."

"Why do you think it's more popular with white than black people?"

"I don't know—'cause white people are more freaky than black people, I guess."

"White people have this myth that black people are sexy."

"They are. But *that's* overboard, that's *way* overboard, that's in the water . . . that's practically *drowning*."

"What about a girl giving you a blow job?"

"If a girl does it to a guy, that's a different story. But a hundred percent black people say this—she would not dare kiss him after that. He wouldn't let her."

TABLE 15   Performed Cunnilingus

	Yes	No
White	22%	78%
Nonwhite	20%	80%

"You think white guys would let a girl kiss them after that?"

"Well . . . that's how a lot of people feel."

Partly from the excruciating courtesy shown to the white interviewer, this conversation seems thoroughly sincere. It was echoed, several hundred miles to the south, by a North Carolina boy: "Down here we mostly say that—not to be prejudiced—but they mostly say that white people do that. We say that white people have been known to do stuff like that."

In at least one case involving an integrated New York couple, the boy acknowledged that his feelings threatened their relationship: "I just don't wanna do it. I just don't want to go into the bit of, in street terms, what they call 'eating.' I just can't do that."

"Something about it you don't like?"

"The whole thing. I just couldn't do it. She has wanted me to do this for some time, but I just couldn't do it."

"Is it the taste, the smell?"

"I'd say both."

"But she really wants you to do it?"

"Yeah. For a while I decided I don't think I will. But I still think about it. Is it actually worth not doing it and losing her at the same time? I still think about that. I'm not totally sure yet."

And therefore, like the girl who felt obliged to perform fellatio, he feels obliged to forgo it: "I would like it if she would, but the way I look at it, in fairness, if I'm not going to do that for her, why should she do it?"

The vehemence in these interviews makes one expect the statistical analysis of the questionnaire to mirror a sharply lower level of cunnilingus, and perhaps fellatio, among blacks. But it reveals no such thing (see tables 15 and 16), and one might pardonably regard the verbalized negative attitudes toward oral sex expressed by blacks as merely, well, lip service.

In talking with all teenagers, regardless of gender, we were left

TABLE 16 Performed Fellatio

	Yes	No
White	21%	79%
Nonwhite	20%	80%

with the clear impression that oral sex was felt not so much as a simultaneous pleasure as an alternating one. A 17-year-old East Coast boy said, "I was in—what do you call it?—cunnilingus, and she was totally in another world. I was enjoying myself, 'cause I dig it, but I was frustrated and I would have liked to say, 'Hey, why can't we try something else?' And I couldn't get it out. And this is a girl I really feel comfortable with, like one of my longtime girlfriends, and I was contented. . . . She had said earlier that she didn't want to have intercourse and I said that's okay. That didn't bother me too much, but sometimes I feel that I'm being deprived, like I'm being used as a tool sometimes."

Or, as a 15-year-old girl more succinctly and poignantly put it, "When you're having oral sex performed on you, you feel kind of lonely."

5

Solo Performances

Oral sex may under some circumstances feel lonely, but masturbation is the loneliest kind of sex. And, except for kissing, the earliest: The average age at which teens start to masturbate is 11 years and 8 months, and 90% of those who masturbate during their teen years start before they turn 15.

It is not, however, a universal experience. Slightly fewer than half (46%) of all boys reported masturbating, and about a quarter (24%) of girls. The percentage of boys who have masturbated rises steadily through the teen years (the figure for 18-year-olds is 60%), but the percentages for girls seem not to be age-linked.

The figures for boys present some difficulty, however, for the rising percentages of those who say they've masturbated don't at all match the data about the age at which masturbation begins. Based on our interviews, in which more than three-quarters of the boys said they'd masturbated, it appears that the rising percentages in the questionnaire represent not an increase in the numbers of boys masturbating but an increase in the percentage willing to *admit* it.

To a surprising degree, teenagers still regard masturbation as in some way shameful. Fewer than a third (31%) said they felt no guilt when they masturbated, and a fifth (20%) felt either "a large amount" or "a great deal." More to the point, it seems to be something that kids just don't talk about. A 15-year-old California boy who said he masturbated, but "not often at all," was asked if there were "some guys among your friends who are known for doing it quite a bit." His answer: "They wouldn't be my friends if they were known for doing it."

An older boy from a Maryland suburb agreed that the subject was essentially taboo.

"What about masturbation, do people talk about that?"

"No, not at all."

"Do you think most people are doing it?"

"That's kind of tough. You kind of look at 'em and you wonder, Does he jerk off or not? You think about it. I figure most people do. It feels good, it can't be hurting you. It's really kind of tough, though, because you don't just go up to a person and go, 'Do you masturbate?' I can't think of any of my friends that ever admitted to me that they do."

Even when kids agree intellectually that masturbation is fine, the reticence remains, as this 17-year-old boy from rural Pennsylvania indicates: "Masturbation to me is . . . I guess it's necessary. I guess it's a necessary part of sexuality considering that it's a part of experimenting with your body to get sexual pleasure. I mean, there are going to be times when you get sexually aroused and there is not a girl around and you have no other choice. Either that or jump in a cold shower. Masturbation, I see nothing wrong with it. I'm sure there is probably not a single one of my friends who can say they've never masturbated. But then again, they probably wouldn't say they masturbate often even if they did."

Among boys, in particular, masturbation has a bad name because it's a tacit admission of not having "real" sex, and one California 13-year-old linked it with homosexuality: "Most of my friends, you know, they think that masturbating is really bad—you shouldn't do it, you know. They think you're gay if you masturbate or something. . . . It's kind of like, don't do it or else they're gonna think you're gay or something." The notion was echoed by a 17-year-old rural black: "That's something we don't talk about. That's something you just don't talk about around the table with the guys. I don't even think you can talk to your own girl about that. 'I masturbate, I get my jollies from that,' I mean. . . ."

"What would they think of you if you said something like that?"

"They'd call me a freak. Like 'You ol' freak, get away.' You'd be like a black clown—nobody wants to be around a black clown. Next thing you know, you have no friends. You might be turning to gay people, they might be your last choice. . . ."

"A total change in your life—"

TABLE 17   Ever Masturbate?

	Nonvirgins	Virgins
Yes	43%	32%
No	57%	68%

"I'm telling you."

"—from telling someone that you've masturbated?"

"What always had me, something like that—I mean, what brings up a discussion of that anyway? Somebody saying, 'Yeah, man, I got me a blow job,' and you be saying, 'Yeah, man, I masturbated'?"

As it happens, kids who admit having masturbated are significantly *more* likely to have had intercourse than those who say they've never masturbated (see table 17). Yet facts don't really seem to have much effect on kids' feelings about masturbation, and boys are not alone in regarding it as possibly shameful and certainly private. Even those who enjoy it (and more than two-thirds—68%—say they enjoy it a medium amount or more) can find the topic awkward, as this exchange with a 15-year-old New York nonvirgin dramatizes:

"Did you masturbate growing up?"

"Yeah, a couple of times, yeah, sure. It's hard for girls to say 'Yeah, I masturbate,' but I did, yeah."

"How do you feel about it."

"It's so personal."

"Satisfying?"

"Yeah, it's satisfying, definitely. Now I can masturbate and I can have an orgasm. Before . . ."

"How do you generally do it?"

"Fingers. Magic touch [laughs]. I find this very personal. I don't like it when some girls say, 'Do you masturbate?' I just say, 'It's none of your business.' But we all know that means yes when someone says 'None of your business.' But we don't discuss it. I find masturbating very personal. . . . It's a wonderful thing that you can be with yourself and not have to have a guy around to have an orgasm. That's good, because when you really need to do something like that and you don't have anybody and you're horny, what are you gonna do?"

In some cases, the awkwardness leads to a sort of jesuitical distinction that obscures the facts. One boy, for instance, reported that he "didn't masturbate, just touched it is all." And a 17-year-old girl with a steady boyfriend said that she had masturbated, but "nothing inside me or like that."

"Just with your finger?"

"You know, not *inside*, just on the outside, I guess, a little bit. . . ."

"Could you make yourself come to an orgasm?"

"Yes."

The ambivalent feelings about masturbation continue despite the general absence of the old myths—going blind, getting warts on your hand, etc.—but one athletic 14-year-old boy did offer a version of *Dr. Strangelove*'s "precious bodily fluids" theory:

"A lot of teenagers masturbate a fair amount; some don't. Which group do you belong to?"

"Those who don't."

"Have you ever?"

"Yeah. To tell the truth, I have."

"But you don't so much now."

"It makes you weak, that's what I heard. My mom's old boyfriend played on a professional soccer team and he said making love or having sex makes you weak—that's shooting sperm, so shooting a lot of sperm makes you weaker and weaker and weaker, and you don't want to walk around school sagging around 'cause you can't even hold yourself up."

For all their private anxieties, however, most teens felt intellectually certain that there was nothing wrong or dangerous in masturbating, perhaps because of the kind of schoolroom education a 17-year-old California girl reported: "They're always stressing in school how it's not bad, it won't stunt your growth and all those old wives' tales. In health class they'll always say how it's good for you, and I never understood why people thought it was bad."

But even when kids feel sure that what they're doing is morally and physically okay, masturbation can cause stress. It is, after all, a learned skill. Ambivalence compounds the problem, and for one Boston boy who had started masturbating early and had never ejaculated, every "failure" was an occasion of panic.

"During the years when you were worried about this, did you talk to anyone?"

"I didn't talk to anyone, kept it all to myself."

"What was that like?"

"It was hard, it was really hard, 'cause that was practically all I thought about. I thought I was sick, or something was wrong inside."

"You never talked to a doctor?"

"Didn't bother, because I didn't want my mother to find out."

"For three years this was?"

"Yeah."

"How often would you try during the three years?"

"Four times a week or so. To see if there was any progression or anything came out, but nothing."

Even success can be something of a mixed blessing, especially for boys. One told us that "one day I did it and a fluid came out—you know, sperm—and I got scared then because I thought something had busted inside."

In general, however, masturbation is more often an occasion for fantasies than for fears, most commonly (57%) about one's girlfriend or boyfriend, although 36% reported fantasies about strangers, 41% about acquaintances, 11% about relatives, a quarter (28%) about rock stars, 44% about TV or movie stars, and 17% about made-up people. In general, boys were more likely than girls to have fantasies—more than three-quarters (77%) of the boys and only about two-thirds (68%) of the girls—but the objects of their fantasies are noticeably different.

Boys and girls were about equally likely to have fantasized about their girlfriends or boyfriends, but boys were much more likely than girls (52% to 38%) to have had fantasies about strangers. At least among teenagers, the oft-repeated notion that women's fantasies are likely to focus on some mysterious figure who will force them to do all the things they won't allow themselves to admit wanting to do seems to be a myth. By a somewhat larger margin (56% to 38%), boys are more likely than girls to have fantasies about acquaintances. Though the sexes are equally likely to have fantasized about rock stars, this, too—given the relative paucity of female rock performers—may indicate a generally higher level of fantasies among boys; they are certainly more likely (by 52% to

37%) to have fantasized about TV or movie stars. The sexes are approximately equal, however, when it comes to fantasies about made-up persons.

With one exception, none of these fantasies appears close to being the sort of obsession that Coles's "Cheryl Tiegs" boy reported. The only fantasies that more than 15% of the kids have more than twice a week involve boyfriends and girlfriends. Here, however, almost a fifth of kids (19%) fantasize at least once a day, and more than a third (36%) do so twice a week or more. Boys and girls do not differ significantly in terms of the frequency of these fantasies, and both genders have *frequent* fantasies about their boyfriends and girlfriends more than twice as often as they do about other subjects. To a certain extent, then, it appears the chicken-and-egg question can be answered: Having a sex partner is more likely to lead to sex fantasies than having sex fantasies is to having a sex partner.

These figures are for all fantasies; our interviews suggest a further difference between the genders about masturbatory fantasies. Boys more often talked about responding to images: Asked if he used magazines when masturbating, a 15-year-old New Jersey boy answered in an almost mystified tone, "Of course." Girls reported responding to words. Some girls, indeed, seemed positively turned off by images, and one college freshman described pornographic movies as "ridiculous. It stops being sexy when it's, you know, you see pores and lots of red stuff and you can't figure out really what it is."

But words seem to be different. One girl reported using Xaviera Hollander's book as an aid; and a 16-year-old Californian, when asked if she masturbated to orgasm, said, "Yeah, yeah, and I *can* do it really quickly, but I always try to prolong it because I think it's more pleasurable that way. And a lot of times there are some favorite passages I have in—what's it called? It's *Fanny Hill*, but it has a different name—*Diary of a Pleasurous Woman* or something like that—and there are some wonderful passages in it I love to read as I masturbate, it's really fun. And I've read them so many times now it's almost like I've memorized them. . . ."

This girl masturbated "like twice a week, and sometimes it's every day," but she was between boyfriends at the time. Most of the teens who masturbate report doing so less when they have a girlfriend or boyfriend—especially, of course, when the relationship includes genital play, oral sex, or intercourse. But in some instances, sex is sex, and a suburban New York girl said, "Inevitably I find that when I have sex more often, any type, I become more interested in it. I get used to not having it for periods of time and become much less interested in it. So [having a boyfriend] doesn't work as any sort of relief, really. Because I found out that when I went away to school, I was used to having sex a lot at home with my boyfriend, and it was really a problem being really horny the first couple of weeks."

She solved her problem by masturbation—a substitute for "the real thing," perhaps, but it's difficult to argue that the substitution is in any way bad. Some boys complained about finding it messy, but except for that, masturbation—as long as a teen doesn't talk about it—is virtually without negative consequences. And as one boy put it, "It's the best contraception there is."

6

Virginity: Keeping It and Losing It

For about a third of all teens masturbation is at best a temporary outlet (and 57% of kids who've had intercourse report *never* having masturbated). For these kids, sex includes—and may be dominated by—sexual intercourse. For each of them, there had to have been a first time.

Most kids, with the obvious exception of rape victims (see chapter 10), planned this momentous occasion. Well over half (57%) talked the matter over with their first partner before having intercourse. And contrary to popular myth, girls are more likely to have had such discussions, hence are less likely than boys to have been "swept away"—by a margin of 64% to 52%.

In only a few cases (5%) did boys or girls report having their first intercourse with a stranger. For about a quarter (23%), the first partner was a friend; for more than two-thirds (68%), it was a boyfriend or girlfriend. Boys appear to have been more casual than girls, however, for about a third (32%) of them describe their first partner as a friend—more than half as many as the 61% whose partner was a girlfriend. By contrast, more than three-quarters of the girls (76%) were with their boyfriends, only 13% with friends. As these figures might lead one to expect, girls tend to be significantly older at the time of their first intercourse, as is borne out by the figures in table 18. These figures are cumulative, however, and by the end of their teen years, during which about half will have had intercourse, the percentages of boys and girls tend to even out (see table 19).

More than half the teens (54%) first had intercourse at their own or their partners' houses; another 15% were at a third party's house. Only 2% first had intercourse in a hotel or motel—not

TABLE 18 Age at First Intercourse

	Age 13 or Under	Age 14	Age 15	Age 16	Age 17 or Older
Boys	50%	15%	14%	16%	3%
Girls	18%	16%	32%	24%	11%

surprising given the ages at which first intercourse took place—
and 15% were outdoors. The traditional trysting place, a parked
car, was actually used by only 12% of teens.

In general, no matter what the degree of planning or of logistic
difficulty, most of the teens regarded their first experience positively.
Only 5% said they were "sorry they had the experience"; the rest
were pretty evenly divided between "glad" (43%) and ambivalent
(46%). Girls, however, were *much* more likely than boys to express
sadness or ambivalence, as shown in table 20.

These figures are particularly interesting since girls were more
likely than boys to feel that their relationship with their first partner
improved after intercourse. Their lingering regret, despite the
improved relationship, suggests that girls place a higher value on
virginity *per se*. About half, for instance, want to be virgins when
they marry, while only a third of the boys want to marry a virgin.
Rather poignantly, 15% of the girls who'd already had intercourse
said they had wanted to be virgins when they married.

To some degree, however, the girls' feelings may be based less
on moral or intellectual beliefs than on the disappointing or painful

TABLE 19 Percentage at Ages 13–18 Having Had Intercourse

	Age 13	Age 14	Age 15	Age 16	Age 17	Age 18
Boys	12%	28%	31%	44%	38%	46%
Girls	6%	11%	26%	30%	46%	53%

TABLE 20 Feelings about First Intercourse

	Sorry	Ambivalent	Glad	No Feelings
Boys	1%	34%	60%	5%
Girls	11%	61%	23%	4%

physical characteristics of their first time. A 15-year-old New York,
asked if she enjoyed it, said, "No, it hurt. I was like 'Aaargh.' "

"Was it what you expected it would be?"

"Not the first time. I was like 'People *enjoy* this?' "

And another 15-year-old, a New York Catholic, said she "wasn't
expecting it to hurt that much. It was like total pain. Even after the
first minutes of pain, it's still like you're too sore to enjoy anything.
I didn't expect that at all."

A large number of girls talked to us about pain, but in many
cases the strength of the relationship made the discomfort easier
to bear. At least in terms of overcoming pain, emotional factors
may be more important than the boy's facility as a lover. An 18-
year-old Long Island girl who first made love to her boyfriend
when she was "sixteen, maybe fifteen," ran into technical difficulties
with her boyfriend's condoms the first time they tried intercourse.
"They weren't lubricated and it was just too rough. Because I'd
never had sex before, we just couldn't get it in." She got fitted for
a diaphragm, and about a month later—though he was presumably
not much more accomplished—they succeeded. "We were both so
excited. We hadn't been able to sleep the night before. I can't
remember that much leading up to it, but we had sex a few times—
I guess about three times—that night. He really enjoyed it; I found
it emotionally nice, but painful. It was like a *good* hurt, but still it
hurt; it was uncomfortable. But it was something we both felt really
good about. We were active sexually for the rest of our relationship."

In some cases, however, the expectations for the event may be
so inflated that virtually any experience is likely to come as a
disappointment. A 16-year-old California girl told us, "Afterwards I
thought, That wasn't what I thought it would be like."

"What did you think it would be like?"

"I don't know. When I was thirteen, we moved to England, and
I was so lonely. We were there five or six months. I didn't have
any friends, so I read all these romantic novels, because I didn't
have anything else to do. So I had this feeling that guns were going
to go off and stuff, and that didn't happen. . . ."

One 15-year-old New York City girl sounded as if no level of
expectation, however low, could have prepared her for the disappointment of her first time. "The first time it was horrible. He was
so excited at the fact that he could first have sex with me that it

was so quick that it wasn't even *anything*." But even in so disappointing a circumstance, the fact that they were a *couple* helped. "It was very quick, but it was sentimental. We cuddled a lot afterwards, which was—I find that to be the best part about making love. Cuddling and waking up in the morning and stuff, that's nice."

She went on to say that their sex life eventually became "wonderful," and it seems that for all the male nervousness that boys (and their girlfriends) reported to us, loving couples can usually get past the momentary clumsiness of inexperience. Especially for girls, however, no amount of polished technique can compensate for a lack of love. Another New York girl, a 17-year-old black, had what at first seemed a perfect experience with a man a few years older.

"So the first time you did it, was it planned? Did you know you were going to sleep with him?"

"Yeah."

"Did you like it?"

"Yeah, it was great. I had a really good time. It was a nice rainy day, in a beautiful loft with a huge bed on the floor. He's a photographer; he was very sensual."

"Did he seduce you or did you seduce him?"

"I don't know. It was kind of mutual. It took a long time. I was there for about ten hours."

"In bed?"

"No, first we talked for about three or four hours. Then, slowly, for about two hours we were in bed. It took about five hours."

"Was it what you'd expected?"

"Yeah."

"Did it hurt?"

"Yeah. He gave me this pain-killer, some prescription thing that you can get out of any drugstore. Tylenol and something. Just to relax you. I was very tight, so it did hurt."

"Did he know you were a virgin?"

"Yeah."

"Did that make him nervous or anything?"

"I don't think so, but I talked to him afterward and I said, 'I understand you might be nervous, because some people are scared that if you have sex with a virgin they're going to hold on to you and not let you go because you're the first or whatever.' He wasn't the kind of person who would call me every day or every other day. He'd call once or twice a week. I had to call him."

"Did that bother you?"

"Yes, it did. I didn't know he was living with this woman, so I didn't understand what was going on. I thought he put on such a great act, being so nice and concerned, and then not showing any concern at all afterward."

Though this girl doesn't regret her physical experience, she felt emotionally betrayed. She did, however, have the comfort of knowing that however misled she might have been, she'd willingly— even eagerly—given up her virginity. Often, that's not the case and one partner or another will be more eager. This seemed to happen almost as often to boys as to girls, but the boys felt less regret afterward; certainly, though they might have felt emotionally trapped, they weren't physically pressured in the way that a 17-year-old Pennsylvania girl recalled having been when she was 15.

"I was baby-sitting one night and I asked him to baby-sit with me and we were just petting and kissing and he tried to get my pants off. And I was really—I guess I was almost in tears and I didn't want to. And he just was so—not forceful as far as hit me and get rough with me, but really putting the pressure on."

"Physically or emotionally?"

"More emotionally. And part physically. Not that it was plain he would force himself on me that way, but then he tried to and I just didn't want him to at all. I think I was really scared about him hurting me or something and I knew it wasn't right. That's the way I've always been brought up."

Finally, however, she gave in. "I don't know if I was tired of saying no or if I wanted to see what it was like. It seems so long ago and I can't remember."

"Did you like it?"

"Not really. Part of me did, but I think if I would have liked him it would have been so much more special. Every time he'd say about having sex, I'd say no. I knew deep down I didn't want to because with him it really seemed dirty. There wasn't anything there—it was just to fool around."

So many other girls described similar situations that the experience of having to face physical force doesn't seem all that

TABLE 21   Parents' Marital Status

	Married	Separated	Divorced	Widowed
Nonvirgins	26%	40%	49%	32%
Virgins	74%	60%	51%	68%

uncommon. Some yield—"I didn't want to take my clothes off and he started forcing me and I was going 'No!' and he was trying to calm me down because I was really upset and then I just said 'Okay' "—but most of the girls who reported being pressured managed to maintain their resistance. Though there's certainly no easy way to explain the difference, we can take a look at the various factors that might be associated with greater sexual activity and see if any seem especially significant.

To begin with, teenagers whose parents are divorced or separated are much more likely to have had intercourse than those whose parents are married or widowed. On the extremes, the gap is almost a two-to-one margin, as shown in table 21.

This gap seems too great to be simply the result of the increased opportunities for privacy kids may find in single-parent families where the parent is employed outside the home, a factor that in any case would not explain the gap between the kids of divorced and widowed parents. Our interviews do show that when the parent is dating or has taken one or more lovers, the teenager regards this as a tacit approval of sexuality and acts accordingly. Also, to the extent that parental advice may be a restraint on teens' sexual activities, parents who have "failed" in their own marriages are taken considerably less seriously (see table 22).

Parental income seems to have no effect on sexual activity, and no part of the country is significantly more or less active than any other. Though urban teens are somewhat more likely to have had intercourse than their rural or suburban counterparts, the association

TABLE 22   Do Parental Attitudes Affect Your Sex Behavior?

	Married	Separated	Divorced	Widowed
Yes	38%	24%	20%	45%
No	62%	76%	80%	55%

TABLE 23   Planned Level of Education

	Nonvirgins (%)	Virgins (%)
Some high school	78	22
All of high school	39	61
Some trade school/skills center	42	58
Some college	27	73
All of college	24	76
Graduate school	23	77
Don't know	28	72

is relatively weak, and area of residence makes no difference at all in the age at which intercourse first takes place.

Perhaps because of the possible consequences of unwanted pregnancy, teens' educational plans do make a difference in the level of their sexual activity. Though the correspondence isn't absolutely linear, plans for higher education are generally associated with lower sexual activity (see table 23).

Not surprisingly, the figures in table 23 are supported by the associations between current school achievement and sexual activity. There is a more than two-to-one disparity between the percentages of nonvirgins among those who report their grades as well below average (54%) or below average (51%) and those who are well above average (21%).

Nominal religion is not significantly associated with a particular level of sexual activity, but the 18% who say they are influenced "a large amount" or "a great deal" by religion are far less likely than the average teen to have had intercourse. Indeed, these kids are more likely never even to have kissed a member of the opposite sex than to have had intercourse (see table 24).

To the extent that religious influence is a reflection of parental values, however, it is worth noting that the small percentage of

TABLE 24   Levels of Sexual Activity among Religiously Influenced Teens

Influence of Religion	Never Kissed	Intermediate	Had Intercourse
A large amount	16%	74%	10%
A great deal	13%	76%	11%

TABLE 25   Alcohol Use and Sexual Activity

	Never Drank	Have Used Alcohol
Nonvirgins	13%	47%
Virgins	87%	53%

kids whose parents taught them that sex is "not healthy and normal" were significantly *more* likely to have had intercourse (38%) than those who learned it was healthy (24%). They were, however, very slightly less likely to have had oral sex.

Though we'll look more closely at drugs and sex in chapter 11, it's worth noting here that occasional use of marijuana doesn't seem to have a major effect on sexual activity; regular use—twice a week or more—is, however, associated with more frequent and more casual intercourse. Perhaps most striking, though, is the association between drinking and loss of virginity (see table 25).

Perhaps because alcohol is the most socially acceptable drug, our interviewers found it associated to a great extent with teens' first intercourse. This was particularly true of unplanned intercourse (kids who were planning to have intercourse but were nervous about it frequently reported sharing a joint or two in order to relax). Sometimes it was boys who were surprised (a 13-year-old who was "kind of counting on fooling around" lost his virginity after his date "had taken booze out of her parents' liquor cabinet so we got pretty drunk"), but it was more often girls. One New York 15-year-old who had not yet even been out on a date told us, "I had a party on Saint Patrick's Day in my house—my mother goes away every weekend and so I have a lot of parties—and so all of us were there, and all our mutual friends and stuff. And four or five people slept over that night, and we were both pretty drunk and sort of just fell asleep together and got more involved as the night went on. I don't think he made the first move; I'm pretty sure *I* did."

But especially because of the importance girls tend to place on continuing, loving relationships, girls can find the aftermath of alcohol-influenced "surprises" hard to bear, as another New Yorker told us. "The first time I had sex was in Florida. Me and my mom went camping alone and we were just hanging out, and the night of the Super Bowl I just got together with somebody. It was kind of weird."

"How old were you then?"

"Fourteen, I think, maybe fifteen."

"It was kind of casual?"

"Yeah, it wasn't good. For the first time, it's a sad story."

"Were you drunk or stoned the first time?"

"I was kind of drunk because of the Super Bowl, and I was into smoking pot then. I guess I was out of it, or whatever. I always regretted it."

"Why?"

"You know, all my friends, their first time is a whole special story—they finally found the right guy and stuff."

"Were you disappointed?"

"Just with myself, after, when I thought back on it."

7

The Pursuit of Sex: Making It Better

No matter what the first time may have meant—no matter how casual or how committed—it can only happen once. And most teens who have had intercourse that first time will continue to be sexually active. Though more than half (55%) of sexually active teens said it had been a month or more since they'd last had intercourse, six out of ten (59%) expected to have intercourse again with their most recent partners. Given the difficulties of maintaining a relationship—feelings go sour, families move—that six-of-ten figure is extraordinarily high. Since almost nine out of ten girls (87%) reported their most recent sexual intercourse had been with their boyfriends, it seems especially likely that girls will continue sexual activity once sex has entered their lives; this was true for only two-thirds (67%) of the boys.

With these facts as background, we can perhaps understand an otherwise startling statistic: Fully two-thirds of the teens who said they had a girlfriend or boyfriend at the time they answered the questionnaire had also had sexual intercourse (see table 26).

There is an indication here that ethics (chapter 2) are not unrelated to actions, and most teenage sex does occur within the context of a relationship. It also changes the relationship—generally for the better. Asked what effect their first intercourse had on the relationship encompassing it, only 12% of boys and 15% of girls said the relationship had become worse as a result, whereas 44% of the boys and a whopping 63% of the girls said it had become better.

This does not mean that teenage relationships, even those that benefit from sex, are any easier to sustain than relationships between adults. They are probably more difficult, in fact, for teens

TABLE 26   Have Girlfriend/Boyfriend Now?

	Yes	No
Nonvirgins	65%	38%
Virgins	35%	62%

have to reckon not only with the unpredictable and fluid personality changes of adolescence but also with sharply varying degrees of parental discipline and support. Certainly an outsider has to expect that although more than half (53%) of 15-year-old girls said they expected to marry their most recent sexual partners, they are destined to be disappointed. (The outsider is supported in this belief by the fact that 82% of 15-year-old boys do *not* plan to marry their most recent partners.) But from the outside, of course, any relationship can look like a soap opera.

From the inside, things are different, as a 17-year-old Pasadena boy revealed when he talked about his recent difficulties with his regular girlfriend. They'd been going out for more than a year, and for the last several months had been having intercourse a couple of times a week, but on the night before the interview, "we had intercourse, and I felt that she was really tense. She wasn't talking all this weekend, and I knew something was bothering her. She doesn't want to talk about it; she's said she doesn't want to talk about it, so . . ."

"And you said you can't stand that?"

"Yeah, it bothers me. But—last night we had intercourse and I didn't feel she was that turned on. She doesn't have climaxes very much. That's something that bothers her and bothers me, too."

"Do you try to do what you can to have her climax?"

"Yeah."

"Manually and orally?"

"Yes. That's what we talked about last night. I said, 'What makes you feel good?' So she showed me."

"What kind of things were they?"

"Stimulating her manually *while* we're having intercourse."

"Have you done this before?"

"Yeah, I read stuff about it, but I—I tried it before, but I didn't know that—that—she hadn't told me that really felt good."

"So last night was the first time after all this time she told you?"

"Yeah, we hadn't done that much."

"What was she mad about, or why wasn't she talking?"

"We talked a little bit about it Friday. She seemed mad after the party, and I was asking her why. Well, one of the reasons was that some girl that was at the party, she said was coming on to me. And I didn't notice this. And that's happened before—she said that some people are coming on to me and I don't notice it. I'm generally pretty friendly and I talk to everybody, you know, at a party or something like that, and I don't, you know, I don't notice if somebody is flirting that much or not."

Jealousy, whether well or ill-founded, can threaten lovers at any age, but the question of sexual performance—of sexual *adequacy*—is especially vexing for teens: 82% of nonvirgin teens said their partners' satisfaction was "very important" or "extremely important"; only 5% said it was only "slightly important" or "mattered not at all." The concern increases as teens grow older: *No* 17- and 18-year-old boys said their partners' satisfaction was slightly important, and only one of the 17- and 18-year-old girls said so. Yet this pattern of concern, which is found in teens of every region, color, and economic status, runs up against a hard fact: Most teens lack the broad range of experience that would allow them to feel certain of their own adequacy. Caught in that bind, they can suffer agonies of self-doubt and lowered self-esteem.

Among boys, premature ejaculation is by far the greatest worry. Fewer than 10% report ever having had a problem getting an erection, and only among 13- and 14-year-olds is there any significant difficulty having orgasms. Well over a third (39%), however, say they've had problems with coming too soon. One 17-year-old, who'd first had intercourse with an older schoolmate when he was a high-school freshman, recalled, "Oh, God, I couldn't believe how good it was, you know, I couldn't believe I had this *woman*—'cause she was really developed, too—and I came, I was coming all over the place in about a minute, and I was real embarrassed, that really made me feel like shit."

Another 17-year-old boy, a New York City black, described early orgasm as "a bad sexual experience." Coming too soon, he said, "really tears everything up." Aware of the problem, he sought reassurance by reading about it, discovered he wasn't alone, and regained some of his self-confidence.

Other kids know there's something wrong, but aren't quite sure what to do about it. A California boy, also 17, said he might have a problem "coming too fast, because all the times I did it [snapping his fingers] that was it."

"Did the girls come?"

"No."

"So it wasn't a very satisfying experience for the girls?"

"They didn't complain. I don't know. I usually call them a day or two after: 'Did you have fun?' They'd say yeah, yeah, and laugh. But they wouldn't tell me if—you know."

"When you have sex with your girlfriend, would you want to make it more enjoyable for her?"

"Yeah."

"Do you know how to go about doing that?"

"No."

Though this will probably be no comfort to anxious boys, our interviews reveal that girls do indeed regard premature ejaculation as a problem. One New York City girl, a 17-year-old dating an older man, said her friends often talked with her "about the guys who are 16 they make love to. It's just like get into bed, fuck, and he'll come in five minutes, and that will be it. That's such a drag. I couldn't imagine that. I'd be left sitting there like 'What do I do now?' They'd be wiped out and you'd be sitting there." And a 16-year-old California girl, generally happy with her sex life, said that her boyfriend "sometimes can only do so much and then he's just pooped. He gets really tired. But I can keep going. That's the only problem sometimes."

"When you have sex, do you usually have it more than once?"

"Yeah, unless we're in a hurry or something. But he sometimes—once it happened, he had an orgasm before I did and I just went nuts, so . . ."

"Did he continue with you then?"

"No."

As one might expect, since it is not unconnected with premature ejaculation, about a quarter (24%) of girls report difficulties having orgasms. Interestingly, and contrary to what boys think, this is not the problem girls most frequently mention; the same percentage (24%) say they've had difficulty becoming lubricated, and more

TABLE 27   How Much Do You Enjoy Intercourse?

	Not at All	A Small Amount	A Medium Amount	A Large Amount	A Great Deal
Boys	0%	0%	19%	28%	53%
Girls	1%	2%	28%	25%	45%

than a third (36%) have sometimes found intercourse painful.

Yet despite their occasional difficulties—and despite the fact that a little over half of boys *and* girls worry either "a large amount" or "a great deal" that they are not good sex partners—there's no doubt that kids enjoy sex (see table 27). And that despite the myth, girls are not lying there thinking of England.

Indeed, in many cases they are not lying there at all, for teenage sex is by no means limited to the missionary position, and the range of turn-ons and turn-offs is virtually limitless. A 15-year-old New York girl described some of the things she and her boyfriend had tried during the preceding few months: "Let's see, he's strong so he can lift me up, so we stand up and we make love. I'll wrap my legs around him and my arms. That's good. And I asked my girlfriend if she'd ever done anything like that and she said, 'No, my boyfriend can't lift me up,' and I went, 'Ha, ha, ha.' It's really *good*, too; if you can get a guy to lift you up, it's really good. We've done the dog position. We've done just sitting up. We've done halfway off the bed, like I'll be off the bed, just sideways. We've done so many weird things, like this way, and sideways, and we've done sixty-nine. But I don't like the way he—he can tantalize me and get me excited by having oral sex, but he can't make me come or anything like that, or—I don't know—yet."

"What's your favorite position?"

"Lately? A week ago I came for the first time from being on top, and I just learned how to really get into that, to like it, so I like that now."

A number of other girls, like this 17-year-old, also said they liked being on top: "I like getting on top especially, which I hadn't done. He considers that *me* making love to *him*, which is kind of right. He brought it up and I was very uptight about doing something new; I thought somehow, I can't do it. Then I thought, Fuck it—so I did it and he got very happy. He got into me."

This girl seemed to like the *idea* of being on top almost as much as the reality—something she shares with a 17-year-old northern California boy who said, "I like the expression on women's faces when they're turned on. When they are maybe at orgasm, they get a really neat expression on their face and that's what I really try to ... when I'm having sex with my girlfriend, that's what I want. I want her to let me know by the expression on her face that she's reaching her peak, she had the best orgasm of her life, and that's what I like to drive for when I have sex."

"How do you bring her off? What's the best way for her to—"

"I think the best way is have her being dominant, to have her straddle me. That's a good way to get her off. She likes it. She likes feeling dominant. We never talk about this—I don't know why we don't. But she likes it. She really does like to be dominant and she gets off a lot—I don't know if a lot faster, but she seems to enjoy it a lot better. And I like it that way. I think it's kind of—it's better than just the flat-out way, the male dominant. I don't care for that. A lot of my friends said they tried anal sex; I just couldn't get into that, even though [my sex-ed teacher] says it's one of the cleanest parts of the body—the anus and everything. From what she said, it's painful, too, so I couldn't see ... If I'm going to give my girlfriend sex, I don't want it to be painful."

The questions of pain and cleanliness come up often in discussions of anal sex, particularly among girls. One 15-year-old said her boyfriend didn't push her to do anal sex, "but he likes to touch me on my anus and I don't like it. I don't know, I'm just very turned off by it. I don't know why. I think it's because I excrete there and maybe I don't feel clean there or something. It's okay if he just touches me—as we're making love, he touches my anus and stuff—but I don't think I'd ever be into anal sex. Maybe some other person could get me into it; I think I'd probably break in half if [he] tried to do that to me."

In general, particularly in noncasual sex, the boys are aware of the possibility of pain and may choose to forgo their pleasure. A 17-year-old New York black told us his girlfriend "said that at first it was painful, or she would say she really didn't get any enjoyment out of it. With our relationship it's pretty much a mutual thing where she gets enjoyment out of it and I get enjoyment out of it.

If both of us can't get enjoyment out of a certain part of sex, then we just don't do it."

In a few instances, however, it's hard to avoid thinking that for some boys, giving pain is a sadistic plus. A 14-year-old from northern California said, "I butt-fucked a chick once, but she said it really hurt and everything."

"How did it happen that you were butt-fucking her?"

"I was kissing her, and I was kissing her down her back and she was on her stomach and I went back and I butt-fucked her a little and she said, 'Oh, it hurts,' and I just said, 'I don't really care about this.' I was just doing it because I'd never done it before, to see what it was like. . . ."

"What did you think would be interesting about butt-fucking?"

"I never did it before."

"Just something different?"

"Yeah. I didn't have to look at her ugly face."

Such callousness is rare, however, and even though it is usually boys who suggest or instigate anal sex, most, like this 17-year-old, wait for consent. "I had led her up to it. We'd had a sexual relationship going on for a while. I sort of played with her butt and everything and sort of led her up to it. I think that's what let her, what put her at ease, and she didn't mind. I don't think she'll do it constantly, but that one time, she didn't mind. She was very inhibited, but she said, 'What the hell, go ahead,' and so I did."

We came across only one instance of a girl instigating anal sex, and as it happens this 17-year-old turned out not to like it particularly.

"I brought him on to doing it, 'cause I'd never done it and I was always curious."

"How did you hear about it?"

"Probably through a porn magazine or something. Or hearing something from my brother about 'getting fucked up the ass,' and freaking out at the thought of it. And I saw in the porn flicks that the girls looked as if they were about to die, so I really wasn't into it. But then I thought, Shit, I might as well try it or I'll never find out. So I suggested it to him, I guess, and he didn't do it right away; a couple of days later, he just gave it a go. We had one night of heavy sex. It was all right. I don't see why people make a big thing about it."

"Did you find it painful?"

"It's painful at first. It's kind of like getting devirginized. It's not pain all the way—you get used to it."

"Did you like it?"

"Not especially. To me it was just kind of making love the other way."

"Did you have an orgasm that way?"

"No. I said to him after, 'I don't think I could have come like that for sure.' "

In general, however, most girls were not even this tolerant of anal sex. A 16-year-old New Yorker said she and her boyfriend had "started to, but it hurt too much. I don't like it—it was very painful, it wasn't fun." And a 17-year-old spoke succinctly for many of our respondents when she pointed out, "I don't seem to have any sexual feeling in my ass," and that it thus seemed pointless to endure the pain.

Indeed, to the extent that any teens were involved in sado-masochistic sex, their attitudes seemed to involve curiosity rather than any particular psychic drive. A 15-year-old girl moved without shifting gears from a discussion of games like spin the bottle to those she was playing with her boyfriend: "One time he tried to tie me up—Why am I saying this? It's so embarrassing. He didn't hit me or anything, but it didn't do anything for me. I was very upset afterwards, because I didn't get off and he did. I'm sitting like this—he tied me to the bed like this, with my arms tied. Not to hurt me, just so that I couldn't touch him. Just like this and my legs like that."

"Your legs were tied to the bed, too?"

"Yeah. It was very strange, because he had to, like, tie this rope back and bring it all the way to the door. The strings were like seven miles each both ways, tied to different things. But it was terrible, it was horrible. I didn't like it at all."

"What didn't you like about it?"

"Because I couldn't touch him. And he got off too fast for me to get off, and I couldn't get off when I was tied up like this. . . . It was no fun."

"Where did you get the idea to do it?"

"His father had a book on sadism. He has all these kinds of books, and he had this book on sadism. We read the book afterwards, but we were just talking about 'Let's try something,' and he said, 'Wow, let me tie you up.' I was like 'Are you *kidding?*' He goes, 'No, let's just fool around.' I said, 'Okay, why not?' Then he always says to me now, 'I wish you would tie *me* up.' He doesn't mind—he *wants* to get tied up—and I say no, because I like him to touch me. It's no fun if you're not touching. I like him to touch me.''

"So you don't think you're gonna do it?''

"No. We also do other things. I mean, he hits me. Not hits me hard, but we'll be making love or something and he'll smack me on the ass. I don't mind that. Not if it hurts me hard, though. If it hurts, then I don't like it, I say stop. Sometimes we'll just kid around and I'll hit him and we'll wrestle. . . .''

"Does it turn you on to hit or be hit?''

"It doesn't turn me on. It just makes it fun because we wrestle in bed and stuff. It's fun. It turns me on because we're both naked and we're playing around with each other. It turns me on, but if I was fully dressed and I was walking around the living room and he smacked me on the ass as hard as he could, I wouldn't get turned on. I'd be upset.''

Most teens certainly seem to share this girl's idea that sex is "no fun if you're not touching.'' Though a couple of girls had masturbated in front of their boyfriends, their motivation seemed at least partly pedagogic. Said one 16-year-old, "He was just curious, just because he wanted to know what I liked, and so he said, 'Why don't you masturbate for me so I can see what you do?' ''

"Did you feel self-conscious about it, or were you perfectly comfortable?''

"No, I felt fine with it, with him. It was really nice, actually, 'cause that way he could see . . . I mean he could *literally* see what it was that I did instead of me trying to tell him. 'Cause it's a lot harder to figure out exactly what a person means. And I don't think he was masturbating. I don't think I've ever seen him masturbate. I'm not sure—I don't think he was masturbating. But, yeah, that was trippy. Unusual.''

For some kids, the particular *kind* of sex is less important than its locale. A number of girls offered variations on the sea-sand-and-stars theme, and a 17-year-old suburban boy said he liked best "making love in really erotic places, places that you would never think of. Like I did it once in a toolshed, at my parents' wedding (my dad remarried and I was downstairs). I was blown out of my mind when we made it down there. I was leaning up against the door and someone walked in; that was embarrassing.

"And I made it in a tree once. I had my foot on this branch, and I was holding on to a branch here and a branch there, and nothing below me, and she had all her weight on me. And in the woods once, in a sewer pipe. I was about thirteen then—we couldn't think of anywhere else to go. In an old abandoned house, and in a brand-new house that nobody had moved into yet. Carpet was there; we decided to go there. On a floor, on a rug, on a water bed—that was wild. In the woods on a blanket. Outside a synagogue, *inside* a synagogue once. I'm Jewish. Right in the middle of the sanctuary, just laid out on the floor.

"I love going to erotic places. It's the same routine every time, practically, just the places make it different. I've always wanted to do it at school. I'd go somewhere like the auditorium. That's one of my fantasies."

"Have you tried to pull that one off?"

"No. But I've hinted."

Most of the teens' searches for exotic locales don't seem quite this inventive, or compulsive; and some—for instance, a 17-year-old girl's version of *The Three Stooges Make Love*—are inadvertently comic: "We did it in the bathroom, it was so kinky. But we had so much fun."

"On the floor or in the bathtub?"

"No, I was on the sink. The bathroom was half the size of this room, maybe. It was tiny. There wasn't room to lie on the floor, and the tub was a small tub. So I was sitting on the sink, and as a result I got the worst bruise on my coccyx bone. I couldn't sit for a week, and my legs got stretched out; I was in pain for a while. I had a great time, and he had a very decent time, even though he's very used to it, having a house to do it in and stuff. It was fun."

"Did you have an orgasm then?"

"Yeah. That's how I hurt my butt. We were really going at it and I had an orgasm and I like fell on the floor. That kind of stank."

Though the female orgasm doesn't usually have consequences quite so spectacular as she reported, most teens felt it was important, and boys in particular seemed to measure themselves as lovers by whether or not their girlfriends had orgasms. Such validation, however, was often complicated by the confusion both sexes felt about what precisely an orgasm is. Some boys, like the 16-year-old suburbanite who spoke of a girl not wanting "to come all over me," seemed to imagine an effect similar to the male orgasm. Others, like this 13-year-old Los Angeles boy, used auditory clues. Asked if his girlfriend had had an orgasm during cunnilingus, he said, "Yeah."

"How could you tell?"

"She was making noises and stuff, groans or whatever."

"You know what a girl's orgasm is like?"

"I've *heard* them before. Like my parents in the next room or whatever."

And an older boy, 17, confidently announced that he'd "found out that women have two types: One kind is like a mental thing— they just moan and groan; then literally coming, that's the second type." He added that he'd had no formal sex education: "All I know is what I feel in the dark and pick up on the streets."

Good information is indeed hard to acquire, for girls often seem to be as unsure about things as boys. Asked if she had orgasms during intercourse, a 15-year-old said, "I think I do. I don't fully understand what it is to have an orgasm, so maybe I'm overlooking it—like maybe I'm expecting something completely different from what it is. I do get a warm sensation, like a thrill through my body at times, like often. An orgasm, I guess, is something different."

And a girl said that once when her boyfriend "was stroking me, I was really spaced out or something, and he said, 'God, I thought you were having an orgasm.' I was just talking to my friends—'Are you really aware when you have one? How many can you have?' I've never asked my mom about it. I guess I'd be scared to."

Once they have a clear sense of what an orgasm *is*, however, many girls expect them. A 15-year-old who had often masturbated to orgasm said she'd never had one with her boyfriends. "Do you ever discuss it with the guy?" we asked.

"Yeah, I always complain to him: 'You go too fast! It's not fair!' "

"And how does he react?"

" 'I can't help it!' "

And some, like this 17-year-old, expect more than one. Asked

"What's the easiest way for you to have an orgasm?" she replied, "Pretty much any way. I don't come just once. My friends tell me they come and then finally they fuck and they both come together."

"You have multiple orgasms?"

"I can't understand how they can have only one orgasm. I mean, it's really good. It'll make you feel good."

"Is that while he's still inside you or while he's stimulating you?"

"While he's inside me, all the time. I don't understand how my friend can have just one orgasm."

Many girls, however, are more relaxed about orgasms, even indifferent to them. A 14-year-old Californian, asked if she'd had orgasms during intercourse, simply said, "No, I think I'm too young. That's the way I feel. It'll happen sooner or later." And a 17-year-old Pennsylvania girl who'd first had an orgasm about a year after she and her boyfriend began intercourse, said she now had them "pretty regularly."

"Is it important for you to have an orgasm?"

"No. I *enjoy* it. When we both feel that we really want to make love, then, you know . . . I think it feels good, too, without an orgasm, and I enjoy it without the orgasm. It doesn't make any difference to me."

"Is it important to him that you have an orgasm?"

"No, 'cause he knows how I feel, that it doesn't mean I'm enjoying it any less. I mean, you know, when I *have* an orgasm, I enjoy it, but I can enjoy sex without having an orgasm."

Other girls—though not necessarily their boyfriends—feel the same way. A New Yorker who said she so far hadn't had an orgasm during oral sex with her boyfriend (though she had during intercourse) said, "He's very concerned about that. For a long time, I didn't have an orgasm when we had sex either, and he was like, 'Gee, I want you to have an orgasm. Do you feel fulfilled?' He was scared that I wasn't feeling fulfilled."

"How did you feel about it?"

"It didn't bother me. I was still enjoying it, and you can only eat somebody for so long before you get really tired. So he was doing his best, and I was satisfied, so it was okay with me."

The likelihood of a girl's having an orgasm is not significantly affected by any of the various sociological measures, though it may perhaps be related to what she learned about sex from her parents. Among the nonvirgin girls whose parents had taught them that sex was normal and healthy, more than three-quarters (77%) had achieved orgasms; among those whose parents had taught them nothing, fewer than two-thirds (64%) had. But it would seem that, in general, conditions within the particular sexual relationship are more likely to be determining than any factors outside it.

Though boys expressed themselves as being more willing to have and enjoy casual encounters, both boys and girls generally felt that sex was qualitatively better when love was involved. "Better with love, definitely," said a 14-year-old Boston boy; and a 16-year-old New York girl said that while she didn't think one had to be in love with a boy to have sex, "I think it's more pleasurable if you love them, if you care about them a lot. Pure sex—if you just see someone to go home and go to bed—it's not that much fun."

8

Parents: Letting Them Know

No matter how gymnastic teenage sex may be, no matter what degree of pleasure or guilt kids get from it, it is in at least one major respect different from adult varieties, for even older teens remain in some ways subject to parental rules and disciplines. Parents can react to the reality of teenage sex in any number of ways. They can be supportive, critical, enraged, deceived, or self-deceiving, but theirs is an inescapable presence.

Because of the vast gap teenagers perceive between their parents' standards of right and wrong and their own (chapter 2), it's very likely that most kids who've had intercourse don't go out of their way to let their parents know about it. A little less than a third (32%) say their parents definitely know, and a few more (36%) say they definitely don't. The remaining third are unsure. Two-thirds (66%) of sexually active teens are sure, however, that their parents approve of their sexual activities "not at all" (48%) or only "a little" (24%). About a quarter (28%) say their parents approve "somewhat," and a very small number (6%) report complete approval.

Though kids may have escaped the double standard to some degree, their parents still seem caught up in it, and sexually active girls are significantly more likely than boys to feel parental disapproval (see table 28).

Though the degree of parental approval rises slightly with age, the association is statistically significant only for boys and isn't strong for either gender. This might seem to imply that parents base their approval or disapproval more on abstract notions of morality than on a specific child's maturity, but this isn't necessarily so. At least to the extent that performance in school is, like

TABLE 28   Parental Approval of Teenage Sexual Activities

	Not at All	A Little	Somewhat	Complete
Boys	37%	22%	36%	5%
Girls	47%	26%	20%	7%

chronological age, a measure of maturity, parents respond to it and are somewhat more likely to approve sexual activities among those who are at or near the top of their classes.

Except in respect to the double standard, religion does not seem to affect parental attitude in significant ways: Regardless of their religion, boys receive about the same degree of approval or disapproval as other boys; girls as other girls. But particularly among Roman Catholics, boys and girls report a sharp disparity (see table 29).

To the extent that the double standard is still in operation, it is particularly difficult for girls because their parents are almost twice as likely as boys' parents to know of their children's sexual activities (see table 30). To some extent the figures may reflect the comparatively later age at which girls are likely to begin intercourse and the need they may feel for parental cooperation in getting certain types of birth control. It is also likely, however, that such parental knowledge has to do with the notable ease of communication among girls and their mothers. Though about two-thirds of boys say it's hard to talk about sex with either their fathers (64%) or

TABLE 29   Catholic Parents' Approval of Sexual Activities

	Not at All	A Little	Somewhat	Complete
Boys	32%	17%	35%	13%
Girls	51%	22%	24%	3%

TABLE 30   Do Parents Know of Teens' Intercourse?

	Yes	No	Don't Know
Boys	24%	38%	38%
Girls	42%	31%	27%

their mothers (67%), a majority of girls (53%) do *not* find it hard to talk with their mothers.

Still, parental lack of knowledge is the rule rather than the exception, and many kids apparently feel that parental ignorance is teenage bliss. For instance, the 17-year-old boy who so enjoyed making love in forbidden places happily remarked, "My parents still think I'm a virgin. They don't know anything."

Many parents do know, of course, but teenagers are not fools and tend to volunteer information about their sex lives only when they already have some reason to believe that they won't be met with chill disapproval. A 17-year-old Boston boy who believed that his mother "would probably have a heart attack; my father'd go into a coma" if they learned he was having sex with his girlfriend was obviously less likely to tell his parents than was a New York girl whose mother had "told me beforehand, 'The second you have sex, the day after we'll go to the doctor and get a diaphragm fitted.'"

Though one may wonder about the parental wisdom of giving tacit approval for sex and letting birth control wait until *afterward,* the girl did indeed tell her mother immediately. The attitudes of parents who hold off any such comments for fear of encouraging their children to have sex are understandable, but such hesitation runs a severe risk of mistiming the moment when parental intervention is in order. For instance, a 12-year-old California girl who'd had sex several times without birth control said that her mother "doesn't think I'm going to start thinking about it until I'm sixteen or seventeen."

"Did you think about telling her after the first time you'd done it?"

"Well, no. I figured she'd really get mad if I told her."

That is not to say there are no risks involved in parents' *presuming* a child is having sex; as we saw in chapter 1, a parent who refuses to believe a child's denials can severely undermine the child's trust. But the negative consequences of this sort of misjudgment seem much less damaging to both parent and child than those that can result from silence. Even when a parent initially presumes too much, conversations based on such presumptions can set the stage for later confidences. A 15-year-old New York girl, asked if she'd talked with her mother when she was first thinking about having intercourse with her boyfriend, said, "No, but she was curious about me because she knew I'd been going out with him and she kept on saying, 'Listen, you need birth control.' And I was going 'No, no,' and I kept putting it off myself. Like, 'No, I don't need it'—very upset, you know. Like, 'Mom, what do you think I am?' I put her off and I guess that was wrong, because I guess that could have been a big mistake, but it wasn't. Lucky for me it wasn't.

"How did you tell her you'd been devirginized?"

"It was really funny because she had just come home from vacation afterwards. She was, 'So what did you do?' I didn't want to say, 'Well, [my boyfriend] was here,' so I kinda said, 'Well, I was with [my boyfriend] most of the weekend. And, mom,' I said, 'I'm not a virgin.' And she was like, 'Wha-a-at?' and I said, 'Mom, I'm not a virgin,' and she said, 'Oh, was it good? Did you like it?' I was like, 'Is *that* all you're gonna say?' She was, 'Tell me, did it feel good?' 'Yeah, it was okay, mom,' you know. It was pretty funny. I just told her very openly. I was more embarrassed than she was. She was, 'Well, we're gonna have to make an appointment immediately,' and she called that day and she made an appointment for me."

"Do you think she approves?"

"She does. She's just afraid now because I am being too . . . She thinks she's being too liberal with me."

Rather more to the point, one would think, is that the daughter's question—"Is *that* all you're gonna say?"—reveals that she, too, may feel her mother is being overliberal. Other parts of that interview, for instance, reveal that the mother is not entirely happy with the nature of the relationship:

"My mother keeps on saying, 'It's gonna emotionally disturb you. If you break up, you're gonna have emotional . . .' She's very concerned about the fact that, see, I'm her only child, so she's very—Now I'm going to his house. His dad is away—his dad just had a baby with his girlfriend or something, and so I'm up at his house a lot, and I say, 'You know, mom, it's better for me up there. I have a better time, there's a laundry machine.' I can do my laundry and watch TV and he makes me dinner. I like to be up there, and I say, 'Mom, I'm gonna spend the night at [my boyfriend's], but she's still at that state: She's very liberal, she lets me do what I want, but she's not *that* liberal to say, 'Okay, go ahead, whatever you want.' She'll say, like, 'How about just on weekends?' And I'll say, 'Mom, it can't be just a weekend relationship.' "

There is an element of inadvertent comedy in such negotiations—the girl, after all, had only recently turned 15—but lying or mutual self-deception is not preferable. It's clear, however, that they are *easier,* and that parents who choose the route of openness take a difficult path. Some of these parents, however, seem to be not so much open as indifferent, demicaricatures whose minds are so open their brains have fallen out. Consider the mother who let her daughter, age "fourteen, maybe fifteen," wander off drunk and stoned to the tent of a 19-year-old man during a camping trip: "My mom was cool. She figured it would happen sometime."

About a year later, when the girl was 16, she began a relationship with one of her mother's friends, a 37-year-old coke dealer who ran a pottery workshop. When he began pressing her to move in with him, she finally told her mother. "It was the worst thing I'd ever had to confess in my life, I think probably ever will!"

"How did she react?"

"I kind of broke it to her very subtly. I'd told her at one point I was seeing [a schoolmate] and after a while she asked me about him, how come I wasn't seeing him anymore. I said, 'I'm kind of not into him anymore,' and she said, 'Yeah? Are you seeing anyone else?' So I said, 'Yeah, I've kind of been seeing [the mother's friend]. And she said, 'Oh, yeah?' Her reaction wasn't bad at all."

At the risk of sacrificing my liberal credentials, I would suggest that polite interest—or, for all one can tell from the daughter's account, terminal boredom—is not the ideal reaction to a 16-year-old's announcement that she's been dating a 37-year-old coke dealer. It certainly seems true that a teenager who tells a parent "the worst thing I'd ever had to confess in my life" not only expects a little more than "Oh, yeah?" but is *entitled* to it.

On the other hand, various strategies of ignorance seem little better. A 14-year-old California girl who'd been having essentially meaningless sex ("I don't *feel* anything") with an 18-year-old neighbor for close to a year said that neither her parents nor her grandmother, who was at home during the day, had any idea what was going on: "God forbid if she knew. It would be awfully gnarly."

Another Californian, a 16-year-old who used no birth-control

TABLE 31 Is It Hard to Talk to Your Mother about Sex?

	Nonvirgins	Virgins
Yes	66%	53%
No	33%	46%

device during regular intercourse with her boyfriend, said her parents knew nothing about her sex life: "I can't talk to my parents about that." A 17-year-old Pennsylvania girl who also had regular intercourse, though somewhat more satisfactorily, said she "might tell her parents in a couple of years, but right now they would get upset and probably ground me for life."

Her secrecy gained her a certain amount of peace and quiet, but there's no doubt that she—and many teenagers like her—was very much bothered by not having someone to talk to.

"You think your values are different from theirs?"

"Yes, definitely."

"If you had a kid, would you let her have sex at your age? What would you do?"

"I'd probably talk to her about it and explain to her how it affects you psychologically also, and let her decide."

"How do you think it affects you psychologically?"

"Well, the first thing I kept thinking about after I had done it was I'm not a virgin anymore, and I almost went crazy."

It seems clear from our interviews that some kids who are planning to enter sexual relationships *want* to be told to wait. But those who can't talk to their parents hear either nothing or a ritualized naysaying that has no bearing on their *immediate* situation—and those who can may find their parents unwilling to take the responsibility for saying anything more than "Be careful."

"Be careful" is by no means bad advice, but it seems distant indeed from the between-the-lines question kids seem really to be asking. They don't want to know whether or not intercourse is "right"—that's something most of them are perfectly prepared to decide—but whether it is right with *this* person at *this* time. The advantage shared by parents who have chosen openness with their children is that there is at least a chance that the real question can be asked—and answered. In that context, it's interesting to note that kids who can talk about sex with their more approachable parent are usually significantly *less* likely to have had intercourse than those who find it hard (see table 31).

The figures strongly suggest that parents who believe that their silence or the threat of their disapproval will encourage their sons and daughters to refrain from sexual activity are surely—and perhaps tragically—mistaken.

9

Going Steady/Breaking Up

There may indeed be ways in which parents can influence their children's decisions about whether or not to begin a sexual relationship, but such relationships, once started, have their own dynamic. A few last for years and eventually become marriages, but most break up. Almost a fifth of boys (19%) and a tenth of girls (9%) said their most recent sexual relationship had lasted a week or less; only 14% of all the teenagers' sexual relationships had endured for more than a year. Breaking up may be just as hard to do as the song claims, but most teens go through the experience at least once.

Though some statistics suggest that breakups may be harder on girls than on boys (79% of girls said they had loved their most recent sex partners, but only 58% of boys claimed to), our interviews indicate that boys and girls are about equally likely to fall *out* of love, and that girls choose to break up just about as often as boys. Certainly the data do not support the notion that boys are after only one thing and will dump the girl as soon as they get it. If anything, girls seem slightly less likely than boys to go through lengthy periods of sexual mourning before starting new relationships.

Breakups or no, once kids start having sex, they tend to continue; only a very few nonvirgins (6%) had gone for more than a year since their last intercourse. The percentages are equal among boys and girls, and boys (15%) were half again as likely as girls (10%) to have abstained for six months to a year. Perhaps because girls are less involved in casual sex than boys, they are more than twice as likely to be involved in an ongoing sexual relationship. Close to half (44%) of nonvirgin girls had had intercourse in the week before they filled out the questionnaire, but only a fifth (21%) of the boys had.

This in no way denies that exploitative relationships exist. As one girl wrote, "My best sexual experience was with a boyfriend I had this year. He played with my breasts and he had his finger up me. I played with his prick and I gave him a blow job. I thought it was okay because he told me he loved me, and I thought I loved him. After a week, I found out I had been used and we broke up. It was also my worst because of the way it ended." But even the most sincere teenage relationships can founder in the ways adults' marriages sometimes do.

In general, kids break up for the obvious reasons: In the words of a 16-year-old suburban boy, they end with "either the girl liking another guy or the guy liking another girl, or else just fights. I've never ended with fights, but a girl liking another guy; she finds out another guy likes her, so she wants a change, you know."

"Does one or the other person usually get upset when it ends?"

"Sometimes. Usually the person that ends up not breaking up."

Human realities are such that the process can perhaps never be without some degree of pain, especially since kids are capable of needless cruelties. A 17-year-old Boston boy who'd been sleeping with his girlfriend for about a year ended it because "she was getting fat, for one thing. I told her to stop getting fat, and then she started getting bitchy: 'Don't tell me what to do,' and stuff like that. So I said, 'All right, see ya later.' "

"Did it bother you to break up with her after a year?"

"Not really, because I liked this other girl."

"Had you already met her?"

"Yeah. She's one of my sister's friends."

"So what was going on at this point?"

"I'd be sitting at home with [my girlfriend], right, and the other girl would come in with my sister, and I would tell [my girlfriend] I was going out into the kitchen to get something to drink and I would go into my sister's room and start fooling around with the other girl. Just playing, you know, pushing her around and stuff like that, walking up to her and whispering in her ear and stuff."

"Was your sister there?"

"Yeah."

"Did you think [your girlfriend] noticed this was going on?"

"I think so."

Teens often seem to make the transition from one relationship to another without shifting gears at all. To some extent they are more or less forced to learn this behavior by the social rules that operate in their early years; in many parts of the country, a boy and girl who date at all are considered boyfriend and girlfriend. As a Boston boy explained, "A lot of girls won't [kiss you goodnight] unless you're going steady."

"When are you supposed to ask a girl to go steady with you?"

"When she wants to, I guess. When you hear about it from your friends, or else when you feel you like her a lot or she likes you."

"You have to go on a few dates first?"

"Nah, not necessarily."

"You could ask a girl you never had a date with?"

"Yeah, if you know her and if you like her and she likes you, and she says yes, then you're going steady with her."

"What does it mean if you're going steady?"

"You know, you're boyfriend and girlfriend."

"That means you're not dating anybody else?"

"Yeah, unless you discuss it or whatever."

"How many times have you gone steady?"

"A bunch. A lot."

The presumption of exclusivity in such tentative relationships makes a chain of serial breakups inevitable, and the lack of real bonds between a couple makes those breakups seem easy. With the notion of "going steady" prevalent in most parts of the country, it's no wonder a 17-year-old suburban boy was able to talk with so little embarrassment about how he got together with his current girlfriend, 'Betty.'

"It was last September, last November. A year ago November. It was the day after a football game; we had won our last game of the season and we had a winning season, so there was a party. It turned into pretty much a . . . not *per se* an orgy, but close to it. You know, it started out kiss-a-cheerleader night and it turned out everyone was kissing everyone else. So I met Betty, and she was going out with another guy and I was going with another girl at the time. The other girl and I weren't really getting along. So I met Betty, and from there we just started getting together, and every now and then we'd go out. One night after I left my girlfriend's house, I went to a dance and I saw Betty and I took her home and I kissed her goodnight and she said she didn't really feel right about it. So it ended up I broke up with the other girl. So right away Betty and I started going out, and we've been going out ever since then."

Later on in our interview, however, it turned out that the antiseptic phrase "weren't really getting along," carried more weight than the boy had initially admitted. "The thing that happened with that girl—one night, it was during baseball season and I was at a game and we were away late. I got back late and I found her . . . She was waiting for me at the school with another guy, and I knew the guy had a reputation for really going after the girls. I got kind of mad, but I didn't think anything of it. Then over the summer he always used to get to me more and more. He'd come over and see her a lot, and it just used to bug me a lot. Then finally one night . . . then she started to lie to me, saying she was going out with her friend and she'd go out with him. She told me all this, and that was that for me. So I started going out with Betty."

Still later, talking about his earlier girlfriend, this boy said, "We went together for nearly two years, and after about six months we really didn't have very much trust in each other. But I guess neither one of us would break up because the thought of not having a boyfriend and not having a girlfriend really kind of kept us together." This certainly sounds a little like "staying together for the sake of the child," but one should not be surprised; many teenage lovers feel their relationship is worth maintaining because it provides them with a certain status.

That is not to say teenagers are hopelessly romantic, for they are certainly aware that a difference of a year or two in age—a difference that would be meaningless to an older couple—may prove determinative to them. A high-school senior who'd gone out with a girl a year ahead of him said that it was his "most special relationship. . . . It meant the most to me. When she went away to college, it hurt a great deal. But that was just another thing I had to learn. . . ."

The terminus may be artificial and arbitrary, but kids know it's incontrovertible. Another senior, who'd had a sexual relationship with his girlfriend for about a year, talked about his college plans:

"I plan on going to college in Ohio, University of Dayton."

"Is she also a senior?"

"She's only a sophomore. We're gonna have to split apart. You can't be unrealistic and say that you're not going to go out with anyone else. The fact of the matter is, I know we'll both go out with other people."

It's obviously difficult for even the most serious and committed teenage relationship to survive lengthy geographic separation, but such relationships often founder for internal reasons as well; infidelity and jealousy are by no means reserved for adults. Such breakups can be extremely painful, as a 17-year-old Phoenix boy discovered when he found out his girlfriend had gone out "with another guy. An enemy of mine."

"Did she have intercourse with this guy?"

"Yes."

"You know about it?"

"She told me about it."

"How did you react?"

"I was crushed. I wanted to kill her. Love and hate are very close."

Despite the fact that a partner's infidelity can at some point hit teenagers with grown-up force, the presumption—even among the youngest teens—of exclusivity virtually guarantees a chain of break-ups, and may trivialize the notion of commitment. A 17-year-old from Boston, in the midst of his first sexual relationship, told us he'd had about "twenty *steady* girlfriends," which he defined as "someone who you go out only with her and she goes out only with you."

"How do they end, these relationships?"

"How does the whole relationship end?"

"You've broken up with girls nineteen times."

"Usually, well [laughs], the last two, they caught me with a couple other girls."

From such relatively innocent game-playing, it's only a short step to the behavior exhibited by another Boston boy. "Tell me more about your social life. You go out with this one girl; is it an exclusive relationship, you see only her, or do you go out with other girls at the same time?"

"Well, actually, it's strange. I'm only supposed to be going out with her, but on the side I've been seeing a few other girls."

"She doesn't know about it?"

"No, she doesn't. I feel guilty about it. *That* I do feel guilty about, sometimes."

"Do you sleep with all these different girls?"

"Two of them I have; the others I just see a lot of times. One of them I like a lot—it's not really much of a thing where you get to kissing or petting a lot, it's just good to talk to her and like that. And it's mainly like that."

"Would your girlfriend be upset?"

"I think so."

"Does she go out only with you?"

"As far as I know. . . ."

Given that "going steady" in some ways *trains* kids for infidelity, it's no surprise that the more committed partner in a relationship may exhibit jealousy or possessiveness. Whether or not such feelings are justified by the immediate facts, they seem natural enough. But they can be damaging, even in an otherwise sound relationship. A 15-year-old New Yorker said she'd broken up with her boyfriend "about two weeks ago because he was getting to be a bit of an asshole, too possessive. I don't like that. I *do* love him, though."

"Do you want to go out with other men at the same time?"

"I do want to have the freedom to know that if I do happen to want to go somewhere with another guy, or *talk* to another guy, I'm not going to have someone hanging over my shoulder saying, 'Hey, that's not fair to me.' "

One senses that many teens are caught in a trap of their own devising. Most share the belief that whatever sexual activity may be appropriate for their age, it is appropriate only in a boyfriend/girlfriend situation. Given the reality of sexual curiosity and sexual desire, their urge to be moral impels them into doomed relationships; and the more teens invest themselves in such relationships, the more likely it is that someone's going to get pretty badly bruised. This may happen, for example, to the boy who, after a yearlong sexual relationship, wants a 17-year-old New Yorker to move in with him. Says she: "I think it might be a disaster, not on his part but on my part. I don't think I'm ready to move in with him now, and not just be friends but sexual . . . Sometimes when I go out—I went to see the Cramps, and I went with him and I just wanted to run around and flirt with a lot of guys and I couldn't do it! It was terrible!"

"So you feel trapped just seeing one guy?"

"That's what I thought I wanted—but once you have it, it sometimes turns out to be a drag."

10

Rape, Casual Sex, Group Sex

Not all teenage sex exists within the context of a relationship. Among boys particularly, there is a good deal of casual sex. Close to a third (31%) of nonvirgin boys have had sex with someone they "didn't really know," as opposed to about a fifth (22%) of the girls. In addition, boys were more than twice as likely (37%) to have first had intercourse with a stranger or friend, rather than a girlfriend or fiancée; only 17% of girls had done so. Such encounters may be an easy and pleasurable outgrowth of friendship, but they can also be hostile and mechanistic. The prime example of the latter sort is, of course, rape.

Fourteen percent of all girls in the survey reported they had been raped—more than a quarter of them (26%) when they were ten years old or younger. In most cases the rapist was someone they knew; more than half the time it was a friend, neighbor, or relative (see table 32).

Somewhat contrary to expectations, city dwellers were no more likely to be rape victims than were girls living in the suburbs or rural areas, and girls from affluent families were as vulnerable as those living in comparative poverty. Girls who reported themselves as doing badly in school, however, were much more likely to have been raped than those who reported themselves as doing well (see table 33).

Because the absolute number of girls in the sample who'd been raped is relatively small, one can't say that these figures are mirrored nationally, but the association is very strong and leads one to consider the surmise that to the extent school performance is a reflection of intelligence, intelligent girls may have a greater

TABLE 32 Identity of Rapist

Boyfriend	Friend	Neighbor	Relative	Stranger	Gang Rape
16%	30%	9%	13%	29%	4%

ability to recognize and avoid potential rape situations.

It is at least equally likely, however, that rape—or even moles-tation—is so traumatic an experience that it cripples its victims not only emotionally but educationally as well. A 15-year-old remembered what happened with her father when she was in fourth grade: "He was drunk and everything and I came home from school and he had taken all the clothes in the closets and put them on fire. He'd axed out the mirrors. And he was just in his underwear and a shirt when I came home. And he goes, 'Come up here,' and I was really scared and I go up and he goes, 'Get in this room.' My sister is in there, so I go in and he locks me in there until he comes back and he goes—he started yelling at me and he said, 'I hate people, I hate all this,' and he said, 'This is what people are going to do to you when you get older.' He just scared me and played around with me, but he was like hanging out—that's enough to scare anybody in the first place."

"So you're saying he didn't put his penis inside of you?"

"Right."

"That he just played with your—"

"Right."

"Was that physically painful?"

"Yes, very much."

". . . Did he move out at that time?"

"He moved out like about a year later."

"So you told your mom at that point, or did she ever know?"

"No. I don't know. I don't think I even told my sister. I didn't

TABLE 33 Percentage of Rape Victims Within School Performance Group

	Well Below Average	Below Average	Average	Above Average	Well Above Average
% Raped	33	22	19	11	0

TABLE 34   Relationship with First Intercourse Partner

	Age at First Intercourse (Boys and Girls)							
	Under 11	11	12	13	14	15	16	17 or Older
Stranger	6%		14%		6%	4%	6%	9%
Friend	69%	48%	34%	19%	16%	18%	9%	17%
Boyfriend/ Girlfriend/ Fiancé	25%	48%	52%	80%	75%	76%	84%	75%

tell anybody. I was too afraid, too embarrassed. I didn't know what to do."

In the intervening years, she twice attempted suicide.

The fact that this girl had been victimized by her own father may have made her less likely to have told anyone, but our survey revealed that the vast majority of rapes go unreported, no matter who the rapist is. Only 9% of the rapes in our survey had been reported to the police, even though almost a third (29%) had been rapes committed by strangers. This suggests that rape occurs *far* more often than police records indicate.

In addition, a question arises about the degree of consent when younger girls are involved in sex. At least some of the girls who'd first had sex when they were 12 or 13 years old (12% of the girls who had *ever* had intercourse) and *all* of the 6% who'd had intercourse before the age of 11 can be said not to have given their informed consent. While one appreciates the civil-libertarian arguments against applying statutory-rape laws to older teens, these statistics indicate that the effort to eliminate such laws entirely is probably misguided.

Rape, whether forcible or statutory, is obviously the extreme form of exploitative sex, but it is hardly the only one. Though most teens believe that intercourse belongs in the context of a continuing (or at least continuable) relationship, it's clear that such relationships are far less common among younger teens (see table 34).

In general, even the youngest boys were likely to have had their first intercourse with someone roughly their own age; only 1% of boys who'd had their first intercourse at age 13 or younger had a partner over the age of 17. For girls, however, the picture is quite different (see table 35), and it is hard to imagine that at least

TABLE 35 Age of Partner at First Intercourse

% of Nonvirgin Girls Reporting Partner's Age as:	Girl's Age Under 11	11	12	13
17–19	39%	×	38%	41%
20+	×	25%	×	8%

some—and probably most—of the relationships that involve wide age gaps are not exploitative.

Except for the question of age, however, casual teenage sex does not seem exploitative in the classic ways. Fewer than 6% of boys had ever had sex with a prostitute, and none of the girls had ever had sex for money (2%, however, had had intercourse for drugs). But certainly some kids are willing to play games with the notion of "love." A high-school senior told us, "Some girls just have to be cared for before they will make love to anybody. I think that's a big thing with high-school kids, at least high-school girls. Love means a lot to them—at least the *word* means very, very much. I think there are three or four girls I care about—I don't love at all, but I care a lot about. But I think if I said 'I love you' and acted like I meant it, I could have sex anytime I wanted with them."

"Do you think a lot of guys use that? Once they know the power of that word, if they say that word, they can get what they want?"

"I think a few do."

This by no means implies that one partner or another is always exploited in casual sex. When it is *genuinely* casual—when neither partner is deceived as to its meaning—it can be a source of almost innocent pleasure, as an 18-year-old girl told us. Two summers earlier, traveling in Europe, she and her friend "met these two guys on a train. We had been walking by, and he leaned out and he said—this was in Germany and they could tell we were, I guess, Americans. They were eager to meet more Americans at this point; they were tired of talking in simple language. So they leaned out and said, 'Hey, come party with us.' They had a bottle of wine."

"They were Americans?"

"Yeah, and we went in. During the course of the next four or five hours, we were together. We would run out at stops and buy lots of beers, so we were pretty toasted by the time we got off the train. We went to an information desk to find a place to stay and found out the youth hostels were filled and the cheapest double they had was fifty dollars. We decided to go in for a room with four people.''

"You and your friend and the two guys?''

"And the two guys. And what happened during those five hours is . . . I found both of them attractive, but I found one of them more appealing and we were kind of flirting. He ran out and picked a flower for me and came back in and gave it to me. Then as we were leaving the train, he gave me a kiss. So we got to this room— it was a huge room . . . it had a big double and two singles, and the guy who had been flirting with me just kind of fell on the double and said, 'Come here, give me a kiss,' instead of what might have been more natural or more obvious . . . to have the girls share the double. But he wasn't interested in that, and I kind of knew what was happening. Then we went out for the evening and came back, and it was fun—he was a funny person. We stayed up most of the night talking, too. I felt a little bit guilty because I had a boyfriend back home, and he was saying, 'You shouldn't at all because it's really nothing, it's really just a good time,' and that's exactly what it was.''

"Were the other two people involved?''

"The other two people we hoped were asleep. We kept on giggling and whispering through the night. I think they had trouble sleeping. Also the other guy—it got really weird. First of all, what was so exciting about the situation a little bit was that we just kept on assuming certain things. Like he just fell into bed and said, 'Come here,' and kind of assumed I would. And we got changed and just assumed that it didn't matter; we could change in front of each other—who cares?''

"The two of you or all four of you?''

"All four of us. And so it was just that people did things that might have been shocking, but everyone just accepted it. And the other two were kind of fooling around, but the girl didn't want to have sex, and the guy got really frustrated and he was—the room was dark, but there was a little bit of light, a blue light from the streetlights outside, and the guy was naked, and he got out of bed, and he was so frustrated he went over to the window and he started climbing out the window—this was five flights up—pretending he was going to jump. So the other guy got out of bed, also naked, to go talk to him. It got to be this thing where—it wasn't an orgy, but it was . . . it had a little bit of that feeling, just being all naked together. And everyone started walking around completely naked. It was fun."

Despite whatever momentary feelings of guilt might operate, about a quarter (26%) of the nonvirgin boys and a tenth (11%) of the girls have had more than one sexual relationship going on simultaneously. About a fifth (19%) of the boys have been involved in group sex, more than three times the percentage of girls (6%). Furthermore, a number of the kids interviewed reported various occasions of group nudity—skinny-dipping, strip poker, etc. The essentially lighthearted nature of such occasions was inadvertently revealed by some comments a boy made about strip Monopoly, "where if you lose, like, let's say for every thousand dollars you lose . . . you have to take a certain thing off."

"Clothing?"

"Yeah. And that's weird. 'Cause, like, it's bad enough you're losing the game."

Actual group sex, however, is of a different order, and though some kids reported enjoying it—or enjoying thinking about it—many were made uneasy by it. A 16-year-old California girl remarked that one of her friends had something of a sexual problem: "He'd have sex with anything that moved . . . with me, with my boyfriend . . ."

"He's bisexual?"

"Yeah. We had an orgy one night, the three of us."

"How was that?"

"Well, my boyfriend fell asleep so we didn't really . . ."

"Was everybody doing things to everyone else?"

"No, it was more like one would rest while the other two were, and we'd go back and forth."

"Did you like it?"

"Well, yeah. I was so drunk and so stoned that I didn't even know what I was doing."

11

Sex and Other Stimulants

Though girls and boys often say they've gotten so drunk or stoned that they didn't know what they were doing, other teens suspect this excuse. One girl, a black 16-year-old from Washington, D.C., said that maybe "once in a while a boy will try to get a girl high to have sex with her, but when it comes down to it, if that girl doesn't want to do it, she isn't going to do it whether she's high or not, I think. So I think it's different, it's separate. I think drugs might have something to do with some cases, but most times it's like, 'We're gonna get high,' not 'We're gonna get high and have sex.' I think that teenagers—I don't think that they want to be under the influence of any kind of drug when they're having sex, because they want to get all the enjoyment out of it, you know, and they might think that if they smoke some herb before they do it, they might lose out on something. Most old people think, My child's getting high and she's gonna have sex too—you know, it's all hand in hand. But it's not—it's totally different, 'cause you can go and smoke a joint in the bathroom, but that doesn't mean you're going to go and have sex right after it."

This sounds, I must say, perfectly sensible, but as researchers have repeatedly demonstrated, the effect of any particular drug is related not just to chemistry and quantity but to set and setting as well. Expectations, mood, and social context matter a great deal, and many teens seem quite prepared, even eager, for the loosening of inhibitions they associate with drugs or alcohol.

More than half the teens (56%) reported having used drugs or alcohol. In order of popularity, the substances were alcohol (50%), marijuana (34%), uppers or stimulants, including "speed" (10%),

TABLE 36   Annual Frequency of Marijuana Use by Age and Sex

Times per Year	Boys at age					
	13	14	15	16	17	18
0	92%	79%	63%	66%	60%	48%
1–11	×	4%	11%	14%	15%	7%
12–51	2%	5%	7%	8%	6%	7%
52–103	3%	3%	3%	2%	2%	7%
104–364	3%	7%	10%	5%	11%	17%
365+	0	1%	7%	6%	6%	15%

Times per Year	Girls at age					
	13	14	15	16	17	18
0	89%	90%	67%	65%	50%	74%
1–11	6%	1%	13%	15%	12%	6%
12–51	4%	3%	6%	8%	18%	8%
52–103	×	3%	×	1%	2%	2%
104–364	1%	3%	9%	8%	7%	8%
365+	0	0	5%	3%	11%	2%

cocaine (6%), downers or tranquilizers (6%), hallucinogens (4%), Quaaludes (4%), angel dust (4%), and heroin (2%). Partly because of state alcohol regulations, it is easier for most 13-year-olds to buy dope than beer. Alcohol use increases sharply with age, but marijuana use does not decline, and though boys are more likely to smoke—intensively—than girls, older teens of both sexes are more likely to be regular users (see table 36).

In general, despite the disagreements voiced at the beginning of this chapter by the Washington, D.C., girl, certain kinds of sexual activity and drug use are strongly related. Among teens who've used alcohol at all, almost half (47%) are nonvirgins; among those who haven't, 87% are virgins. For simple marijuana use, the association is similar, though not quite as strong. Heavy marijuana users (those who smoke twice a week or more) do seem to be notably more active sexually than their more moderate or abstaining peers (see table 37).

Though the rate of marijuana use is not significantly related either to the age at which kids begin intercourse or to whether their most recent intercourse was with a girlfriend or boyfriend,

TABLE 37   Annual Marijuana Use and Virginity

Times per Year	0	1–11	12–51	52–104	105–364	365+
Nonvirgins	19%	34%	61%	45%	70%	80%
Virgins	81%	66%	39%	55%	30%	20%

heavy smokers are more likely to have a greater number of sexual partners, to have had intercourse with a stranger, and to have had more than one sexual relationship at the same time. These tendencies are, as table 38 demonstrates, quite strong, and without trying to enter the debate about whether there is any such thing as "promiscuous" behavior, we can certainly say that heavy marijuana use is associated with behavior that most teens consider morally wrong.

In chapter 2 we saw that only 5% of teens thought sexual intercourse with a stranger was all right for a boy, but fewer (3%) believed it was okay for a girl. Though there is a gap between action and ethic (about 8% of all teens have had sex with strangers), heavy smokers stand out markedly among their nonvirgin peers. In addition, though fewer than 18% of the teens who've had intercourse have done so with six or more partners, 28% of heavy smokers have. As a 15-year-old New Jersey boy said, "Whenever I get high, I always get horny."

Many boys also believe that if drugs or alcohol don't actually make girls horny, they do make them more compliant. A 17-year-old Boston boy complained that he'd had only "about four or five" hand jobs, because "girls, see, when they're about fifteen to sixteen or seventeen, they don't really like to fool around too much because they don't know too much. They think, Ooh, that's gross, and stuff like that."

"Is it a problem getting them to give hand jobs?"

"Yeah."

TABLE 38   Annual Marijuana Use and Sexual Intercourse with Strangers (by % of nonvirgins)

Times per Year	0	1–11	12–51	52–103	104–364	365+
Yes	17	20	33	31	41	46
No	83	80	67	69	59	54

"What would you have to do?"

"Actually, I'd have to get them drunk."

A 14-year-old California boy, asked whether girls were "easier" when they were high, agreed: "When they're drunk, it's easier. When they get high, it's kinda easier, too, 'cause they want to do stuff more. They won't go further, but they'll do the lesser stuff easier. But when they're drunk, they don't know what they're doing."

A number of girls confirmed that they were certainly perceived as—and may have been—more vulnerable when drunk. A California 14-year-old put it simply: "If you're drunk, most guys like to take advantage of a drunk girl." But a Maryland 17-year-old suggested there might be a certain amount of self-deception on the girls' parts.

"Do you have any idea whether drinking and drugs make kids more likely to get involved sexually?"

"Definitely. That's the common excuse."

"Which more?"

"Drinking."

"Drinking in particular?"

"Yes. And the common excuse is 'Oh, we . . . I was drunk. I didn't know what I was doing,' which is a lie. It's just an excuse. They might have been a little bit less inhibited, but the feeling was there regardless."

There is, however, a distinction between feeling and behavior; kids can be horny without acting on it, and being "a little bit less inhibited" can certainly affect behavior. As an 18-year-old college girl said, "I've found that I've messed around with people only because I've been drunk and they've been drunk," and a 15-year-old said that being slightly drunk made sex "much easier."

That it's easier doesn't necessarily make it wonderful. As a 16-year-old California virgin said, "People have things they're self-conscious about, and drinking and drugs, your sense of judgment is the first thing to go. When you go out, you may say, 'I'm not going to have sex with just anybody tonight,' but if you've been drinking, all your sense of judgment is gone, and you figure, 'Why not?' Drugs and drink make it seem more natural, because people aren't as tense."

"Do you like that, or do you wake up the next morning full of regrets?"

"Yeah, that happened once. We had a party in my house, with my parents and all their friends and their kids, who are my friends. It was like two parties going on all at once. They got a band for us. We were really drunk, and the drummer of the band and I, I was hanging on to him and he was going up my dress right in front of my dad and I was too drunk even to know anything."

"Did your parents get mad at you?"

"Yeah. They didn't want to do anything while everyone was there, but they got really mad after everyone left. I felt awful. I woke up thinking I must have come off like a slut to everyone who was there—people that he works with and everybody. I was really embarrassed."

It's hard to assess the degree, if any, to which the drummer "took advantage of" this girl, for the urge to *epater* one's parents is ever strong. But some cases are not so ambiguous. A 17-year-old Pennsylvania girl recalled events that took place several years earlier.

"I don't feel comfortable with myself for having sex with him, because it just happened, and we were doing a lot of drugs then. . . ."

"When you were thirteen. What kind of drugs?"

"A lot of pot and speed and downers and . . ."

"Speed and pills and cocaine . . . ?"

"No coke, just a lot of pot and drinking, beer and sometimes wine, not very often."

"Did he have it or did you have it?"

"He had it."

"How old was he?"

"He was a senior."

"And you were . . ."

"Well, no, he would have been a junior and I would have been in eighth grade."

"Did he get the liquor and other stuff?"

"Yeah, he found a way."

"The drugs, too—did he get them, or did you?"

"No, he got those."

"Did you try them first with him, or had you tried them before?"

"I tried them once before, and, you know, I didn't get off the first time, and then I think I just thought, Well, I'm really neat—

TABLE 39   How Drugs Affect Intercourse

	Make It Better	Make It Worse
Marijuana	29%	11%
Hallucinogens	4%	8%
Downers	3%	10%
Angel Dust	3%	5%
Uppers	10%	4%
Quaaludes	6%	4%
Cocaine	8%	4%
Heroin	0	4%
Alcohol	27%	11%

he's a senior and I'm in eighth grade and I feel really neat. Now, you know, I really feel bad and I kind of hate myself, so now I just want to forget it."

For most kids, however, the combination of sex and drugs is by no means a melancholy experience. Not only are marijuana and alcohol linked with more frequent sex, but sexually experienced teenagers generally think they lead to improved sex (see table 39).

In general, boys are slightly more likely than girls to think marijuana makes sex better; girls are more likely to think alcohol does. Girls are also more than twice as likely to think uppers improve sex, though the percentage of girls thinking so declines steadily from age 15 on, while the percentage of boys remains relatively constant. Despite the fact that about a quarter of the teens believe marijuana or alcohol improves sex, only 12% say they smoke "always" or "frequently" before intercourse (81% say they smoke "sometimes" or "never"), and only 14% frequently or always drink.

In the interviews, the kids tended to be relatively mild about the extent to which either marijuana or alcohol affected their enjoyment of sex. Some girls, however, were extremely enthusiastic about Quaaludes. A 15-year-old New Yorker said, " 'Ludes put you in a dreamy feeling. It's like this whole dream of just on a fantasy. It's really great." Another said, "It's written up as to be a sex drug, and it really is, actually. It makes you so horny. It makes you so unaware. I could never hold myself up when I was on Quaalude; my knees'd just shrink in—you feel like a rag doll. It would make you very horny and very tingly and you just want to lie down." Indeed, the only complaint about the drug was that it sometimes was too effective. A 17-year-old girl said, "I did a Quaalude one time, and it was, like, the worst experience."

"Was it really? Some people say Quaaludes are great for sex."

"Well, it was great for me. I was—pow!—so horny I couldn't stand it, but it really turned my boyfriend off."

"He did one, too?"

"No, he didn't. He doesn't do any drugs besides pot."

"So what turned him off?"

"I must have gotten so aggressive that he couldn't stand it. It was on my birthday. I went to school and I was romping around the park near the school, and I remember going up to him and throwing myself at him and I think he didn't like that. And then we went back to my house and it just didn't work, he wasn't into it. He didn't find me attractive in that state."

Though a couple of the younger boys complained that marijuana made them feel paranoid and tentative in their sexual moves, boys more commonly complained about alcohol-related loss of erections; indeed, one said he no longer drank on dates because of previous bad experiences. Several girls had also noticed the problem. A Pennsylvania 17-year-old said, "You know what alcohol does, especially to the male part. Forget it. There's no way." And a 16-year-old New Yorker said, "It's no fun to have sex when drunk. First of all, a guy *can't* have sex when drunk. And when I'm very drunk, all I want to do is go to sleep—'Get offa me!' "

Despite the fact that use of certain drugs is associated with heightened levels of sexual activity, it should be remembered that more than a third (35%) of teens said *no* drug made them enjoy sex more, and almost half (48%) said none made them enjoy it less. For such teens, drugs are—in the sexual arena—an irrelevance. Indeed, a number of the kids echoed a 17-year-old California boy's comment: "You should be able to have sex when you're not stoned. It's sort of like hiding."

12

Birth Control, Pregnancy, and Abortion: Facing the Consequences

Thus far, we've been looking at sex the way most teens do: as a source of physical and emotional pleasure. But as 16% of the girls who'd ever had intercourse were reminded when they became pregnant, it is fundamentally a mode of reproduction. Older girls were even more likely to have become pregnant; nearly a third (31%) of the 17-year-olds and more than a fifth (22%) of the 18-year-olds had been pregnant. The overwhelming majority of these pregnancies (86%) ended in abortions.

Though teenage pregnancy is almost always an extremely unhappy business, teens are apparently willing to take their chances with it. Well under half (40%) used birth control during their first intercourse, and though the percentage rose with the level of experience, only about half (55%) said they normally used any. These figures are a little high, for of those who said they used birth control during their first intercourse, more than a fifth used withdrawal (18%) or the rhythm method (3%). Somewhat dishearteningly, about the same percentage reported using withdrawal (17%) or rhythm (4%) as their usual method (see table 40).

Given that kids seem aware of the consequences of pregnancy (virtually all those we interviewed regarded it as a disaster), one has to ask why the percentage using birth control is so low. The most frequently cited reason (15% of boys, 13% of girls) was the teens' belief that it interfered with sex. Several others reasons were cited as well, as shown in table 41.

Among the kids whose parents had taught them that sex is healthy and normal, about two-thirds (63%) normally practiced birth control. Among those whose parents taught them nothing,

TABLE 40   Type of Birth Control Used

	First Time	Most Recent Time
Rhythm	3%	4%
Withdrawal	18%	17%
Condom	62%	54%
The Pill	11%	45%
Diaphragm	3%	4%
Foam	1%	4%
IUD	0	2%

only half (50%) did. But among the kids who had learned most about birth control from their parents, only about a quarter (28%) used any method of birth control during their first intercourse, a much smaller percentage than those who learned from books or media (50%), their partners (49%), or school (45%). In terms of regular use, with one exception—among those who learned most about birth control from their parents, fully 91% practice it—where teens learned about birth control seemed to have no effect on whether they used it at all or on the method they chose.

Though the kids cite many reasons for failing to use birth control, genuine ignorance about the reproductive process seems to occur only among the youngest kids. A 17-year-old who'd first had intercourse four years earlier said his girlfriend used to tease him: "She used to call my house and say, 'I'm having a baby.' "

TABLE 41   Reasons for Not Using Birth Control

	Boys	Girls
Hard to use	4%	3%
Too expensive	4%	1%
Can't get it	8%	8%
Parents will find out about it	6%	11%
Someone else will find out	3%	4%
Too young to get it	4%	2%
Don't know how to use it	2%	4%
Too embarrassing to get it	5%	11%
Don't have intercourse often enough to use it	13%	18%
Interferes with sex	15%	13%
Don't believe it's right to plan for sex	7%	11%
Birth control is morally wrong	4%	2%
Afraid of physical side effects	3%	11%

"Afterward, you mean?"

"Yeah. Sometimes she used to play like that 'cause we were both kidders. We used to always play all the time."

"Were you using birth control?"

"Thirteen? I didn't know what it was. I never even heard of it before. Thirteen. I didn't know anything could happen at thirteen."

"You thought maybe she couldn't get pregnant or you couldn't get her pregnant."

"That's why we just played around. I betcha if we knew it was capable of happening, we wouldn't have played like that."

"What about birth control now?"

"Oh, I definitely use it."

And a California 12-year-old, who said she hadn't used birth control when she'd first had intercourse because she hadn't yet had a period, didn't use it her second time either, "because I had my period, but it wasn't coming regularly, so nothing could happen."

"You'd started menstruating but you still couldn't get pregnant?"

"No."

"Do you know about birth-control methods?"

"Some of them. Not really."

Older girls, particularly from small towns, more often cited embarrassment as a reason. A sexually active California 16-year-old said she never uses birth control and that her boyfriend doesn't know it.

"He doesn't? What does he think you're on?"

"The Pill. You see, I haven't gone down to Planned Parenthood and I was going to, but I didn't. So don't tell him."

"Why didn't you?"

"I'm afraid. I really am, of an exam and just . . ."

"You've never been to a gynecologist?"

"No. And my mother won't let me. I don't understand why, but . . ."

"Have you asked her?"

"Yeah, but she says, 'Oh, you're too young. You don't need that yet.' "

"And she, of course, doesn't know you're having sex?"

"Yeah."

A 17-year-old Pennsylvania girl said that with her first boyfriend, when she was 15, "the only thing we'd do was the withdrawal method."

"He wouldn't actually ejaculate inside of you?"

"Right. That was the only type, which really isn't that good."

"It is possible to become pregnant."

"Yeah."

"Would it have been difficult for you to get birth control at that time if you'd wanted to?"

"Probably not. I was going to go down to Family Planning a couple of times, but I heard some really kinky stories about that, so I didn't really want to go."

"What kind of stories?"

"Just weird. That they're weird people down there. I was never down there, but I knew girls who had gone down there and I don't know, they didn't like it so much. So then I was going to call a doctor on my own, and I—I don't know. . . ."

"Can you do that without your parents finding out?"

"I don't know. They would probably have known about Family Planning if I had gone down."

"You think so?"

"Probably. They probably know people. I don't know. See, they know just about everybody, so I don't know."

A 16-year-old California girl looked back on an earlier romance during which withdrawal had been the only birth control they'd practiced and said, "I did worry, but I didn't do anything about it. I would tell him to make sure, but he'd always say I didn't have to worry about it. Now I look back and see I was so fortunate."

"Did you ever ask him to use condoms?"

"He just thought that was kind of unnatural. . . ."

"And you never thought of pills?"

"I would have been too embarrassed to get anything."

In some cases, it must be admitted, the girls' embarrassment or fears of unpleasant consequences if their parents find they are using birth-control devices seem entirely justified. A 17-year-old boy from a Washington suburb who regularly used condoms said, "Just the other day a girlfriend of mine, who I've been going out with for about two months now, decided she wanted to go on the Pill because we're having sex a lot. I said, 'You don't have to—at least, don't do it for me. I'm no reason. If you want to, that's fine, but don't do it for me. Do it for yourself.' She said okay. I had never had sex without a rubber; I thought, well, here's a chance I might try it.

"Her parents found the pills. And her parents—her older sister set such a model of the perfect daughter that it's hard for this girl to follow in her steps. Her sister had straight A's, she goes to Temple, big-time virgin till she's married—all that good stuff. And this girl . . . So they blew up and she called me the other day and told me about it. Her parents said, 'Okay, you've got two months to find another place to live.' "

This surely sounds like an unpleasant scene, but the consequences of yielding to embarrassment or to fear of one's parents can be even worse. A 15-year-old New Yorker who'd been fitted for a diaphragm with her mother's knowledge said, "My gynecologist asked to have, since I was underage, a parent's permission, but I think it should be made easier for kids because I think there's some people that can't tell their parents and they need birth control, and in that situation—I'm gonna use [my friend] again: She found it hard to tell her mom for the first time and she stalled a long time before she got her diaphragm, which caused her abortion."

Of course, it is not strictly true that the girl's fear of telling her mother she needed birth control caused her to have an abortion; it simply contributed to her becoming pregnant, and she *chose* to have an abortion. Still, the connection is intuitively correct. The "squeal rule" proposed by the Reagan administration—and still, despite court setbacks, a live issue in many states—would require government-funded clinics dispensing birth-control devices (virtually all such clinics get tax money) to notify the parents of any teenager seeking prescription birth control.

It seems unlikely that such a rule will produce the results its proponents desire. As we've seen, even without a squeal rule, teenagers are far too likely to have sex without birth control. While it's possible that limiting the *practical* availability of birth control by means of a squeal rule might marginally affect teens' sex practices by causing kids to opt for oral or anal sex rather than intercourse, this would hardly seem a giant leap forward in national morality. It's far more likely, however, that the imposition of a squeal rule would be followed by an increase in teenage pregnancies, and a corresponding increase in abortions and illegitimate births.

TABLE 42   Regular Use of Birth Control by Family Income (in thousands)

	Under $6	$6–12	$12–18	$18–24	$24–30	$30–36	$36–42	$42–50
Yes	59%	33%	63%	45%	74%	53%	74%	79%
No	37%	58%	27%	47%	22%	47%	26%	21%
Don't know if partner								
is	4%	9%	11%	7%	3%	×	×	×

Since no one claims that this virtually certain outcome is desirable, the only rationale for a squeal rule is a punitive one—a belief that girls especially should be punished for having sex. This is not a particularly attractive argument—indeed, the more polished advocates of the squeal rule deny any such motive—but it is the only one the facts allow.

To the extent that the squeal rule and its local variations are to be debated as public policy, then, the question must be framed as follows: Granting the desirability of meting out biological and emotional punishment to teens who have intercourse, is increasing the likelihood of unwanted pregnancies the appropriate way? There are at least three grounds for answering the question in the negative.

First, to the extent that such a public policy strikes hardest at those who are forced for economic reasons to use publicly supported clinics rather than more expensive private physicians, it would exacerbate the already existing link between use of birth control and family income (see table 42).

The figures, troubling enough in the present situation, become intolerable when pregnancy is viewed as a state-directed punishment. If the "crime" is equal, then as a matter of equal protection the likelihood of punishment must also be equal.

Even if the use of pregnancy as a punishment weren't economically discriminatory, it would still fail the test of equal protection; for owing to their comparative fertility (a condition meriting neither praise nor blame), some teens would be more likely than others to be punished for identical acts. Apportioning punishment via the gene pool—sentencing, say, blue-eyed bank robbers to 20 years, brown-eyed to 5—is indefensible.

Finally, on a less theoretical basis, there is the fact that the overwhelming majority of teenage pregnancies are terminated by abortion. Many people, of course, find any abortion morally reprehensible, but even those of us who are pro-choice find abortion undesirable as a method of birth control. Any policy that would cause teens to turn toward abortion in greater numbers is surely misguided. And the alternative, an upsurge in the birth of unwanted children, is certainly cruel—for these infants are likely to be the *truly* punished—and perhaps discriminatory along racial and economic lines as well. As one 17-year-old rural black put it, "Minorities always end up getting in trouble. 'What's your problem, man, why you crying?' 'Man, I gave a girl a baby.' White people can get out of that: 'Hey, get her an abortion. We'll keep it quiet, you know. Get her an abortion.' Minority people, it's 'Oh, my God, we haven't got the money. That doctor's talking about five hundred dollars and we don't have five hundred dollars. I think it's cheaper to keep the baby—that'll be on insurance, hospitalization.' "

The indefensibility of the squeal rule hardly means that present public policies affecting teenage sex ought to stand unchanged. To the extent that the state has any legitimate interest in the extremely difficult task of reducing teenage sex, strict enforcement of the existing alcohol laws might prove more effective. To the extent that there is a mutual state interest in the more achievable—and unambiguously desirable—goal of reducing teenage pregnancies, public policy should make birth-control devices more, rather than less, available. Such efforts should be focused on girls, both because they are generally more likely to suffer the consequences of unwanted pregnancies and because they are much more likely than boys to avoid birth control for reasons of embarrassment, ignorance, fear of their parents, or the belief that "planning" for sex is wrong.

Public-policy questions aside, the discovery of an unplanned pregnancy is a traumatic moment for teens. For better or worse, it is likely to change and often to end the couple's relationship; and especially in cases where pregnancy is the first indication parents have that their child has been sexually active, it affects the parent-child relationship as well. Finally, to the extent that the pregnancy becomes more or less public knowledge—as it is likely to—it may change the child's social status.

TABLE 43   Abortion Okay If . . .

Girl has been raped	63%
She is unmarried	24%
She cannot support child	38%
She doesn't want the child	37%
Other reasons	12%
Never	25%

In all cases, however, pregnancy poses immediate moral and practical dilemmas. Should the teen abort the baby? Where? How? If not, should it be kept, or given up to adoption or foster care?

In general, teens are relatively conservative about abortions. A quarter (25%) say it is *never* acceptable, and well under half (38%) approve abortion when the girl would be unable to support the child (see table 43).

Judgments about the morality of abortion are relatively unaffected by age, family income, or place of residence. Religion does matter, however: Catholics (24%) are only about a third as likely as Jews (64%) or as those of no religion (62%) to approve abortion for a girl who doesn't want a child. Race also has some impact: Blacks are more likely than whites to approve of abortion in such a situation by a margin of 50% to 35%. The gap is even more marked between virgins and nonvirgins: Slightly more than half (50%) of those who've had intercourse would approve of abortion when the girl doesn't want the child, but less than a third (31%) of the virgins would.

In our interviews, however, none of these demographic factors seemed to influence the seriousness with which kids addressed the moral question; cavalier answers on either side were unusual. A 16-year-old Pennsylvania girl who'd had a pregnancy scare described her feelings at the time:

"We really thought about that a lot, and I probably would have had an abortion because I'm really into sports and everything and the only way I'm going to college is if I get a scholarship. . . . [Talks about being "scouted" in her particular sport.] If I would have a baby, I'd have to give up my sports and stuff like that and I probably wouldn't get to college then, and I'm not sure, like I said before, if I'd be satisfied with not going to college, if I just had to stay home. I know later I would like to have kids after I'm out of college. I really like babies and kids, I really think they're nice. And that's why it was really a hard decision for me when I did think I was pregnant, if I should have an abortion or not."

"Did you tell your parents about it when you thought you were?"

"No."

"Would you have told them if you were pregnant?"

"I probably think I would have. Not right away, but I think I would have later on."

"How do you feel about abortions in general?"

"They're not right for every woman, but it's her right to decide what she wants, 'cause for some women they're all right and for some others they're not. See, some women think they're killing their baby, and I think that after the first twelve weeks—I don't think I would have an abortion after the first twelve weeks. . . ."

"You would go ahead and have the baby?"

"Yeah, if it was after twelve weeks. 'Cause then I feel like it's starting really to become a baby. Before that, I feel that it really isn't a baby, the first twelve weeks, it's just starting out. But after twelve weeks I kinda—it's starting to look like a baby more and it's starting to get bigger. But some women, they feel that it's a baby right away, and they'd probably feel so guilty if they did have an abortion, like they killed their baby, that there would be too much of an emotional strain on them, and I don't think women like that should have an abortion, 'cause it would make them feel too bad. It's up to the woman to decide, 'cause lots of times abortions are for the best. If the baby's not going to get a good life or something like that and you're going to be bringing the baby up in a bad situation, it probably would have been better just to get rid of the baby."

Often, teenagers attempting to come to grips with the moral issue focused almost automatically on the woman's situation. A 15-year-old virgin from Queens, New York, said, "I'm against abortion, but it depends on the situation. For a person who doesn't want the child, like a rape case or something, it's okay. But a person who goes out to have sex and wants sex shouldn't be allowed to have an abortion. If the pregnant child is really young and it could harm them, they should have an abortion. Depends."

Despite the number of contradictory phrases and impulses in what this girl said—and contradictions are understandable because the subject is difficult—she was clearly voicing the idea that for some kids abortion is an easy escape from consequences they *ought* to face, or foresee and try to avoid.

In general, boys were much more apt to voice such a concept than girls—at least partly, perhaps, because it is not they who have to face the consequences. A 15-year-old Boston boy said that if he got a girl pregnant, "I'd definitely have her keep the kid. No abortion. For a girl who's going to get hurt by it, if she's real young or something, I believe in it for that; but if the girl realizes what she's doing, if she realizes that she's going to get pregnant, she knows that she's going to have the kid and she still goes on with it, she should take the responsibility to have it. If she's going to have intercourse and get pregnant, she should keep the kid." And a 17-year-old Pennsylvania boy said that if he'd gotten his girl pregnant, he wouldn't have wanted her to have an abortion: "I'd be against that."

"So, a tough situation?"

"Yeah. I wouldn't have married her, but I'd be against an abortion."

Girls, obviously, were less likely to feel this way. Sometimes their judgment seemed shaped by concern for the potential child: A 14-year-old rural girl said, "If you're that age—say, a teenager—and you let the baby live, it's just about killing them anyway."

"Why is that?"

"Well, you don't have the proper care for them, it's worse. It's better to just end their agony right away than to let them starve to death or something like that. I'm not against abortions at a teenager age. For a grown-up to have an abortion, yeah, I am then."

A 14-year-old said, "I don't think it's right of people to say abortion isn't right. If you're poor, the last thing you need may be another kid. Abortion shouldn't be something you depend on, so you go all the way every week, but it should be something you can use in an emergency." Typically, even though this girl was a strong defender of the right to abortion, she recognized the morally difficult nature of the question—for instance, that rights could be abused.

Other kids—especially those who focused less on the situation of the prospective baby than on the situation of the pregnant girl— saw the question in an entirely different light. A 16-year-old California girl was thus able to see the choice *not* to have an abortion as a moral failure. "For a girl in high school, if she has no ambition whatsoever, she just wants to become a welfare mother, that's fine, go ahead and have a kid. But other than that, you can't go to college and take a kid along."

Typically, girls tended to see abortion as something you *had* to endure if you were pregnant, and though they were grateful the option existed, they were troubled by it. A 14-year-old New York girl said abortion was "necessary, and I think it's okay because if you're pregnant, it's a way out. If you're fifteen or sixteen years old, there's no way you can have a kid, and I think it would be better for the kid if you had an abortion, because there's no way you could handle it. But it would do a real mind trip on me because to me, even though people say the baby isn't a person yet, I still think it's killing my own baby."

"Would you ever have an abortion?"

"If I was pregnant, yeah."

"Do you know anybody who's had one?"

"Couple of my friends at school."

"How do you feel about that?"

"I think they're nice people. I don't think anything bad about them."

"How do you think they feel?"

"Awful. They went through such a thing. . . . So it's taken them a very long time to recover from it, not really physically, but mentally."

As this girl indicated, the difficulties involved in reaching a decision about abortion are merely the beginning of the pain. A New York 15-year-old described her abortion, at the Eastern Women's Center, as "very good. They counsel you before; then they take you in and get you ready; then you just go in. . . . But it bothers me. It'll probably bother me more in about two years. It'll probably hit me. . . ."

Her abortion, early, was by suction; in cases where the girl is afraid to tell her parents or indulges in wishful thinking, the process itself can be more painful. A 14-year-old California girl, whose boyfriend left town late in her third month of pregnancy, finally told her mother and was admitted to the county hospital for a saline abortion. "It hurt—you have no idea. I was sitting up there—I was laying up in there first. First you start to leak, and there were a lot of Spanish people in there, 'cause those are mainly the only people who have this kind of abortion. There was a Spanish woman in there along with me, and she told me, 'Don't worry, don't worry.' And it *hurts,* it hurts more than your regular labor, but I broke my water bag and everything. I had expelled everything, so I was cooler there the next day, because they usually have to get the afterbirth out and I had already expelled it."

"Was your mom with you?"

"No, she had left. It was about an hour after visiting hours. Then they cleaned me out so I wouldn't have any parts of the baby that would grow and make me bleed. And that hurt. The whole thing hurt. You got to go—go first when you first find out, and that way if you're just one month pregnant, all you go is just zippety-doo-dah and not even go in the hospital, you just stand on the examination table and it's all over. But with me, I didn't tell. It hurt—oh, Christ, you hurt all in here. It hurt me in the shoulder, and you hurt in your head. And they kept giving me shots, and the problem was with me, I was in labor too long, and they had to give me suppositories—the doctors, every three hours, and those things hurt—to make the baby come out faster. I have—I'd like—to get all this off my chest, so I'm glad you asked me."

Getting it off one's chest is hard, for many girls are ashamed to talk about their experience, and when they are willing to talk, they may suffer negative social consequences. A rural boy said that in his class, "eighth grade, there was a girl last year that got pregnant."

"What was the reaction to that?"

"She really blabbered it all over the school and the boy really got mad."

"The boy who made her pregnant got mad?"

"Yeah, 'cause he didn't want anyone to know. She blabbed it all over the whole school. I don't think the boy felt too highly of her. I don't think anybody did, really."

"What did she do with the baby?"

"She had an abortion."

"Did it affect her reputation?"

"Yeah, I guess. In high school, you know, all the seniors and juniors are after her now because they heard about it. They think everybody can get everywhere with her, so they go after her."

Hers was a typical, though not universal, situation. The girl who'd had her abortion at the Eastern Women's Center went to a graduation party two days later. "Our school is very small, 110 kids, so everything that happens to you the whole school knows. So of course at my graduation everyone was coming up to me and asking, 'Are you okay?' It was amazing because it was all pure concern, not, Oh, my God, an abortion, the sleazy bitch. It was very nice, very concerned. I got a lot of calls later, too. It was a very nice feeling. I had a lot of support."

Nonetheless, she soon broke up with her boyfriend. Although one girl said she thought her pregnancy "might have brought us a little closer; going through that together and making a decision like that when you really care about somebody, no matter what the conditions are, no matter how old you are—it's hard," pregnancy generally terminates a couple's relationship. Most last through the abortion, but few survive for long afterward.

In the one case among our interviews where the pregnant girl did not have an abortion, the couple are still together, but the relationship is severely troubled. The couple, Washington blacks, had been living together for two years (since she was thirteen, he seventeen) when the girl got pregnant. Two years later, still unmarried, they were still together, but the father was regularly and flagrantly unfaithful, and the girl, by then seventeen, generally uninterested in sex. The father's financial contributions were fitful, so the girl worked part-time after school every day. Despite their problems, however, the girl was unquestionably a fighter, and unquestionably in love with her daughter.

"What grade are you in now?"

"Twelfth."

"Do you plan to graduate?"

"Yes, I plan to graduate. I hope so."

"Do you find high school different for you because you have a child?"

"It was a little different. I got pregnant when I was in ninth grade and I went to school at [a Catholic school]. I had trouble with a lot of people talking about me when I was pregnant, and I don't live with my mother, and people that talked about me said I was going to drop out of school. Even my mother said I was going to drop out of school when I was going to have the baby. It was kind of hard, me doing my homework and getting up and going to school. But I haven't dropped out. I've managed to keep on going. It's kind of hard and it's expensive and . . . for her to have the things she's supposed to have, it's expensive. I can't hardly get the things that I like, I want to have. I have to buy for her first."

Even though this baby had been planned for, wanted, these were hard and painful choices, and they meant, among other things, that the child was at a neighbor's all day. One admires the mother greatly, but one feels as well that no child of fifteen or sixteen should have to make such choices—not in this country, at any rate. One wishes the social conservatives who are trying to limit women's access to abortions and to birth control might have similarly exerted themselves on behalf of this young mother. But they haven't, and they won't.

13

Homosexuality

Teens who indulge exclusively in homosexual sex are, of course, spared the risk of pregnancy. But they face other problems that may be at least as severe, for their peers' attitudes toward homosexuality remain overwhelmingly negative. Though half the teens (53%) thought it was okay for two girls to have sex together if they both wanted to, three-quarters nonetheless felt that such actions were "disgusting." And again, though about half (49%) thought it was okay for two boys to have sex, more than four out of five (84%) said that such boys were disgusting. Boys and girls were equally intolerant of male homosexuality, but boys (68%) were notably less likely than girls (84%) to find lesbianism disgusting. Of course, lesbianism has long been a staple of male-targeted pornography—indeed, it regularly appears in glossy *Penthouse* and *Playboy* pictorials—and our interviews revealed that for at least some boys it was more likely to be titillating than disgusting.

But when we approached the question in a more practical way, girls actually turned out to be *more* tolerant than boys. Asked what they would do if a same-sex friend told them he or she was gay, only about a third (35%) of the boys, as compared to half (50%) of the girls said they would remain friends. Additionally, boys were more than twice as likely, by a margin of 32% to 16%, to say explicitly that they would break off any such relationship. Indeed, in our interviews, many boys but no girls expressed what might be called an irrational hatred of male homosexuals. A 15-year-old San Francisco boy said, "I hate gays . . . I think all my brothers do, too. They really—it just doesn't seem right. They're a disgrace."

"Are you personally experienced with them?"

"No way."

"Have any guys come on to you or propositioned you?"

"No."

"Why do you think it's bad?"

"It's not normal, I think. There are so many of them and they're all sissies and they talk funny and they dress funny and they look funny and they act funny, you know. It just doesn't seem right."

Another San Franciscan, 14, said, "I hate the motherfuckers. In SF—maybe it's just because I grew up in SF basically, but we go out and beat faggots up all the time 'cause I hate faggots."

"What do you hate about them?"

"It's wrong . . . I beat their fuckin' asses. I hate faggots."

Boys also seemed much more afraid than girls of being identified as gay, even when their sexual experiences and fantasies had been exclusively heterosexual. A 16-year-old from rural Pennsylvania talked about his best school friend: "We get kidded a lot about that. We go driving around together and, you know, if I get tickets to a basketball game, I'll ask him to go and it's the same way with him. And you should *hear* the stuff that we get kidded about. They say—Well, about five weeks ago, he went down to Florida for a week. Well, then the week after he got back, I was going down. And they'd say, 'Why don't you two go down together 'cause I hear Florida's a great place for that kind of stuff?' . . . It's gotten to the point where we look at stuff like 'We can't do that because . . . we can't.' Like we were gonna do this one act—they're having like this 'Gong Show' thing and we were gonna do something in school and he said, 'We can't do that, because, you know, people might think something.' "

Though this seems like relatively mild stuff, such fears seem warranted. A 17-year-old from a Boston suburb saw his best friend emerging from a gay bar, asked him about it, and discovered his friend was gay. "Still your best friend?"

"He's not my best friend now."

"Because of this homosexual thing?"

"Not really. Because I moved. I haven't seen him for a while. Last night was the first time I seen him in like two or three months."

"Did he ever tell you about the stuff he does?"

"No. I just go, 'Keep it to yourself. I don't want to hear about it.' "

"But you were upset at first?"

"A little bit. I was thinking that he might be giving me a reputation or something. 'Why are you hanging around with that faggot?' You know."

"I know a lot of guys your age are real faggot-haters."

"If I'm with my friends, right, and we see a faggot, we'll tease him, but I just do it because—I don't do it to be mean, actually; I just do it so my friends won't think that I'm queer. Because if, like, I say, 'Leave the guy alone, he hasn't done nothing to you,' they're the type of people who would say, 'Oh, you must be a faggot, too.' "

"Do they know about your friend who is a homosexual?"

"Yes."

"And they know you're his friend?"

"Yeah."

"So how does that affect you?"

"Not really. They know that I've moved and can't possibly see him."

"What if you hadn't moved?"

"Still be the same. As long as he didn't come down. They'd probably bother him if he came down, came down to the house, wherever we were."

"So he stopped coming around afterward, after you found out?"

"Yeah, it bothered me, 'cause they used to really pick on him, hit him, punch him around, stuff like that."

"How did they find out he was homosexual? Through you?"

"Yeah. I just figured, Might as well tell them."

"So he had all these friends—"

"Yeah."

"—and then he just didn't have them anymore."

"Yes. He's got other friends, you know."

"Do you feel bad about that?"

"A little bit. I told the kid, 'I can't protect you, because they'll think that I'm a faggot.' But I still like him."

"But you're the one that told he was a faggot."

"Yeah."

"Does that bother you?"

"No."

"You just figured they ought to know?"

"Yeah."

With friends like that, it's no wonder that many teens are reluctant to admit even the faintest hint of homosexual feeling. Though about a third (31%) of teens said they knew a homosexual, and almost one in ten (9%) said they had a gay friend, only one of the more than a thousand teens who answered the questionnaire considered himself a homosexual (3% said they were bisexual, and 97% heterosexual). Unless one assumes that gays are a hundred times friendlier than heterosexuals, these figures must indicate vast underreporting of sexual preference by homosexual teens. Examination of the questionnaires bears this out; for instance, a rural California 17-year-old—one of the handful of boys that age who had no more than kissed a girl—had had oral sex with two different boys during his adolescent years, but still listed himself as heterosexual.

About 5% of teens did say they had participated in some sort of homosexual activity during their adolescence, however, and about a fifth (20%) had participated in same-sex sexual play as children. Contrary to widespread similarities in the kids' moral beliefs about heterosexual acts regardless of regional, class, or religious differences, there is a much smaller degree of consensus about these homosexual activities. Though urban, suburban, and rural kids were about equally likely to say they'd remain friends with someone they discovered was gay, higher degrees of tolerance were associated with higher income levels, and blacks (34%) were notably more likely than whites (22%) to say they'd cut off the friendship if they learned a friend was gay. As we have seen, the gap between the sexes was especially wide in this area, and it would seem that for girls the bonds of friendship are strong enough to overcome the moral uneasiness they might feel.

To a major degree, however, it seems that attitudes toward homosexuality are strongly related to how well kids know anyone who is gay, since such knowledge is associated with tolerance. Kids who knew any homosexuals and those who didn't were about equally ready to call two girls who'd had sex together "disgusting," but those who had gay *friends* differed sharply from the majority (see table 44).

TABLE 44   Lesbians "Disgusting"?

	To Those Who Have Gay Friends	To Those Who Have No Gay Friends
Yes	51%	80%
No	49%	20%

    Similar differences appeared when the question was asked about boys. Though all the kids tended to be more liberal when asked if—regardless of whether they found it disgusting—consensual homosexual activities were morally okay, kids with gay friends were again more tolerant. When the question was asked about girls, the margin was 79% to 49%; about boys, 72% to 45%. Urban teens (13%) are more than twice as likely to have gay friends as suburban (6%), and more than three times as likely as rural (4%). That suburban teens are somewhat more tolerant than either urban or rural kids may be related to their generally higher levels of income. Finally, tolerance was closely associated with the kids' educational plans: Those who plan on high levels of schooling show notably more liberal attitudes (see table 45).

    Despite the evidence of changing values, and despite the efforts of various gay activist groups to provide support for high-school kids in some parts of the country, homosexual teens remain likely to face at least strong disapproval and sometimes brutality from their peers. This does not mean, however, that teens are closed to the notion of exploring homosexual feelings. A 15-year-old New York girl said that one afternoon when she, her boyfriend, and another friend were sitting around her apartment "really drunk . . . I don't know how it started, but I started making out with a girlfriend of mine, and my boyfriend also saw. He came back in and he asked me if I was a lesbian, and he was very upset about the idea of my being a lesbian, and that got me really pissed off,

TABLE 45   Okay for Two Girls to Have Sex Together?

Plan to Finish:	Some High School	High School	Trade School	Some College	College	Graduate School
Yes	44%	44%	51%	52%	54%	60%

because I don't think there's anything wrong with it, because we've known each other since we were like nine years old. I think we both always wanted to do it just to see what it was like, and it was very pleasant for me. . . ."

"Was it kissing or touching?"

"Both. I enjoyed it very much. It was nice. People are always talking about how males and females are equal, they should be able to have equal jobs and everything, but I think on the emotional level, I think females are a lot more sensitive. And if I was to have a relationship with a female, like one of my friends, I think that we would have a really good relationship, because we know each other. We know how we feel, and we'd be more sensitive to hurting each other. We wouldn't do it as easily."

Perhaps because of the greater intolerance among boys, male homosexual experiences tend to be more clandestine, less personal. A Boston 16-year-old said, "The first guy I ever kissed—I hope this isn't grossing you out—was a bartender in the place where I worked, and I didn't even know he was gay. When he got up from the seat—we were sitting in a booth—he lifted himself up on my knee, so I got an idea. We went driving around the circle once and we did it there. It was winter."

"How old were you then?"

"Fourteen. I went with him and his friend. I stopped going there two years ago because I heard someone calling my name once, from a car, and I felt, 'They know who I am, they know I do it.' "

"Doing it consists of blow jobs and kisses?"

"There wasn't much kissing then. Blow jobs and beating each other off."

"What about anal sex?"

"I don't think they do that there."

"Do you see any guys now?"

"The bartender I see once in a while. I wave to him. He knows my family."

"When's the last time you had sex with a guy?"

"Two weeks ago. This artist who did paintings—I ended up talking to him in his shop. I told him I was kind of getting into modeling, which is true, kind of true."

"You met him that day?"

"Yeah. I ended up saying, 'I'll model for you.' So I went up to his studio. He had a place outside the Square. He was working in a store and he had all these life-size portraits of naked men. They all looked angry. I got such an impression of anger, it was unbelievable. He used a lot of blues and purples. I like art, and I could see a lot of the anger that was put into his work. They looked kind of suffering. It was like I could learn a lot from him just by looking at his paintings. He's never sold one, and they should be sold; they're good, there's a quality to them.

"And he never got to paint. We got into something else. He's the first guy I've ever had intercourse with. Every time before that, they'd always done it to me, which I didn't like."

"You mean anal sex? So this time you were the active guy and he was the passive?"

"He asked me what I wanted, and I said, 'I've never been fulfilled in fucking somebody,' so he let me."

"Which do you like better?"

"I like doing it, but I've only done it once. I like doing them both, but not really. I don't like getting fucked, 'cause it hurts. I know it must feel good to them."

"When did you first fuck, or get fucked?"

"My brother. When we were little. Not really little. Still—he still does it."

"Do you still do it?"

"I don't like to. I always have to give, and he always receives."

"He's eighteen?"

"Yeah."

"Does he see girls, too?"

"He's the one with the *Playboy* books and goes out with girls and all. He's really into that."

"Does he have sex with girls?"

"Yeah, mainly girls. I think he just takes his horny things out on me."

This boy had had several other furtive sexual encounters, including one with his parish priest, but wanted a more personal relationship. "I work in a clothes store now, because I like clothes, and I met this kid there a couple of weeks ago who left an impression of being really nice and friendly. I could kind of get across that he wanted to be a friend. I don't think there was anything sexual involved. I'd hope there would be, but I don't think there is. I'd like to be his friend really bad. He held a suit, so I got his number and name, and he ended up being my best friend's sister-in-law's cousin. So last night I called her to tell her he said hi. She said say hi to him. I don't know how to get started. I have his number and I'd like to call him, but 'How'd you get my number?' "

"Would you want to call as a friend or a sex partner?"

"Both. But really as a friend—or really as a sexual partner. I don't know."

"How do you think you've been affected in the last few years by the books on homosexuality?"

"Haven't read any."

"What about the gay rights movement?"

"There is one? I'm not aware of it. I know there's one supposedly somewhere. Is there an organization that has anything to do with gay teenagers? I just want to meet somebody that's like me."

"I don't have the number now, but I'll get it for you."

"It's just that who wants to do it with old guys? The youngest guy I've done it with was my age, but he was put away for a while. The next-youngest was twenty-one. I want to do it with somebody my own age, so we can both enjoy it, so we can be friends. I want to be both friends and lover, or even friends."

"You didn't think there was a gay rights movement?"

"I knew there was one, but I didn't think it was that strong. I thought it might have been this little rented room and on the door it said it."

Listening to kids like this, one wishes gay rights organizations were *more* active, had *greater* outreach. But it's also true that this kid's first sexual experience, when he was 14, was with two older men, in the sort of parked-car quickie we would unhesitatingly call "exploitative" if he'd been a 14-year-old girl. Paralyzed by the fear of bad publicity about "recruiting"—which fears might in many cases turn out to be justified—gay organizations have little choice but to wait for kids who want their help to come to them. On balance, this is probably the best policy, but it doesn't stop one from feeling sorry for the many confused and lonely kids this boy represents.

14

The Next Stage?

Whatever its delights or miseries, however inventive or conventional, teenage sex comes to an automatic end when a kid turns 20. Whatever happens after that is a different book. Yet kids *plan* for the future, and the shape of their futures—and, in a sense, of all our futures—is to some degree shaped by the hopes, dreams, and fantasies of their teenage years.

To the extent that planning does have an effect on reality, it looks as though the institution of marriage will survive for the next generation or so: 87% of the teens surveyed (83% of the boys, 91% of the girls) plan on getting married. These percentages aren't affected by the kids' ages, nor—somewhat surprisingly—by their parents' marital status. (Children of divorced parents in our sample were three times more likely to describe themselves as homosexual or bisexual than children of married parents, but the raw numbers are too small for statistical validity.) Reassuringly, to those who fulminate against teenage sex, plans to marry are not significantly related to whether or not a teen has had intercourse.

Though a significant minority (42%) of teens want the woman to be a virgin when they marry, a majority (53%) think it's a "good idea to live with somebody before marrying that person." Since the percentage of those wanting to be or to marry a virgin bride declines significantly with age, the notion of living together before marriage will probably become even more established than it is now.

The idea that couples should thus try things out is, understand-ably, most enthusiastically endorsed by the children of divorce (see table 46). It is also no surprise that nonvirgins should approve of

TABLE 46   Okay to Live Together before Marriage?

Parents:	Married	Separated	Divorced	Widowed
Yes	50%	63%	69%	57%
No	50%	37%	31%	43%

the idea more strongly then virgins. But there is general national approval. Only in the solid South and the mountain states does a majority disapprove of couples living together; and though rural teens are more conservative, urban and suburban teens are virtually indistinguishable. A 15-year-old New Yorker may have spoken for most American teens when she said, "I'd live with somebody before I'd marry them, of course." A 17-year-old suburban boy put it this way: "You might as well live with her a while, because if you marry her right away, you just find out things that you could have found out while you were living with her. See, that way you don't have to go through the agony of a divorce, in case you got kids or something."

Based on the pain kids expressed about breakups that hadn't included living together, even adults who've never broken up with someone they were living with might find this boy's vision over-optimistic, but it's one that many of the kids share. To the extent that one dares predict the future, however, it seems likely that this generation of teens isn't going to find its greatest difficulty with the *concept* of marriage, but rather with the institution's dynamic. Almost a third (32%) of the boys thought it would be "better if women work at home while men pursue their careers," but only a fifth (20%) of the girls agreed. Indeed, 82% of girls thought women "should be allowed to do anything men do whenever physically possible."

We are, all of us, in for interesting times ahead.

III

Interviews

As noted in the introduction, the interviews we undertook served two purposes: They helped Mathtech design and word our questionnaire, and they provided us with anecdotal evidence to enrich our raw statistical data. Many of these interviews have been cited in Part II, but most examples were necessarily brief—and, of course, were chosen in order to illustrate a particular fact or trend yielded by the statistics. In this section, however, we want to give the teens a chance to speak in a context where their words would be free from our judgments (though not, I would hope, from the readers').

The interview excerpts that follow are arranged as much as possible to follow the subject-matter order of Part II. Names and identifying geographical references have of course been changed, and the interview excerpts have been edited for readability.

Fifteen-year-old Suburban Male

Q: Did your parents ever talk to you about sex? Never?

A: No, my father just said to me once, "You're getting older now, you better watch it." I knew what he meant. Like, I hope you don't ever get a girl pregnant.

Q: That was the beginning and the end of your sexual discussion with your parents?

A: Yeah. The birds and the bees. [Laughing.]

Q: Do they ever talk about sex between themselves?

A: No, I never heard them, never. But my mom's open about it, you know.

Q: What does she do that's open? Give an example.
A: She always says, "If there's ever anything you ever want to know, just ask me."
Q: She has said that?
A: Yeah.
Q: Did you ever ask her anything?
A: No.

Twelve-year-old Urban Female

A: We talk about my mom's boyfriend.
Q: She has one?
A: Yeah. She's not very young. And so we talk about Harry sometimes, a lot of times.
Q: She likes to talk about him with you?
A: Yeah. It's nice.
Q: What kinds of stuff do you talk about?
A: Oh, he's in the middle of a divorce, so we talk about how his ex-wife-to-be, I guess you would say, is very mean to him. She stole his dog, broke into his house, and all that stuff. And we talk about some other things.
Q: Like what?
A: Like about sometimes I bring it up about they might get married. They're on vacation now. So we talk about that, she goes, "Oh, God, I hope I get those reservations," and all that stuff.
Q: Do you have any feelings about those kinds of conversations? Do you like to talk about her boyfriend more than the other stuff?
A: Oh, it's—it's okay to talk about him. She gets all kinda . . .
Q: Silly?
A: Yeah.
Q: Does he ever come over and stay?
A: Oh, yeah. Not overnight, but I think once he did when they were out real late.
Q: How did you feel about that?
A: Well, at first I didn't like it and I cried about it a lot.
Q: About him staying over?
A: Yeah, because my parents were divorced when I was only a year and a half old, so I never see my mother with a man,

right, so when they first started going out together I cried about them going out together. I don't know why I did that, though. Because I thought that he was taking her away from me and stuff like that. So I kinda got very upset about it. But, yeah, he comes over and all.

Q: Do you ever talk about that? Does she ask how you feel?

A: About him?

Q: About him coming over and . . . The time he spent the night, did she ask you anything about it?

A: Um, it was a long time ago; um, I can't remember. Well, it's like they went together and I said, "Are you staying in the same, what do you call it, motel room?" and she said, 'No, because that would interfere with his divorce." But it wouldn't bother me if they did.

Sixteen-year-old Rural Male

Q: Do your parents ever talk to you?

A: Yes.

Q: What have they told you?

A: Well, like maybe I'll be going to a party or something and my mother will ask certain questions and she'll say, "You know, certain stuff is wrong," and they'll talk about it. I'll say, "They might be drinking there," and she says, "Well, you know I don't like you to do that," and "You know that's wrong"—and so I don't.

Q: You don't drink?

A: Right.

Q: Because you know that's wrong?

A: Actually, I don't really like the stuff. I haven't tasted anything I've liked. I've tasted beer before, but I don't like it. And there are many times when I could have had some, 'cause, with my dad being a baseball player, they've got loads of it in the clubhouse and you can . . . He doesn't drink too much, but when he was playing, every once in a while on the way home from a game he'd take one in the car with him and if I wanted to I could have asked him for drinks and stuff like that.

Q: Is it partly because of your religion that you don't do it?

A: Well, they're—I wouldn't say that they're really strict, but they come down on me pretty hard, you know, they give me the impression, they stress it so much that I know I'm afraid to do it because of what they would think.

Q: What they would think or what they would do?

A: Both.

Q: What do they tell you to do or not do about sex?

A: Well, my mom usually brings up examples, like when you're watching TV shows she'll see something there like some girl is pregnant and they have this whole situation with the guy and the girl that are still in high school. . . . She goes, "You know that you shouldn't do that, don't you?" She uses that [TV] as a way to talk.

Q: Things that she sees on TV?

A: Uh-huh.

Q: TV becomes a tool?

A: Yeah. Like there are certain shows that she doesn't like 'cause of stuff like that. I mean, what I say is, I tell her I know wrong from right and just because they have it on the TV show doesn't mean that I'm going to go out and do it. I explain *that* to her and I say there's no reason why I can't watch a certain TV show just because that has it.

Q: What shows might she object to?

A: "One Day at a Time"—she doesn't like that. It was on right after school when I'd come home and I'd be really tired and I'd lay down on the couch and watch that and she says, "I don't like that show."

Q: That's the one with the divorced mother and two daughters?

A: Yeah. The two daughters, the older one, she's going out with all different guys and stuff like this, she wants to get married to a man who's in his forties, and on the show she's eighteen, and Mom just doesn't like the way they run the daughters' lives on the show. I guess it's 'cause that's not the way she would do it.

Q: Does your father ever talk to you about it?

A: No.

Seventeen-year-old Urban Male

Q: Did you ever play something out in your mind, put yourself into a scene somewhere, imagine what it would be like?

A: Yeah. Like my friend, he's talking about a girl built, just way out there, everything. He used to talk about coming home, and she'd be in a negligee, he done came from a hard day of work. He takes his briefcase, throw it over to the couch, and she'd lead him on with her negligee, lead him into the bedroom. My other friend, when he comes home everybody's gonna be nude. He always had that idea . . . he even talks about it now. When his wife come home everything is always off. They just sit, eat dinner nude. Something like that, you know. I used to think he was kinda wild.

Q: What about you? What main things did you think about?

A: I used to think about taking a girl and going to a drive-in or something like that, I'd park the car, and you can take the seat and fold it back and make it into one of those beds. "What are you doing? What are you doing?" "You're gonna find out." [Laughing.] Yeah, man.

Q: Ever do anything in a drive-in?

A: Who, me? Most of the time when I go to a drive-in it's a family outing.

Q: You don't do it at those?

A: [Laughs.] No, you don't do it at those.

Q: What about family? You say your uncle gave you your first rubbers. Where did you learn about it, when did your parents tell you about sex, did you ever talk about it?

A: No. I don't know. I guess people figure you're gonna get it off the streets. Guys talking and stuff, when you're young, then it's "I guess it's too late to tell him, he already knows," you know. Some parents say, "I'll wait till he gets to be twelve or thirteen, then I'll tell him." By twelve or thirteen he could tell them, tell his parents more than they know. "Say, Daddy, did you ever try tongue-kissing?" "Where did you get that from, boy?" Everybody I know, their parents won't say anything about that. They'll talk about protection—"You keep yourself protected. I'm not supporting no baby, you know. I make enough just for y'all, not enough for a little junior. I don't want to be an early grandfather."

Q: So your parents and your friends just kinda told you to stay out of trouble.

A: Yeah.

Q: Did they tell you how to stay out of trouble in any way?

A: They kinda figure you could get it off the streets. Yeah, some do. This white dude was always talking about how he's not gonna give any girl no baby. He's gonna have an affedectomy or . . .

Q: A vasectomy?

A: Yeah, a vasectomy. He was gonna get one of them, right. Is that where they . . .

Q: It's tying the tubes.

A: Yeah.

Q: So you can still come but you're kind of sterile.

A: Yeah, that's what he used to talk about all the time. I'm gonna get one of them, right. That way I can be with any girl I want to. But he changed. Everybody told him about being a father, he started to think, Wait a minute, I wanna be a father, too. I don't want to adopt any kids when I'm old and stuff. He's always talking about crazy stuff like that. We'll be sitting around when we have nothin' better to do, talk about them fantasies, yeah.

Q: What about books and movies, porno movies, dirty books?

A: Oh, yeah. A lot of people got subscriptions down there. I think we probably got more subscriptions than any other state.

Q: What?

A: *Playboy.* "You see this poster lately," you know, "That's the new one, man? Put it on the wall, man." I remember one time I had a poster—Miss April, right; nice-looking, right. So I didn't know how my mother's gonna take it. So I put it on the other side of my closet—you know, the side where you open it up. I can see it but nobody else can see it. For some reason my mother came to clean up one day. So she looked in my closet and she said she didn't see it until she turned around and saw a "butt-nekkid"—that's how she said it—a "butt-nekkid woman" in her face. She called me all the way from outside, I was playing football. So I came all the way inside and she said, "What is this butt-naked woman doing on the wall?" I said, "Everybody else is doing it." "Just because everybody else is doing it you don't put no butt-naked woman on the wall"—you know, ripped it off the wall, ripped it all up, you know.

Q: She got real upset?

A: Yeah, she took the stuff serious. So I never put up any posters or anything. She know I look at the books, right, but she don't want no posters, so when people come over or company or something like that, "what you got there, a kid who puts posters on the wall and fantasizes while he go to sleep or something like that?" That's why they put it up on the wall, anyway. Used to get a naked woman, get a little black light, you know. You turn off the light, but you just change the face of somebody else you know.

Seventeen-year-old Urban Male

Q: If you could live now, or be a teenager in the sixties, which would you choose?

A: Now. 'Cause, from what I get—most of my friends' parents are all from the sixties and fifties, and they're really strict and stuff—so what I really get, I guess that parents back then must've been *really* strict. Be in bed by a certain time, no more than holding hands, stuff like that, no pot.

Fourteen-year-old Urban Male

Q: Do you think times are different now?

A: Of course they are. I think they're real different.

Q: You think it's more permissive?

A: What's permissive?

Q: Like liberal.

A: More liberal, yeah.

Q: Kids do stuff younger?

A: Yeah, I think. 'Cause I didn't grow up then so I don't really know, but I think, 'cause my dad said that he never even fucked a girl till he was seventeen, and he's thirty-eight now. So I think.

Thirteen-year-old Suburban Female

Q: On weekends, do you ever get together with guys?

A: Nope.

Q: Do you want to?

A: Nope.

Q: You're not interested in boys.

A: Nope.

Q: How about in school?

A: Nope.

Q: How come?

A: I don't see nothin' in it.

Q: Have you ever been interested in boys?

A: Nope.

Q: How about with your friends?

A: They like them, I don't.

Q: Are you different than your friends in that respect?

A: Uh, yes.

Q: Do they give you any trouble about that?

A: No.

Q: Why don't you tell me your opinion on why you don't see anything in boys?

A: . . .

Q: What do you think is the difference between you and your friends. What do they do that . . .

A: They play with them a lot. Tease 'em and call 'em names and hit on 'em.

Q: You're in seventh grade?

A: Right.

Q: Any boy-girl parties?

A: A lot.

Q: Do you go to them?

A: Some of them.

Q: What happens when you are there?

A: Just dance.

Q: Do you like to dance?

A: Sometimes.

Q: Do you like to dance with boys?

A: No, not really.

Q: What do you have against guys?

A: Nothin'. I just don't see nothin' in 'em.

Q: How about older boys? Do you like older boys?

A: No.

Q: You think boys just mean trouble?

A: No, I just don't like 'em.

Q: Did you ever have a bad experience with a boy?

A: No.

Q: Did your mother tell you to stay away from them?

A: Yep.

Fourteen-year-old Suburban Male

A: Girls are totally different. They're screwed up. They have so many ways of thinking, you think one minute they think one thing, you ask them, and then the next, they always think all kinds of stuff—I never know what they're gonna be like. 'Cause girls are always different. One will think this way, another will think this way.

Q: You think guys think the same way you do?

A: Most guys, I think, think like I do. Most guys, I think, wanna fuck a chick before they get married, definitely. I think.

Q: And some girls?

A: Most girls, I think, want to before they get married but not when they're young. I heard something like 60% of chicks fuck before they get married. I wouldn't even want to marry a virgin, you know, because . . .

Q: Would you want to sleep with a virgin?

A: Sure, I wouldn't mind.

Q: A while ago men thought they wanted to only marry virgins. . . .

A: Why? It sounds stupid to me.

Q: A woman who's really pure . . .

A: Well, I *don't* want a woman who's pure. I wouldn't marry a virgin. I'd ask her to go out and fuck somebody first.

Q: You would?

A: Yeah. I want her to be experienced, to know what's happening, to be on top of things. I want her to know all kinds of things to do and stuff.

Q: Sexually?

A: Yeah. And also, if they're gonna wait until they get married, how thrilling can they be? If they're gonna wait till they get married, they can't be very sexy or anything.

Fifteen-year-old Suburban Female

Q: Have your friends ever done anything that was real kinky?

A: Kinky. I believe so. Yes. Um—oh, wow—um, yeah, like, should I say what they did? Like, I have one friend, the guy went down her pants and she says okay, you know, and it's third base, okay, and she did the same thing to him, which I think . . . I couldn't do that, you know, I just couldn't, I don't know why.

Q: Did she talk about it?

A: Uh-huh. She talked about it and I thought, how could you. I said, "Icchh, yuk," she said, "Well, 'cause he wanted me to," but . . . I think it's really important to be able to say no.

Seventeen-year-old Suburban Male

A: Yeah. I fell in love the minute I saw her.

Q: You did? How old were you when this happened?

Q: It began in like eighth grade. And I've only really cared about her from that time on.

Q: You sound quite certain about this.

A: Yeah.

Q: Adults often say it's only puppy love, and—

A: I know, and I don't believe that. Why can't a child love just as much as a grown-up? Emotions are emotions.

Fifteen-year-old Suburban Male

Q: You say you think it's okay for girls to want sex as much as boys, but even so there's this . . .

A: Now, it's like, I think it's unfair 'cause a guy can't really get a bad reputation. He *can* get a bad reputation for going too far with a girl, to try and force her, but you don't usually hear of guys getting a bad reputation. Of course, it's the guy that makes the first move, right. Most of the time. I don't know. I think it's bad if a girl will fuck around with some guy here and there, every other guy that comes by—that's my definition of a slut.

But if you're going out with somebody and say you fucked her fifty times a day. That's different if she wanted to. You know what I'm saying?

Seventeen-year-old Urban Male

Q: When you have sex now with your girlfriend, do you worry about your being a good lover at all?

A: It don't bother me. It bothers her. She thinks, Oh, am I good enough for you? and things like that.

Q: What does she worry she's not good enough at?

A: Making love. Because it's her first few times.

Q: But it was your first few times, too.

A: But I don't worry about it. I'm not supposed to.

Q: Why is that?

A: Because I'm a man.

Seventeen-year-old Suburban Male

Q: I asked you before about your expectations because sex is glorified in the culture now much more so than when I was your age, in movies, even TV shows, and it's built up to be quite a fantastic thing. Keeping that in mind, was it what you'd been led to believe?

A: No. It was supposed to be the greatest thing on earth.

Q: You feel it was cracked up to be that thing?

A: Yeah. And that's what my expectations were. But it wasn't.

Q: How close did it come?

A: Well, I have several favorite things. I enjoy sex, but I don't enjoy it any more than I do good food or backpacking or music or traveling.

Q: Well, your experience of sex is more limited than your experience of those other things.

A: Right. I may grow to appreciate it, just as you grow to appreciate good food.

Seventeen-year-old Suburban Male

A: Her parents found the pills. And her parents—her older sister set such a model of the perfect daughter that it's hard for this girl to follow in her steps. She had straight A's, she goes to Temple, big-time virgin till she's married—all that good stuff. And this girl . . . So they blew up and she called me the other day and told me about it. Her parents said, "Okay, you've got two months to find another place to live." First of all, I said, "I doubt that very seriously, I doubt parents can just kick a kid out." And she was hyper and she was crying. So that's the way they look at it. Instead of getting mad at a kid for that, sex is a part of life, sex is something that can be enjoyed. I'm not saying you should have sex every two seconds. But they should . . . instead of looking at it like sex is dirty, you shouldn't be doing it—"I didn't do it until I was twenty-five and married"—they should look at it like, Here is my young daughter. She's going to have sex; at least she is responsible enough to take the Pill, at least she's got enough common sense. But they don't think of that. I think they're looking at it wrong. I think that's very responsible of the girl to make a decision like that. She could be like a lot of foolish girls and not take the Pill at all. Say, "Come on, make love to me without a rubber." That's stupid. I'd get madder at that kid. But her parents don't understand that, don't see that. But I guess her parents are very Victorian. Her mother once said to the girl that "Sex for me is nothing. I let your father because it's something for him." That's pretty bad shape. But the daughter, she knows sex is fun. We have fun all the time we have sex. I think that's putting a heavy burden on that girl, 'cause sex is not wrong and parents shouldn't come out and say it is, 'cause it isn't. There is a time and place for everything, but you shouldn't make sex bad.

Q: Why do you think parents feel that way?

A: Because they are scared. They are scared that their kid will get pregnant. It's like stealing. You tell a kid jail is so terrible, that you can die in jail, they wouldn't steal. You tell a kid sex is so bad—it will make you pregnant and it will make you die in hell—that they won't want to have sex. I can understand that. But it screws up the rest of their life. What happens when they get married—she ends up sitting back and saying, "Okay, husband, go ahead," and that's no fun. Unless the guy is really weird and gets off on girls that don't have fun. I can't understand that.

Seventeen-year-old Urban Male

A: You know white people have been pegged for a lot of stuff, you know. You know, eating and playing and orgies. You guys do it up, don't you?

Q: Well, that's what you pegged us as. . . .

A: We just do it straight as normal, you know. Maybe get into a little breast action, but other than that, we've been pegged as straight guys. Now, they say Chinese people they make love quick, I mean it's over with, man. They say Chinese people make love in ten minutes, it's all over. I remember we used to talk about that—"Chinese people make love in ten minutes." Richard Pryor [sound of fast Chinese]: "That's it, buddy." "Hey, wait a minute, I paid you fifty dollars." They say white people, they don't know what stopping is. White people could go a whole week. They say white men have the urge, they come home and throw their suits off. The drawers are out there by the door where they came in, T-shirt in the hallway.

Q: Do you think it's basically true about different races and what images people have—from what you know, do you find it's basically accurate or real?

A: Only thing I can go by is what people say, and I hear white people talk about it more than black people do. As a matter of fact, I hardly hear black people talk about oral sex and stuff, orgies and whatnot. I hear a lot of white people talk about orgies and stuff like that. So I guess I sort of pegged them as . . . Chinese people making love real fast. Spanish people, man, they gotta talk a month before they can get it on. . . . "I've been going with you for six months, won't you give me a kiss," something like that. But they always say minorities always end up getting in trouble. "What's your problem, man, why you crying?" "Man, I gave a girl a baby." White people can get out of that.

"Hey, get her an abortion. We'll keep it quiet, you know. Get her an abortion." Minority people, it's "Oh, my God, we haven't got the money. That doctor's talking about five hundred dollars, and we don't have five hundred dollars. I think it's cheaper to keep the baby—that'll be on insurance, hospitalization."

Q: That's basically how it goes down?

A: I'm not prejudiced or nothin' like that. But white people, it's "Let's keep it quiet. I give you a thousand dollars, you get the abortion, you don't see my son again," and it's all over with, right. They see you about ten years later, "How you doing?" White people is pegged as playing more than blacks. Like, a white guy can marry a white woman, and next year he's got a girl on the side, you know. My mom sees the soap operas, so she swears she's an expert on it. "Don't tell me. I look at 'Days of Our Lives.' I know what's going on with white people." My cousin had to do a research paper, so he did it about soap operas, white people's lives, as far as doctors and nurses. Like nurses, the only way you can advance is go to bed with a white doctor, something like that. He can move her up in rank. Next thing you know, a first-year nurse becomes a head nurse, you know. All she knows is twenty medical terms. . . .

Q: Do you think people really get affected a lot by what they see on TV?

A: Sure. This white guy I know swears black people's lives are just like on "Good Times," we always suffering, we don't have a meal on the table, we don't have no steak, anything. We kill some watermelon, right. You can't stop us from tap-dancing, right. He'd say, "Man, don't tell me, I used to look at 'Good Times,' you all can barely scum up any money. . . ." We say, "Yeah, we look at them soap operas, and your daddy got somebody on the side." Movies and stuff. White people always seem to come out on top in the movies and black people don't, you know. As a matter of fact, I always think whites kind of consider themselves as superior.

Seventeen-year-old Suburban Female

A: Well, you know, like "Roots" came on and people saying whites used to do the blacks wrong. That was then; they ain't doing *us* like that. I'd like to have a white girl be my friend, because they know more and they can teach you. But see, black people, they dumb and they curse. They so dumb. White people, they can help you and they'll talk to you. They help you with your vocabulary, they know how to talk better. Then when you go for a job, you know . . . I would like a white friend 'cause black people they just curse. They going downtown, going out to the mall and buying all these forty-dollar pants and it still don't look right. White people, they got these big beautiful homes and everything. Black people got dirty houses, and roaches running all around and everything.

Sixteen-year-old Suburban Male

A: Yeah . . . When I was in ninth grade, I felt that the seventh and eighth graders hate me . . . because there were two kids in my grade that didn't like me, and there was one kid in the grade below me and I felt every time I walked by the kid they all made fun of me or said something against me. And then kids' brothers below them said stuff to me, called me names and everything. I didn't have any friends in junior high.

Q: Sounds pretty awful. You must have been glad to get out.

A: So as soon as I got into tenth grade, I thought, Great, I'm in tenth grade. My ninth grade year was okay, I only had two kids in ninth grade who didn't like me, I didn't really care about some of the girls. They were a bunch of bitches. When I finally got into tenth grade, I felt, Well, half the grade is going to be East Junior High and half the grade is going to be West, so I have all the West kids to work on, and make friends, you know. So I said a lot of hellos, I tried pretty hard to make friends, and put on a bit of an act—I'd do what they wanted me to do. But I grew out of that. I'm trying right now to be who I am and do what I want. I was made to feel low to be in acting class, though.

Q: They assumed you were homosexual or something?

A: They'd put you down just because you were in acting— anything having to do with the arts, forget it. Especially in my school, where everything is regulated around sports.

Q: If you're not in sports you're a faggot?

A: Yeah. It was hard for me, and I had a few talks with my sister, who I never knew till I was in tenth grade. I knew her but I didn't know her. She was thirteen years older than I am, and I never talked to her. I first talked to her in the summer of my ninth grade year, I told her a couple of problems and she really helped. There was so much I'd kept inside myself for so long, and if you let out to one person, half of it is off you and you get someone to talk to. So that grade was good. Eleventh grade, last year, was good. I was on the swim team. I knew all the people on the swim team.

Q: So you're an athlete after all?

A: It was swim team, and no one liked it. It was a co-ed swim team, which is the only way I would do it. If it was all boys I wouldn't do it because I'd always be picked last and I hated it. With the girls, they couldn't really compare me. They could say, "At least he's not as bad as her." There's always someone lower than me that they can resent. I feel that everyone's higher than me sometimes. My sister always said that she thought I was higher than everybody else. She said sometimes I act like a snob, but I didn't mean it. I always keep things inside me, I don't know what to say, so I just shut up and smile.

Q: Someday you can leave Meadow High.

A: I want to stick with it. I wanted to go to another school, because I knew the seventh and eighth graders were coming up who were going to be the ninth and tenth graders, who I thought all hated me. Last year went really good, none of them said a thing, I didn't have any trouble with anybody, except for the same two kids in ninth grade, who had nothing better to do than pick on me, that's how I felt. Nothing really physical. I was really scared. I never got into a fight since I was in fifth grade. Now I think I should have gotten into a fight sometime. But when you were in junior high, you compared yourself with everybody, you had to fight somebody to say you'd fought him. When you get into high school they're all a lot more mature. So far I haven't had anything happen this year, and I don't expect anything bad to happen, and I'm going to have a lot of fun.

Q: What kind of fun?

A: I'm going to be in a variety show that we're going to be putting on, going to try to be in the senior class play, that'll look good in my résumé. I did a slide show a couple of Saturdays ago, I got paid thirty-five bucks, and made a lot of connections through my acting group. I have a lot of fun in plays. And the people, the kids. I usually look down to the right or to the left, or don't walk down the same hallway, but these past two years I've been everywhere. I look at anybody I want, I say anything to most people, I say hi and kid around and who cares if they hate me to death, I'll still smile.

Q: Why should they hate you?

A: I don't know.

Fourteen-year-old Rural Male

A: I'm not shy with most girls, really. With some girls I am.

Q: Why would you be shy with some girls and not with others?

A: Some girls that are really big shots in school, I guess you're shy with them. The girls that really act like hot stuff.

Q: These girls your age?

A: Yeah.

Q: Does it matter that you're a ninth grader, does it really change . . .

A: Yeah, it matters a lot. Well, the girls in my grade. When you're a freshman in high school, the eighth grade girls are in another school, the ninth grade girls like the upperclassmen, that's why. Next year, well, the ninth grade girls come in. You don't see many freshmen going out with freshmen.

Eighteen-year-old Urban Male

A: Most girls, if you want them to be yours, you have to be theirs. They want that. There's a real sexual revolution these days, I'm sure *you* know. I think girls are really turning around and coming from the same side, they're looking at their own values and saying, "I want to get it, too; I'm horny, let's do it; come on, take me out; let's go fuck," stuff like that, they're coming from that angle, they'll come and say, "Hey, what are you doing, you're not communicating with me, what are you going after these other girls for, am I not enough for you?" Stuff like that, that you would say or another guy would if his girlfriend was disinterested, didn't want to go to bed with him, talked to other guys, stuff like that, you know, things to make you feel unsure. You feel nervous and unsure of your relationship. You feel like kind of paranoid about how you feel about it. But the sexual revolution is under way, a lot of girls can really pick and choose now, whereas before they were waiting to be picked or chosen, which has changed the virginity ratio a lot, I think, because the right guys for these girls, the good girls that didn't want to have sex with someone that was just a Casanova or something, the big stud in school, would have to wait, they would have to wait a long time, they would actually have to wait a long time, but now they're kind of giving the word out, you know, "Hey!"

Q: Are girls calling up guys more for dates and stuff now or is that not really changed?

A: That's not really changed a whole hell of a lot, I'd say in the last ten years it probably hasn't changed a whole hell of a lot, but then again the last five years or so are all I really know about. I get called a lot, but just to notice them, just "Let's talk," you know. Just to show an interest, you know. I think too many girls feel still uptight about asking, "Do you want to come do this?" Girls will ask me if I'm going with them, you know, if they're, like, my girl. . . . It sounds really ridiculous, sounds almost like I'm going back on what I said a few seconds ago, but girls that I'm going out with real close, you know, that I'm real tight with, they'll ask me out, you know. A lot of things I like is when you're real close to somebody they can—they know your situation, you know, if you're poor. Hey, like, I play sports, I can't work, I don't have a lot of cash, I have, you know, five bucks a week to eat and whatever, and a girlfriend I know works all the time, you know, and she'll—I'll say, "Hey, what do you want to do?" She'll say, "Want to go to a movie?" "Yeah." That's great.

Q: Do you think most guys still feel the pressure to come up with the bucks if they're going to go out?

A: Yeah; it's a real drag, too. I was turned away from movies so many times because I didn't have the bucks. I met a girl not too long ago from Tech, she was really nice. She was really turned on to my body, which kind of gave me a funny feeling. She was—I don't know, I liked it, you know. We were talking at a party, drinking, and I told her I was a wrestler—no, I was talking to another guy, as a matter of fact, so it came out real good. I didn't say, "Hey, I'm a wrestler!" This guy said, "Hey, you're a wrestler, aren't you?" and I said, "Yes," so I guess it came out real good. She dug that, she just wanted to feel my body. I got her name and everything and she said, "I'll be back in another week, why don't you give me a call." And I did and I said, "Hey, I'd really like to take you out, but I just don't have any money," and she said, "It works out okay, you know. I have to get up at 7 A.M. and leave, anyway," and I said, "Okay, if I get there, I'll give you a call." So it worked out real good and I didn't feel bad about it, but I did feel obligated to call her because I didn't want to lose her as a prospect, you know what I mean—like, you know, if you're ever in town, what the hell, the more numbers and names you got, the less lonely you'll be.

Fourteen-year-old Urban Female

Q: When you were seeing him regularly, how often did you have sex?

A: I don't know. Once or twice a week.

Q: Where did you do it?

A: At his house.

Q: He has his own house?

A: No, he lives with his parents.

Q: Did his parents know about it?

A: No, they were at work.

Q: It was during the day?

A: Yeah.

Q: Did your parents know?

A: Know about all this? No.

Q: Your grandma, either?

A: Oh, God forbid if she knew. It would be awful gnarly.

Q: So did you like sex with Bob?

A: No. I didn't *feel* anything.

Q: Did you ever have an orgasm?

A: No. I think I'm too young, that's the way I feel. It'll happen sooner or later.

Q: Did you try different stuff with him, did you try oral sex or—

A: Yeah.

Q: What did you think about that?

A: Well, I knew him, so I guess it was better, 'cause I knew him.

Q: You doing it to him or him doing it to you?

A: Do I have to say?

Q: No, not if you don't want to.

A: Well, I want to help you, but I just don't—

Q: If it's embarrassing, we don't have to talk about it.

A: I don't know. It's just that I have a fear of my mother having cows. She'll find out and she'll have a spastic attack and I'll get into trouble.

Q: She'll never know. We interview so many kids across the country and none of them are identified by name.

A: Okay. Now, what was that question again?

Q: Oral sex.

A: Well, he didn't want to do anything to me.

Q: Did you want him to?

A: No, because it's not really all that big, but he wanted me to do him, so I had to.

Q: Did you like it or did you just feel that you had to?

A: It wasn't horrible.

Q: It wasn't horrible?

A: It was not horrible. You kind of like it after a while. You kind of get into it.

Q: The first time, did you like it? Was that the first time you'd done oral sex to a man?

A: Yeah. I had to muster my guts; he'd been trying to get me to do it for about two weeks. And so all of a sudden we were on the couch and next thing I know I was just there. It was all right, you got to get used to it. So I got used to it, then I really didn't mind.

Q: Then after that did you do it a lot?

A: Yeah, he liked it, so . . .

Q: Did you like regular sex? Actual intercourse?

A: I really didn't care. I mean, if he wanted to I wanted to. . . . But if I didn't want to and he wanted to, I had to.

Q: You did feel like it was an obligation of the relationship?

A: Sometimes. And then sometimes I'd ask him.

Q: You felt like . . . horny.

A: Yeah, I was all horny, and so yeah, I'd ask him once in a while.

Q: What do you like about him, this guy Bob?

A: I can't stand that name. Oh, I don't know.

Q: Like what initially attracted you? Was it his looks, personality—

A: Oh, he's cute.

Q: Good-looking? What's that to you?

A: Let's see. He's got pretty eyes, nice hair, he's got a cute behind, and I don't know, he lifts weights.

Q: Good body?

A: Yeah. That's about it.

Q: Do you think you're in love with him?

A: Yeah. I am. As long as my mom isn't going to find out, yes, I am.

Q: Does she not approve of him?

A: No, really, 'cause he's kind of like on the dark side, you know what I mean?

Q: He's black?

A: Yes.

Fourteen-year-old Urban Male

A: On Saturday I'll go out and party. You look young, so you'll understand. We'll go out partying on Saturday, and Sunday I'll go out and party, and I get a day off on Wednesday and I'll get some friends and we'll skateboard and stuff, friends around my house. Usually when I go party and stuff, it's with my other friends, from ballet. I have two different kinds of friends.

Q: What's the difference?

A: The kids around my house are all kinda punks and the kids at ballet, they're not straight but they kinda all have morals and my other friends don't have morals, kinda.

Q: When you go partying with your friends around your house, what do you do?

A: Get stoned, get drunk, have a good time, pick up chicks and stuff. And if I go partying with my other friends, we'll go out and drive around and, good ol' American kind of fun, go to a concert or something.

Q: Those are the ballet friends?

A: Yeah.
Q: Do they smoke dope?
A: Yeah.
Q: Both groups of friends smoke dope?
A: Yeah. I don't know anybody who doesn't.
Q: Do you do any other kind of drugs?
A: Not really. Coke sometimes, but that's too expensive. I don't want to get into anything heavy. I just do it for fun; coke's real fun.

Sixteen-year-old Suburban Female

A: I had a really bad relationship with this guy. I liked this guy the first part of school all the way till March, and he only liked me as a friend. And I started liking some other guy in the middle of March, and this guy and I had become good friends. Then he called me one night, I was surprised. I thought he was just calling as a friend. He kept calling, and finally we got together, and the first night we were together it got pretty far. It embarrasses me to say how far. It was absurd. This was the first night I'd ever been with him, and the other times I was with him, he *never* took me out. He was always coming over here and fooling around. That first night we smoked dope; after that I decided not to get stoned with him anymore.
Q: You thought you might get sexually involved if you got high?
A: Yeah. But even after I told him I didn't want to fool around, he still kept wrangling around and it got really bad. I would ask him to go to parties with me, and he would always come up with excuses, and finally he stood me up for the third time, and I called him up and said, more or less, that we should cool it. Then he didn't call me back after we had another long fight on the phone. I called him back, and I said I didn't think this was working out, and he said he still wanted to be friends. I said, "Friends, fine." And he said, "Later." I said, "Later. *Much*." I was just so mad. Still, I didn't think I'd been used. 'Cause I thought he did like me at one time and no one knew him the way I knew him. All this. Finally, a friend told me he didn't really care about me. He lied to me a lot. I just thought how stupid I'd been. I never screwed him, but it went very far, too

far. And it's like, since then, I'm very cynical. It's very rare that
I'll be alone with a guy, I'm so scared that they'll try something,
and I just don't know what to do.

Q: What happens when you say no to a guy?

A: Well, it only happened with this guy. When I said no, he just
started tickling or something like that and it'd just eventually
get there.

Q: Was he the first boyfriend you'd had?

A: Yeah, the first guy that ever paid attention to me. That's why I
was so caught up in the whole thing. I was like, Oh, wow, I've
got a boyfriend, lucky me. And it was so full of shit, because he
didn't care about me at all. My friend and I were talking about
it, and she said, "I'm sorry it happened, but you got a lot of
experience out of it." The next time I get involved in a relationship, it's going to be more on my terms.

Q: What would be your terms?

A: A ring through the nose.

Q: For you or the guy?

A: For the guy. First of all, I've decided that I'm not going to screw.
I know that's a very vulgar expression.

Q: That's fine. Did you ever screw this guy?

A: No. No. I came very close, I was thinking seriously about it. It
frightens me to think about it now. God, how could I have ever
wanted to do it with him. I've decided only after a real serious
relationship that I feel secure in that I would think about it, and
do something about birth control, and then do it. I wouldn't do
it unless I really wanted it, it was right for me, I wasn't doing
it to keep the guy, it had to be what I wanted.

Q: Do you feel you might have done it to keep the guy?

A: I think I might have. It was the first guy that had ever walked
into my life, and I was ready to do anything.

Q: Did he ever really put any pressure on you?

A: No.

Q: He didn't really push you to have sex?

A: No, he knew I was really strongly against that.

Q: You'd talked about it?

A: Yeah. I said maybe if the relationship got really serious I might
do it, but not at that point.

Q: Did he ask you? How did it come up?

A: When we talked on the phone he was always talking about sex. Now I look back and I can see all these lead-ups to it. Now I know that's what he wanted, but then I thought he just liked me for me. He did bring it up, and I'd say, "Don't get your hopes up, don't hold your breath, you're not going to get it for some time." I'm really glad I didn't give it to him, or I'd be feeling really cheap now.

Q: Do you think he feels he would be cheap?

A: No, that's part of our sexist society. Guys can go around and screw a lot of girls, and they look macho, but when a girl does it she looks like a slut.

Q: Is that the attitude at your school?

A: Yeah. I think it's really stupid. At this age, most guys are real idiots. All they care about is being able to say, "I screwed her and her and her." And they're users, and they don't seem to care what happens to you afterwards. So I'm very careful. One night I was with this guy, I was just friendly to him, not warming up to him sexually, and some friends were going to be fooling around in his car, and he wanted to get to the car because he was very possessive about it. All my friends yelled that I should follow him, but I thought, No way. The next night he was flirting with another girl, and one girl came up to me and said, "You know, you had your chance." That's not the kind of chance I want.

Q: Can you imagine going with him to his car and just sitting and talking?

A: I could imagine it, but could he?

Q: What would he do?

A: Probably make some moves.

Q: What would you do?

A: I'd probably go along.

Seventeen-year-old Suburban Male

A: I think that's one big thing with high-school kids, at least high-school girls. Love means a lot to them. At least, the word means very much. I think there are three or four girls I care about. I don't love at all—I care a lot about. But I think if I said, "I love you," acted like I meant it and showed that I did, I could have sex anytime I wanted with them. I think I can now, anyway, because I care for them. But if I said, "I love you," right off the bat . . . That's very important for girls. It should be that way. We guys can be very cruel.

Thirteen-year-old Urban Male

Q: Anything you'd like to talk about that I haven't covered?

A: Oh, there's one question that everyone's been dying to know— if people French with their eyes open or closed.

Q: That I should ask other people?

A: Yeah, you should ask the other kids you interview.

Q: Do you French with your eyes open or closed?

A: Closed.

Q: What do the other kids do?

A: Most everybody Frenches with their eyes closed. We sort of noticed that girls French with their eyes open and boys don't. We were just wondering.

Fourteen-year-old Urban Male

A: And then later on, though, I did eat her out and it didn't smell as bad.

Q: You got used to it or . . .

A: I don't know. It just didn't smell as bad.

Q: Did she like it?

A: Yeah. She didn't want to tell me. I asked her and she didn't want to tell me because she was embarrassed and stuff, but I could tell she did. She liked it better than the other stuff. Then somebody called, a friend of mine, and I tried to get her to jack me off, but she kinda would and kinda wouldn't.

Q: She would touch you, but . . .

A: But she was scared.

Q: Was that the first time she'd done it?

A: Yeah. Usually it's the first time . . .

Q: Did you tell her what to do?

A: Well, we were just talking and I took her hand and put it down there, and she got the idea.

Q: Did you have an erection?

A: Yeah. Just kissing her I got an erection. Of course. I didn't get anything hardly because she didn't do anything, and that's usually how you have to do it, 'cause the girl usually won't ever start and she'll never do anything. So you have to take her hand or move up if she's gonna give you head. Usually they never do that.

Q: Has anyone ever given you head?

A: Yeah. But girls my age never do that.

Q: Who did that?

A: I met some girls at the ice-skating rink. We go to the ice-skating rink a lot and they're kinda older, too. But they never do that.

Q: Girls your age just won't give head?

A: No, never. They're scared of that or something.

Q: Did you ever ask one of them to do it?

A: Yeah.

Q: And they just say no.

A: They say no.

Q: What do you think it is about it that gets them?

A: They're just not used to it, I guess. They'll get into it when they're older. I wish *I* was older.

Q: So the first time someone gave you head, was it at the ice-skating rink?

A: It wasn't at the ice-skating rink, but I met her at the ice-skating rink. I met her with some friends and we went up and we were in the park and I just moved up and stuff.

Q: A little messing around earlier?

A: Yeah, we were doing stuff.

Q: So did you like it?

A: Yeah.

Q: Did you come?

A: Yeah, I did. It's better than being jacked off.

Q: How come?

A: It feels a lot better.

Q: It feels better?

A: Yeah. Being jacked off, it's not nothing hardly, it doesn't feel like anything hardly.

Seventeen-year-old Suburban Male

Q: What about oral sex, how do you feel?

A: It turns me on. I think oral sex is . . . a lot of people think it's filthy. Black people, they—from what I understand, they can't stand it. They have a saying: "You shouldn't eat what you fuck." But if you can stick your dick in it, why can't you stick your tongue in it? It's just stuff like that. I've learned that the genitals and the vagina are two of the . . . some of the cleanest parts of the body. It's a lot cleaner than your mouth. So there's really nothing wrong with it, and it's very stimulating, it's a really good way to get off. It's very interesting.

Q: Do you think most girls enjoy going down on guys? Do they have trouble with that?

A: A lot of the younger girls, the first time they do it, they have a real hard time. They're not so sure about it, they don't know what to do. They're just very shaky on the subject. I guess a lot of my friends try to keep away from younger girls because of that and I can see why. It may be a hassle, but then again, she may be something really special to you, so it may be worthwhile teaching her.

Q: Getting high to have sex, is that common?

A: Not among the group I hang around with. I guess some of my friends feel more sexually aroused when they are drunk. Some of my friends get stoned. Even some of my friends with steady girlfriends, they'd even go ahead and cheat on a girl when they're drunk or stoned, but I don't know. I'm really not into it. I find sex is a beautiful thing, and if you can't enjoy it straight, then there is no reason to enjoy it at all. What's the use of doing it, if you can't do it when you are straight. Unless you have a problem, if you can't get it up unless you're drunk, go ahead and do it. But different strokes for different folks. I like it straight so I know what I'm doing. So I can perform to me . . . Instead of being sloppy and just doing it, do it right. Do it when you're sober. So you have control over your body.

Q: Do kids think at all, like they used to, I want to marry a virgin? Or I want to get married as a virgin?

A: That starts off for ninth and tenth graders, I found out. They all start off with that, you know—"I want to be a virgin, I want to get married as a virgin. I'm saving myself for my husband." Somehow or another, they get taken advantage of around eleventh grade. Some get taken advantage of younger. Some of 'em feel bad because they are not a virgin, because of just the fact that their friends have all been taken advantage of. I say taken advantage of because I find out that most of the girls who are sexually active in the ninth and tenth grade have been taken advantage of. I say taken advantage of because seniors and freshmen do it. They'll catch 'em drunk at a party or something.

Q: Senior guys and freshman girls?

A: Senior guys taking advantage of sophomore and freshmen girls. I call that taking advantage of the age gap. . . . If you could see some of the sophomore and freshmen girls at some of the parties I've been to, you'd understand. It doesn't take them very much to get drunk, and to make it with the crowd, they have to drink as much as everybody else and when they're that way, anybody could take advantage of 'em. Usually the juniors and the seniors get to the girls before anybody does. Mrs. Ross has told me a couple of times that girls who have taken her life science class have been taken advantage of by boys when they are intoxicated. I just couldn't do it myself, I just couldn't take advantage of someone who's drunk, because I've got a feeling . . . if I'm going to have sex with somebody, I want them to get pleasure out of it and I want them to want it as much as I do. I couldn't do it to someone screaming and yelling, "Don't do this" and "Don't do that." I just couldn't do it. It's just not my thing.

Sixteen-year-old Urban Female

Q: How often do you see Jeff?

A: Every single day.

Q: Every single day?

A: Well, we go to school together and we have all our classes together.

Q: And then outside of school, too?

A: After school he comes over sometimes and on weekends every single day we see each other. Friday nights we go out and Saturday nights we go out and Sunday afternoons we have lunch together and we do our homework together.

Q: What if somebody else asked you out on a date—would you go?

A: No, I don't think so.

Q: You're just not interested?

A: No. I really like Jeff.

Q: Do you think you're in love with Jeff?

A: Yeah, I do.

Q: And you thought you were in love with Brian, also?

A: I think I was just so infatuated with him. He was rich and smart and he was just . . . an Elvis Presley type.

Q: Brian's not around anymore, so that's why you don't . . . ?

A: No, he's there when I need him. It got to the point when we would be really upset we'd call each other and see each other and we'd talk and make each other feel better.

Q: But he knows about Jeff now?

A: Yeah, sort of. He doesn't really care; he's got his own girlfriends and stuff. It's not really that important to him.

Q: Did you have a monogamous relationship with Brian or was he seeing other girls?

A: He was seeing other girls.

Q: Did that bother you?

A: It did sometimes. When I was really in love with him, it did. But then when I started going out with other guys it didn't bother me anymore. I felt, Well, whatever.

Q: Did you start using birth control with Brian after the first time?

A: No, I haven't used birth control.

Q: You never do?

A: No.

Q: Do you sleep with Jeff now?

A: Yeah.

Q: How often?

A: A lot. The problem is he doesn't know that I don't.

Q: He doesn't? What does he think you use?

A: The Pill. You see, I haven't gone down to Planned Parenthood and I was going to, but I didn't. So don't tell him.

Q: Why didn't you?

A: I'm afraid, I really am, of an exam and just . . .

Q: You've never been to a gynecologist before?

A: No. And my mother won't let me. I don't understand why, but . . .
Q: Have you asked her?
A: Yeah, but she says, "Oh, you're too young, you don't need that yet."

Seventeen-year-old Suburban Male

A: The exhilarating things that I really like I've done with other people, just physical things where we just start rolling around and you know you're on top, I'm on top, I love it. I love that kind of stuff. And with her it was the same way, we could do that and we could say—it was really cool one time, we were laying around in a sleeping bag out camping, with other people around, they're all snoozing, and we were talking to each other and she said, "I'm just starting to feel more comfortable with you, so I can tell you what turns me on," and that really makes me happy when the girl tells me that because that's kind of what I want to do, I want her to enjoy sex with me, and when she feels comfortable enough to tell me . . . She said that and I said, "That's wild." She was telling me about how I could stimulate her clitoris with just my hands, you know, and I thought that was great. Really, nobody would say that unless you were close. Who would want to say, "A little higher here," something like that, you know, who would say that? I've had very gratifying relationships with girls that I see frequently but not all the time and we get to know each other through physical means, and maybe party together, something like that, but we really don't hang around together all the time.

Seventeen-year-old Suburban Male

Q: You were going exclusively with her?
A: Just her. For a year. And we were in love, at least we thought we were and that's good enough. Everything was fine, we enjoyed our relationship. But now that I look back on it, there is a lot I missed. There is a lot I had then that I miss now, but I just want to do something different.
Q: What about sexually between you two, were you happy with your relationship?

A: Yeah. We went out for about a year and a half and we didn't have sex until, I guess, at least five months into the relationship. We had sex, but we didn't have intercourse. She was always trying to tell me you can have sex and not have intercourse, it's just not as much fun. But we were happy. When we had intercourse we didn't have it that much because she was always tentative and scared, more so than I. She was always a pessimistic person and I'm a very optimistic person. And so we didn't have it that much. There was always a lot of caring and always a lot of love involved and it was fun, we had a good relationship. Naturally, I, being an optimistic person, thinking nothing would go wrong, wanted sex more than she did. But I always cared for her feelings and I never wanted to push her. We had a good relationship.

Q: Were you able to tell her what you liked sexually?

A: We never *said* anything like that. We could say *anything* to each other—we talked about masturbation, homosexuality, everything, we always told our feelings—but we never said anything like that. I think basically because we were both good in bed. We both sort of had a feeling what the other would like, so nothing really needed to be said. We were both imaginative and curious. So there were no hang-ups there. It was pretty fun.

Q: What did you enjoy most?

A: Intercourse. Just laying in bed with her and thinking about it was enough, and then going to town. That was the best part. I think it was the best for both of us mostly because there were so many emotions. When you have a relationship with one on one for so long, there is so much caring involved. When you have intercourse, there are so many emotions. She told me once that when we do make love to each other, that she feels so much love, it's one of the best feelings in the world for her. That's just . . . how can you beat that?

Sixteen-year-old Urban Male

Q: Has a girl ever had an orgasm when she's been with you?

A: No, she pulled my hand out, she started saying stuff like "Get your hand out of there." She didn't really know, I guess, what was happening. So she pulled my hand out.

Q: You think she stopped it when . . .
A: Yeah, when she was on the verge of it, whatever. I've read in
   Penthouse and shit like that, but I guess when she was on the
   verge of it she probably decided she didn't want to, it's probably
   embarrassing, you know, for her.
Q: Did she say anything about it or are you mostly guessing?
A: When we were doing it? Yeah, she said, "Get your hand out of
   there," whatever. I go, "Why?" and she explained. She didn't
   say "orgasm," she just said, "Pull it out, pull it out, I think
   something's happening." She didn't even know what was happening. [Laughs.] She knew what was happening, but she didn't
   know any name for it, whatever.
Q: She was afraid of it?
A: Yeah.
Q: She didn't want it to happen?
A: I'm not saying she didn't want it to happen. She didn't want
   me to . . . You know, she probably didn't want to, I guess, come
   all over me, you know. She'd be embarrassed because I might
   think of something.

Fourteen-year-old Urban Male

A: I can't figure out where the clitoris is. They're supposed to be
   like a little cock. *I* can't find it. I've felt all over girls in their
   cunt and I *can't* find it!
Q: And you think that's the crucial point to find?
A: That's where it says it is. It says—yeah, I know it is, because
   anything you talk about, that's what is supposed to get a girl
   real hot and shit, but I can't find it.

Seventeen-year-old Urban Male

Q: Would you ever masturbate if you came home frustrated?
A: No, because I started doing that once when I was eight and I
   just had all kinds of horrible guilt feelings and . . .
Q: Why?
A: I don't know. You feel that you're the only one who's doing it
   and then later on when I got older I found out there were other

kids who were doing it also, but when you're younger you think you're the only one doing it, and also they have different things, where parents always warn against doing this, you know. . . .

Q: Did your parents ever tell you not to?

A: I had a situation where my mother was telling me about how my grandmother, her mother, had told her not to do that. Told her about the evils of it. My father did the same thing. Actually, I think they were trying to get a message across to me in doing this. . . .

Q: What did they tell you would happen to you?

A: They said all kinds of things. I mean, you'd get VD and all kinds of jazz like that. Later on, I found out all this was a lie. We have some books at home, *The Joy of Sex*, *Everything You Always Wanted to Know About Sex*, some title like that, and I read up on it, and they said it was a lie, that the only thing that happened through it was that you would get some type of enjoyment out of it; that was it. They said the only thing that is wrong is adolescents usually feel guilty about it. With my family being religious, they just totally were against that type of thing.

Q: What religion?

A: Roman Catholic. And it's crazy, 'cause, like, when I was younger I used to be an altar boy, and I hated that after a while because they expected you almost to be perfect. They had this idea that somehow you were supposed to . . . where other kids wouldn't totally listen to their parents, you were supposed to. And my friends who were also altar boys didn't like that, either. Because the parents expect more of you, it seems, because of that.

Q: So you felt guilty masturbating?

A: Yeah. After a while.

Q: Did you enjoy it, though?

A: You have an enjoyment, but I think the guilt was worse. You have a plus-and-minus situation, and it was more of a minus because you felt guilty about it for a long time, thought about it for a long time. You might be watching TV and everything and you'd just suddenly think about it, and you don't want to think about anything, you don't want to do anything, and you just feel bad from that. And I think when it came to my parents, they had never known anything about me doing anything like

that, they had never caught me doing that or anything like that.
I know a friend of mine was caught doing that—

Q: In the act?

A: Yeah. It was kind of funny, what happened, 'cause, like, they had yelled at him and everything else. He called me right after it happened, but it was kinda funny what happened.

Q: What did they do?

A: They grounded him for it and they kind of got after him for a while, but from what it seemed, they never mentioned it again. It was like this sinful idea, "How could you?" and so forth. "Where did we go wrong?"

Q: Did they actually walk in when he was doing it?

A: From what he told me, yeah. He wasn't too bright. Instead of going in the bathroom, he was in his room. So his mother, you know, I think had come from the store and had bought some new clothes and she went in there and he's in the act and she yelled and she said she almost had a heart attack, and I think that's funny. With me, I'd never been caught 'cause, like, I would do it either when my parents were out or I'd go into the bathroom.

Seventeen-year-old Rural Female

A: Oh, I was baby-sitting one night and I asked him to baby-sit with me and we were just petting and kissing and he tried to get my pants off. And I was really, I guess I was almost in tears and I didn't want to. And he just was so . . . not forceful, as far as hitting me and getting rough with me, but really putting the pressure on.

Q: Physically or emotionally?

A: More emotionally. And part physically. Not that it was pain, that he would force himself on me that way. But then he tried to and I just didn't want him to at all. I think I was really scared about him hurting me or something and I knew it wasn't right. That's the way I've always been brought up.

Q: That sex was . . .

A: Well, before I'm married. I really didn't want to. With Bill I didn't want to. Bill was like—he was supposed to be real big with all the girls. The school from where he came from, it seemed like every girl he took out he had sex with. And I didn't like that idea, either. I wanted it to be something special, when I had sex with a guy, and all these things together I think really bothered me and I didn't let him then. He kept getting real mad and things like that.

Q: In what way—would he yell at you, get cold . . . ?

A: Well, yelling and he said it a few times, about me being gay.

Q: Saying you liked women if you didn't like him?

A: I don't think he thought it, I think he just wanted to make me feel bad, just to say things to make me give in.

Q: Did it make you feel bad when he said that?

A: It hurt, but not to the point to give in. Just to make me mad and think I don't want anything more to do with him. And all my friends knew it, too, how bad he was for me, and they'd always tell me. And I just blocked it out. And I just—I don't know why I did it. . . . I don't mind talking about it, but when I think back, it was like a wasted two years or something like that—that's the way I always look at it.

Q: What about the first time you had sex?

A: I guess it was at his house. I guess I finally just thought that it didn't matter. I don't think he was really that forceful. I just think I just kinda gave in.

Q: Did he know you were a virgin?

A: Yeah.

Q: And did he like that, the fact that you were a virgin, or did he think that it was kind of a nuisance?

A: He never really said. But the way I looked at it, I just felt like one of the girls or something. And that's what bothered me so bad. But I don't know if I was tired of saying no or if I wanted to see what it was like. It seems so long ago and I can't remember.

Q: Did you like it?

A: Not really. Part of me did, but I think if I would have liked Bill it would have been so much more special. Every time he'd say about having sex, I'd say no. I knew deep down I didn't want to because it really seemed dirty with Bill. There wasn't anything there; it was just to fool around.

Sixteen-year-old Suburban Female

Q: Did you ever have an orgasm?

A: Yeah. I did.

Q: Like, all the time would you have orgasms, or . . .

A: No, not all the time. I can remember two times I didn't. But that was all right, too. I didn't really feel bummed out because I didn't have an orgasm. Because it was still really enjoyable, anyway. I do feel—I always hated it when I was younger and I was with a guy and I knew they were really getting off on it and I wasn't. That always made me feel really shitty. Because guys can get off a lot faster than girls can, or at least it seems that way with me. And it takes me a long time to get as stimulated as I do, and it takes a whole lot of different stuff. It can't just be one thing that triggers it off. It's got to be a whole mixture of different stuff. And I used to feel like, with a lot of guys, they would get so turned on so fast, and in a way I used to kind of look down on them for not realizing that I wasn't. It was sort of like I wanted them to help me get off too, and I didn't feel like they were always doing that.

Q: Would you ever say stuff to them or . . .

A: Yeah, I would, and sometimes they would try, but they would try in kind of a half-assed way just so that they wouldn't want me to be unhappy, but they weren't really trying to make me enjoy myself either, they were just so involved in their own experience. And so that was a real yucky feeling.

Q: You think it was their ignorance or their self-absorption or both?

A: I think it was both. And I think if they had realized literally what I was thinking, it probably would have bummed them out too. And they probably would have stopped and said, "Well, that's really bad, I don't want you to feel that way." But it's really hard when you're at a certain age and that's happening to you to really react to it, because you still want to please them. So it's complicated.

Seventeen-year-old Urban Female

A: I went to this Frisbee tournament a while ago, with a girlfriend of mine and this guy, and it just started out as a ménage à trois and then she left an hour later because I guess he asked her to leave or something. I felt awful, I didn't want to face her the next day, then I just went up to her and she gave me a hug and everything.

Q: Was she a friend of yours?

A: Yeah.

Q: And the guy?

A: No, never saw him before. I was just very attracted to him.

Q: How did it turn into a ménage à trois?

A: It was funny. He mentioned it, and I was very attracted to him. When I found out that she was staying with him in his room ... They weren't boyfriend and girlfriend—they were just spending a weekend together in a dorm. Everybody stayed in the dorm on campus, where the tournament was held. And the person I was there with I didn't really enjoy. We'd known each other a long time and we'd never had sex, and now it was like, "Why don't we have it?" I didn't like that, and I couldn't get into hanging out with him. So that night, it was Kevin and Janet. I had got really sore from doing a lot of free-style and playing some Frisbee golf, and Kevin said, "If you want to come over to the room, I'll give you a massage." So I said, "Sure." So that night he came out into the hall and waited for me. Everybody was in the hall, it was party time at night, people would hang out and throw disks, it was fun. He called me in. He said, "Why don't you come in?" So I said, "Sure." So I went back to the room for my massage and she was massaging me also.

Q: You had clothes on?

A: Yeah, clothes on, undrugged. So I was enjoying it and I just relaxed and we just starting getting very touchy and close and just started kissing and massaging.

Q: She was involved in this, too?

A: Yeah. And then we just all got together. It was fun.

Q: Was everyone fucking each other?

A: Yeah, kind of. It wasn't like "Your turn now." It was a nice, flowy thing. Nobody was ever left out. Somebody was always being stroked, or whatever. It was nice.

Q: You liked it. Did you feel weird about her?

A: Yeah, just when she left the room. I felt weird the next morning, like what is her reaction going to be—I thought she might be pissed. But she wasn't. She was very nice, she hugged me and said everything was cool.

Q: Why did she leave?

A: He mentioned something; he whispered in her ear. I tried to listen but I couldn't, and the next minute she just got up and it wasn't like she was pissed. She just said, I'll be out for a little while, I'll see you two later.

Q: Did you then fuck with him?

A: Yeah. Two more times. It was really nice, he was very nice-looking. It was good.

Seventeen-year-old Urban Female

A: But that whole scene up in the park—it was awful. It was so boring. They'd get stoned and do nothing and space out. A lot of my friends got into acid, and I tried it once or twice. I hated it. I was scared to do it a second time. The first time I was kinda forced into it. Not forced, but I went to the country with three girlfriends and we wanted to get some pot or Quaaludes for the weekend to have fun but we couldn't get any, so one girl got some acid. I had never taken it, it was the most powerful— "green blotter." We were in a nice house, but we were stuck in a room the size of this one, with a big bed. It didn't hit us until an hour or so later, I didn't feel it so I took more; I took half and an hour later I took the other half, so I'd just taken a half. Once it started I was like sizzling away, I couldn't believe it. But I didn't want to freak myself out, that was the last thing I wanted. I felt weird because we were all stuck in the tiny room, and before we knew it the place was covered with clothes, we were trying on everything and laughing, we couldn't stop laughing. Meanwhile her father was right next door, but we didn't look stoned, so we faked it in front of him. He had no idea what was going on. I didn't enjoy it at all. It was so powerful, though, I was sizzling away, and I felt so drained out when I'd come down. I was like, Holy shit, what have I just been through, I was so spaced out. I kept thinking about all the things I'd seen, which were really neat, which weren't real or anything.

Q: Do you ever take drugs now when you have sex?

A: No, not *for* sex. I usually just take them during the weekend. The only drug I do is coke. I drink wine or beer occasionally, but no alcohol.

Q: Do you think they make sex better or worse?

A: Coke? No, a lot of times after I'd taken a little or so I couldn't get into it, because I wouldn't want to do anything but just sit there. Other times you can get into it because you can put your mind into it, and you have extra energy. Wine I can always have sex with because it makes you tipsy, it makes you tingle. I've heard that men can't get hard when they take coke; it's something about the nervous system, or something. That's what I've been told. A friend deals to a lot of Wall Street people, and down there it's a whole sick scene, they leave their wives in New Jersey and get a call girl for a night, and they buy a gram and then they can't get hard.

Q: Have you ever had any experience with impotence, when some guy couldn't get hard?

A: No; I'd take it so personally if they didn't. Unless it's a drug or something that was in the way. I used to smoke pot a lot, but it would space me out so much.

Q: So now you don't?

A: No. No pot, no cigarettes, no coffee, no soda.

Q: Clean living.

A: I eat a lot of pasta. I've been eating so much lately 'cause I've been feeling shitty.

Q: That's good for you.

A: I don't take Quaaludes anymore.

Q: Did you ever have sex on Quaaludes?

A: Yes.

Q: How was it?

A: I can't remember too well. At the time it was great. I guess it's written up to be a sex drug, and it really is, actually. It makes you so horny. It makes you so unaware. I could never hold myself up when I was on a Quaalude. My knees'd just shrink

in, I'd feel like a rag doll. It would make you very horny and
very tingly and you'd just want to lie down.

Q: So no problem having sex on a Quaalude?

A: No problem at all.

Seventeen-year-old Urban Female

A: When we first had sex, I used birth control. But I wanted to get
pregnant.

Q: What did you use?

A: Orthos, the twenty-one pack, the OR.

Q: The first time you had sex, you were on the Pill?

A: No.

Q: How soon after the first time?

A: I'd say about in that August I got some pills.

Q: And you started having sex when?

A: In June.

Q: Two months. What made you decide?

A: When I had sex, I was thirteen. I was turning fourteen in the
next month and I got on some pills 'cause I didn't want to have
no baby. Then we got so close together and everything was so
good and everything. And I just felt I wanted to have a baby. I
stopped taking those pills.

Q: Did your lover know?

A: Yeah; he wanted me to stop taking them, too.

Q: Both of you decided?

A: We moved in and he asked me if I ever wanted to have children.
And I told him yeah. And he asked me when. I said, I was
ready to have children anytime. And I stopped taking the pills.

Q: Did you talk to anybody about it?

A: No.

Q: Did your mother know?

A: No, she thought I was still taking them. See, I kept my pack, I
just punched one out every day to make 'em thought I was
taking them.

Q: So she knew you were having sex?

A: Yeah, I told her. When I first started, I told her I didn't want to
get pregnant. So I told her that I wanted to take pills. Plus, he
had used a rubber the first time we had sex. He told me he was

going to get up and go to the bathroom, and he went to the bathroom and took the rubber off—it was my sister's house—and my sister found it. And I guess she must have told my mother. But I told her, too.

Q: And she took you then to get the pills?

A: I went by myself.

Q: How did you know where to go?

A: Because the school I go to, there's a clinic right next to the school, so I just went over there. See, I had my period when I was eleven and when I was twelve I used to have cramps. My mother took me over there and I had to get checked and get these pills that regulated my period then. So I knew what birth control was.

Q: Did you ever have any sex education in school?

A: No. We never had no sex education in school. Took health, but that was only on VD and syphilis.

Q: From your own experiences, you'd know about birth-control pills?

A: Yes. Nobody never talked to me about it.

Q: Your mother?

A: No.

Q: How did you learn about how babies are made?

A: I went to a parenthood class when I was pregnant.

Q: Before that you didn't know?

A: Well, I knew how you got pregnant. . . .

Q: How did you find that out?

A: I don't know how I know that, I just automatically knew. But nobody never teached me nothing about my body. Before natal-care class. They recommended that in school, and I signed up for it.

Sixteen-year-old Urban Female

Q: Why do you use a diaphragm?

A: Because I've watched a lot of my girlfriends use pills and I've seen them get the side effect of that. I've seen my friends' breasts just like explode, it's unbelievable. I think that if something chemically can do that to you . . . Drugs is different 'cause chemically it does things to you that you want it to do to you, but not birth-control pills. That's putting you in a pregnant state all the time and that's just something I don't believe in. I think the IUD is dangerous 'cause it can infect the inside of you. I just found that to be the simplest.

Q: So you like the diaphragm?

A: Yes, we get along very well. I found no trouble with it at all. The three B's. My gynecologist told me, "Remember your three B's."

Q: What are the three B's?

A: Something like "behind the backbone, between . . ." I forget what they are now, but I know them. It all fits in right.

Q: You went with your mother to a doctor?

A: Yeah. My mom called for the appointment and everything, and she came with me. My gynecologist said, "What is your status and what is your situation?" She's so personal. I said, "None of your business, just give me the diaphragm."

Q: Do you think it's easy for kids to get birth control?

A: Since I was underage, my gynecologist asked to have a parent's permission, but I think it should be made easier for kids because I think there's some people that can't tell their parents and they need the birth control. I'm gonna use my friend as an example: She found it hard to tell her mom for the first time and she stalled a long time before she got her diaphragm, which caused her abortion. I kept on saying, "Listen, I'll come with you. You can't just hang around and stuff." She eventually got it. But immediately my reaction was "Before I ever make love again, I have to have a diaphragm." I think it should be made easier for underaged people to have them. I don't think chemically it should be given; foam or diaphragm, but not pills. I don't think they should allow pills for kids my age.

Q: You think it's okay for kids your age to have sex?

A: Again, under the proper conditions, yeah. You can't stop some-body from having sex. Like the poverty-stricken kids, they grow up with seven hundred brothers and sisters all sleeping in the same bed. They don't know anything else, except go out when you're young and have a good time, and that's what you do. I don't think it's right and just and stuff, but I think that's what they do and they should have birth control in that case. I don't think it's right that kids should just go out and have sex. I think they should have an understanding with their parents and their parents should have an understanding with the person that they're with. My mother totally communicates with my boy-friend. She says, "If I want her home you're responsible for her to be home. It's gonna mean a healthier relationship because I'm not gonna let her go out. . . ."

Q: Tell me about your relationship with your mother. Is she the one that you first learned about sex from?

A: When I was little she was very into making me know about it. I was the bad kid of the group because all the mothers were saying, "Would you tell her to stop telling our daughters about sex?" My mom used to literally give me sex lessons when I was little. Not like . . .

Q: How to . . . ?

A: Right. She would draw pictures for me. She always gave me books, like little cut-out books and stuff. When my girlfriends were over, they'd ask questions. My mom's very free. She'd walk around the house nude and stuff, and my girlfriends were always like watching, and I'd say, "Mom, my friends are coming over, can you put some clothes on, you know?" If my girlfriend would ask a question or something, my mom would draw pictures and sit with us and answer. But all the parents were very against that because my mom was so "They should know—they have to know." And my friends' parents would be like "No, no, you can't tell them that."

Q: You always felt free to ask her.

A: Yeah, anything, anything.

Q: When you were thinking about sleeping with David, did you discuss it with her?

A: No.

Seventeen-year-old Suburban Male

A: Well, I myself use a condom. But taking sex-education courses, I found out that the condom is not 100 percent foolproof. So I figure if me and my girlfriend are going to have sexual relation-ships more heavily, I'm going to tell her to go to maybe a contraceptive counseling course and sign up for the Pill. If she doesn't want to do that, I'll just say okay: "We don't have to have intercourse, we could just foreplay."

Q: It doesn't bother you to use a rubber? A lot of guys say you lose feeling.

A: That's bull, that's a bunch of bull. I've never done it without a rubber and I probably never will. I will when I want a child, but you know I'm really not going to put the chance on a girl. If she's not using ... I got to have the trust in her that she's using that contraceptive. If she's not using a contraceptive, I'm going to use a condom. But there's always feeling in the condom. I mean, if there was no feeling and if it's not right, then why would you ejaculate? It's stupid, it's a stupid saying, it's just a myth.

Q: You don't feel like it's a big deal, it interrupts things?

A: It's got to, but it really shows how much you care for the girl you're out with.... If you're really caring enough that you don't want to get her pregnant, then you should take the time to go ahead and pull it out, but then again there are other contraceptives. You can go ahead and have her be on the Pill. But then again, you got to make sure she's on it. You've got to know she's on it. You've got to have a trust between the two.

Seventeen-year-old Suburban Male

Q: What do you use, a rubber?

A: Yeah. I've used ... let me think what else. The perfect thing for me would be if some of these promiscuous ladies I see would be on the Pill. Another girl that has been in a course type of thing about contraception, and she would use foam and I'd use a rubber. Not that that was wild.

Q: Have the rubbers ever gotten in the way?

A: Yeah, it kind of got in the way at the beach, when I was at the beach, 'cause they broke. Not while I was coming or anything, but right before, you know. You just "God, this feels too good to stop—okay, let me go put another one on." Really getting into it. Other opinions have told me that they really shouldn't stop any stimulation at all. But I would disagree.

Q: You think they do?

A: I really do. I don't know why, but from my own experiences, which probably haven't been that vast, three years probably

I've been fairly sexually active, using rubbers all the time, and I know they damper things. It doesn't bother me to pull out with a rubber because that's only momentary, it kinda almost makes you hotter, you know, waiting for it. And another thing, it has another advantage—if you're ever scared about prematurely ejaculating before the girl has . . . I feel like I can go a lot longer. Because you don't touch anything wet, anything warm, you're inside a rubber, unless it's lubricated and that's not really warm, you can get temperatures through them but it's not the same feeling, you know. When a girl is really hot and really wet, and you put your cock in her, it feels like . . . you slide right in, you know, it's a lot better. And I like it a lot more. I think rubbers are . . . that's why people shy away from them. But then again, you know I like being able to fuck longer—twenty-five, thirty minutes, you know. I love that.

Q: Is that a common feeling among your male friends—"I don't like to use rubbers, I like skin on skin," and all that?

A: You hear a lot of that, of course, but it seems my friends kind of respect the right for girls to say, "Do you have a rubber? We're not going to fuck unless you have a rubber," and they'll be prepared because they know that happens, you know, and I'd rather have one and not enjoy it, and I think that should be the standpoint girls make, 'cause they need to watch out for themselves. I think *they* should carry them, too.

Seventeen-year-old Rural Male

Q: What birth control did you use?

A: A condom.

Q: Did you just happen to have one? How long had you had that condom?

A: Probably a couple of months.

Q: Just to have it?

A: Oh, yeah. I bought it thinking that eventually I'd be using it.

Q: And did you know how to use it?

A: Oh, yeah.

Q: And the rest of the time you'd always use the same thing?

A: No.

Q: What'd you use?

A: Nothing. Just pulled out, came out. . . . That's another thing that kinda got me scared, you know. I didn't want anything to happen, like her getting pregnant or anything. That kinda got to me. So that's another reason. . . .

Q: Why did you stop using the condoms?

A: Oh, gosh, I don't know. Just didn't go to buy 'em.

Q: Other guys don't like using condoms. . . .

A: It wasn't that. I just didn't go buy them.

Q: Did you figure pulling out was safe?

A: Uh-uh, I figure it'd be risky.

Q: But you did it anyway?

A: You can get carried away.

Sixteen-year-old Urban Male

Q: You know any gays?

A: Yeah.

Q: Where do you know them from?

A: I know a girl, a friend of my sister's. I had an experience with a kid in seventh grade when I went on a trip, touchy-feely, plus my brother, who I grew up with in the same room. All three of us used to do it, and then it ended up two of us.

Q: You masturbated each other?

A: Yeah, and then we started getting to blowing each other. But we were pretty little, and then a lot of stuff.

Q: When was this?

A: Junior high, all through junior high. The kid made me depressed, because he was the ugliest kid, and he was fat and walked funny. He had all these *Playboy* magazines, and when I went over to his house we'd look at them, and I wouldn't touch him because he was so gross-looking. I still see him, I say hi once in a while. He's a nice kid, but everything else from there is awful, so ugly and everything. So you think if he's like that, then I must be like that, I must be a goon 'cause I'm gay. When I did it I felt that way.

Q: You think he's really gay?

A: I don't think so. I think he's just very horny and he needs something.

Q: This was also in junior high?

A: It was in ninth grade. Tenth grade and eleventh grade, I just saw him once in a while. I always felt that when I got to be a movie star he was going to blackmail me. Over here, along the river, there's a place where they hang out sometimes, just to get blown during their lunch hour or whatever. Guys do it to you, you do it to them. And this kid and I were just riding through; we were curious, you know. I had, before that, experience with my brother.

Q: The kid in junior high?

A: I was with another kid.

Q: You'd also experienced it with him?

A: Yeah. So we got into the place, and we were bike riding around, looking at things and looking at the guys, and this guy approached us and said he would give us ten bucks each if he could blow us. My friend, I guess, really wanted to, so we both did it. The guy did it to us and he paid us ten bucks. So we made out on ten bucks and had a thrill. He said we were handsome young men. It could have been a bunch of bull, but at the time it . . .

Q: Sounded good to you?

A: Sounded good to me, but I didn't want my friend to know that I'd tried it before. So we did it, and my friend and I ended up doing a little ourselves afterwards, and it became really bad. Not that we went really far. I would do something to him, but he wouldn't do anything back. He just took and wouldn't give. That ended our friendship.

Q: What grade was this?

A: Ninth grade. I don't say hi to him in the hallways at all. He'd come over and want me to blow him or something. I wouldn't. So our relationship ended. I finally realized what a boss he was, and I didn't really like that at all. And none of my family liked him. I liked him, my parents didn't like him. I think I like him just because I resented my family. I finally realized what he was really like, and we stopped completely.

Q: You ever go back to that place on the river, or do that again for money?

A: I never did it for money, I never wanted to. Just one time. Even though I said I only went to feeling a girl's chest, I can go further, if you want me to say it. Okay, here comes my big list.

I've gone pretty far. I haven't met anybody my age—I met one kid my age so far, but he was put away for a while. I didn't know that until he told me later. He was kind of crazy for a while. So I was thinking, here's another one who's crazy, I should be crazy, shouldn't I? I went back there a couple of times, and there was this one guy that I'll never forget, that I met there, who's really good-looking.

Q: This is by the river?

A: Yeah. I kept walking by with my bike. He just leaned up against a tree, and I leaned up against another tree, and I didn't think anything would happen, because he was good-looking, and he was big and everything, and I didn't think he'd want to have anything to do with me. At the time I was fourteen, and I thought I was really ugly, and I'm not saying I'm really handsome or beautiful, but then I was really ugly, plus skinny, plus I didn't know how to play sports and my family was down on me, I had a lot of pressure. No one knew about it. I used to cry at night because I didn't have any friends. Well, this guy was twenty-one, he was in college, a history major, and he was really nice. He was good-looking. We just talked and then we sat on the bench and talked some more. And then we went back and he met somebody he knew, and I finally gave in and went with some other guy. Gave in because he was bugging me. He wanted me to do something with him. So I went with him, and his friend goes, "Don't go with him, he's a creep."

Q: The guy who said don't go with him is the guy you liked?

A: Yeah. And I said, "Then who am I going to do it with?" And he said, "How about me?" I didn't think he'd want me to and he ended up following me, and the guy thought we were going to do a threesome—the guy wasn't mean or anything, he was a nice guy—we tried to tell him no, and then the guy I liked and I talked again, and we had just started to do stuff, when some of the old guys came around; it's really a dumb place to go. If you're gay, don't go there.

Q: I won't.

A: The old guys would watch people, and beat off while they watched them, because it thrilled them to death. They didn't want to get involved, they just wanted to sit there and get a thrill. It was sick.

Q: Did you go to the bushes or to people's apartments or something?

A: Bushes. He said, "I'd invite you back to my apartment for something to eat." I said, "You would?" I didn't know that happened and people did that.

Q: You felt this kind of sex had to take place in the bushes?

A: Not really. I didn't think it went any further than the bushes. He said, "But I'm just jogging," and I thought, He's not jogging. I bet he has his car over there. He just doesn't like me enough. So we'd started and this old guy came over and started beating off, and so we walked away, and this other guy came over, and because we were babes in the woods, we were a little scared and we didn't know if we should do it, and he said, "Let's not." So we just talked. He said, "Meet you Thursday." So I went to the wharf that Thursday to meet him; he said he walked his dog there. It was raining. So he never met me there, and every Thursday if I'm ever around there, the wharf, I always look for him. Did he look like that? Was that him?

Q: Even though it's been three years.

A: Yeah.

Q: You really liked this guy?

A: I liked him that much. He was really nice, I couldn't get over him. I didn't really understand. So I went back to the place another Thursday, but I never saw him again. I still feel strongly that I'm going to meet him again someday.

IV

Reconsiderations

ROBERT COLES

This *Rolling Stone* survey no doubt tells us what certain young people are quite willing for it to tell us—and thereby surely tells us a lot, because all one need do is ask what American youths of earlier generations might have offered in response to such a survey. For that matter, we ought to wonder what American youths of earlier generations would have made of such a survey—the confusion, the surprise, the disbelief, the horror, the outrage! The mere fact of the survey, in a sense, tells us a lot: We have come to this moment in our collective social history, in our nation's cultural life, and—some would with great energy and conviction argue—in our moral record as God's children.

I can imagine youths in every one of our 50 states being delighted and intrigued by the questions asked—youths quite aware of the *Rolling Stone* magazine, not to mention the rock group, and youths less aware but in any event pleased for this chance to make statements, to vote, and, not least of all, to think about sexual matters—and, in doing so, learn about themselves. But we should remind ourselves of the regional character and complexity of American life and, even within any given region, of the differences of class and religious faith and ethnic background as they come to bear not only on political attitudes but on personal values, including those that have to do with one's sexual life and, just as important, one's *proclaimed* (to oneself, never mind others!) sexual life.

Many people simply are not in the habit of talking to one another about such subjects as sexuality; they and others may also not be in the habit of formulating psychological abstractions or categorizations into which they gladly or sadly fit themselves or others. The poll or survey is a familiar feature of our contemporary life—and yet for many it is a difficult hurdle, for moral or religious reasons, when linked to the privacy of sexual behavior. In other words, one has to believe that the more conservative part of the teenage population may be less represented here because of a reluctance to participate.

An additional concern, also methodological, has to do not only with the limits of sampling but with the matter of fear and intimidation (and maybe humor and an inclination to irony) as they affect even (maybe especially) the most interested and enthusiastic participants in a survey such as this one. Again and again the college students I teach have told me that in filling out questionnaires they have caught themselves succumbing to a kind of "herd instinct"—that is, offering answers they thought they "should," or which they thought others might be providing as answers, or which they wished (oh, wished long and hard!) were their genuine responses. There is, then, the possibility of deliberate undermining— the result of nervous fear, or of an aroused wit, anxious to give itself playful vent, or of plain malice, which can be ascribed to the workings of apprehension, shame, resentment, envy, and no doubt ten or so other quite "deep" motives.

Along with those whose religious or cultural scruples mandate an immediate refusal to participate, or an evasive or distorted response to a sexual questionnaire of this sort, there are others who may find themselves unable to deal with it because of certain personal qualities—for instance, this kind of taciturnity: "I don't like much to say things about myself or others, thank you!" When pressed a bit, the same youth put it this way: "No, not even to myself; I don't bother myself with myself!" He lives in a Boston suburb, not a rural town of the South or the Southwest.

One must also keep in mind that adolescence is quite commonly a time of rapidly shifting patterns of behavior—mood swings; wild alternations between idealism and self-indulgent materialism; spells of ascetic renunciation and outbursts of insistent sexuality; moments of sociability and moments of withdrawal; episodes of politeness and episodes of rudeness and worse. So it is with some older people, but as we get into our twenties we tend to settle down, picking and choosing our way through various possibilities, or—since conscious choice is not always possible—falling into one or another manner of doing things.

Among young people the fluctuations are almost "normal"—hence the overriding cautionary need for patience and skepticism. No youth's answers to any questionnaire—not even to any doctor's careful, extended line of questioning—will necessarily tell us what the outcome will be for that youth's sexuality. To call upon Anna Freud again: "I have talked with an adolescent one day and had X decision in my mind about her sexual nature and future, only to see the same adolescent two or three days later (even one day later!) and feel very different; I then change my decision altogether; it is Y, not X, I tell my colleagues!"

As one reads other parts of this survey—for instance, the data on school sex-education courses: the relationship between a youth's taking them and that youth's sexual activity—one is once more in the presence of irony, to say the least. Mr Stokes's comments are helpful; they remind us that sex-education courses vary in their structure and intensity and sophistication, and also in their usefulness to students. There are, one gathers, not a few students who are quite able to sail through a sex-education course and still not do very well in answering the factual questions posed in this survey. Are we to declare the courses a failure? Are we to question the psychology of the respondents: an "ignorance" that defies education and therefore suggests an element of psychopathology—a lapse of memory or a "block" of some kind that operates in such a fashion that what has been taught, and presumably learned, does not come readily to mind? Moreover, many parents are decidedly uneasy about sex-education courses in school—or are outright opposed to their presence in a given school system's curriculum. I rather suspect that not a few students also find such courses unnerving as well as of great interest—a challenge, sometimes, not only to ignorance but to their social or moral or religious tradition.

Nor, again, is the issue of class or regional background to be ignored when it comes to thinking about any data on sex education—and this survey has taken such "variables" into account. Young men and women who live in our crowded urban slums have rather different sexual lives from those young men and women who live in pleasant, well-to-do suburbs or in the countryside beyond. Not only do sexual experiences differ, but sexual attitudes, or, to be more precise, moral attitudes toward sex—how one ought to behave under various circumstances—also happen to differ. There is, as these respondents make clear, and as Mr. Stokes suggests, a moral aspect to sexuality, and some of this survey's data can be helpful in comprehending the ways in which that moral energy, it can be called, does its work.

Mr. Stokes notes, for example, that "most teens regard their peers as in some ways conservative." The survey has told him that "44% of all teens thought their friends would be 'shocked' to learn that they were having sexual intercourse." The texture of any one youth's moral life, as it bears down on (or uplifts!) his or her sexual life can be exceedingly complex. As one must keep emphasizing, and as some of the apparent inconsistencies in this survey also suggest, one can be morally severe even while not living up to the letter of one's own set of beliefs, and one can be morally relaxed and still in daily life be fairly restrained if not puritanical sexually; and of course there are all sorts of intermediate positions with respect to these and other possible polarities.

It is interesting, as one goes through other facets of this survey, to consider the importance young people continue to attach to the word *love*, and to the requirement that sexuality be preceded by some kind of explicitly stated affirmation of mutual commitment, however brief in nature. Perhaps such preconditions of young sexuality are in some cases shams, more lip service to an essentially unheeded morality: *love* as a word used to justify passion, and to pretend commitment when in truth two young people want merely to have a "good time" for as long as that time feels "good" to them. On the other hand, cynicism has to earn its own credibility—a caveat for survey research, as well as for the so-called in-depth approach to human psychology. I've spent weeks, even months, talking with young people who themselves (in moments of utter, even overwrought, candor) don't quite know how to distinguish between self-serving rationalizations and one or another honorable effort to adhere closely to the tenets of a moral code, a religious conviction.

I have already dwelt on the important and impelling role of fantasy in adolescent sexual life. The statistics are high—72% for the fantasies in general; 94% about TV or movie stars; 28% about rock stars; 17% about made-up people; and 57% about specific boyfriends or girlfriends. For what it's worth, I think all these figures are low. It is questionable whether any human being doesn't have some degree of fantasy life, and I have yet to hear a person discuss his or her fantasy life without a sexual reference, however symbolic or disguised. Even so-called latency children get intensely involved with certain other people, and one hears in their posses-siveness and attachment and jealous rages overtones of passion—and one detects an aspect of sexuality in their fantasies, as told or as put into artistic form (drawings, paintings, sculptures), or as conveyed in stories evoked by games.

With teenagers there can be an extremely determined effort to curb fantasy life, push it out of the readily available consciousness. How successfully even the most obviously controlled or "uptight" person of any age manages to do this is perhaps a matter of definition. Dreams persist. Daydreams may be markedly censored or actively resisted, but one doubts they are ever banished *in toto*. The issue may well be neurophysiological—the brain's bioelectric insistence that in one way or another, however briefly and furtively, fantasies assert themselves. And when they do, one wonders whether such powerful forces in our personal lives—the desire for food, for sex, for sleep—are not in some manner going to be symbolically or quite directly and concretely rendered.

As for the use of actors and actresses, we have already met Cheryl Tiegs in this context; and along with other psychiatrists, I hear from youths about an assortment of fantasied lovers who live or work in the Los Angeles studios. I suspect actresses are more in demand for sexual fantasy than actors, probably because men, as the survey shows, seem more likely to wander, in fact and in fantasy. I have noticed that young men are certainly more willing to talk without prompting about their various involvements with television or film stars than are young women, even those anxious to be known as "liberated," free of various sexual stereotypes. Again and again I hear such quiet, private liaisons of the heart ridiculed as "sick" by young, bright, clearheaded women, whereas their male counterparts have no shame or embarrassment in even boasting about their particular Hollywood "affairs." Perhaps these latter youths are the ones who still cling to the old sexually connected stereotypes.

A family's strength affects its young members' sexual lives, this survey tells us—to no one's surprise, one assumes, and to the relief of many of us. We are flooded these days with advice for parents, those whose children are quite young and those whose children are substantially older. Teenagers are supposed to be a major "problem" for so many earnestly confused, even alarmed, fathers and mothers. The phrase *terrible teens* haunts those whose sons and daughters are five or eight or ten years old: the awful news to come soon enough. Publishers have surely not lost much money on "advice books" directed to those parents whose ignorance, vulnerability, and anxiety surely prompt this market. I once received a letter from a father who said he was on the verge of killing his "teenage son and teenage daughter" because they were, in his words, "sex-obsessed"; he demanded that I "tell" him what to do, and send my words of wisdom back "by return mail, meaning right away."

One may be tempted to laugh at such a communication, until one reminds oneself how deeply distressed so many parents are—hence what sad and hurt lives so many young people must endure: the sexual obsessions, among other obsessions of their parents, a constant source of family anguish, if not real personal danger.

The survey's statistics show that children who come from marriages that have lasted are more likely to be sexually restrained during adolescence. While much is made nowadays of sexual "liberation," there is another side to teenage sexual life—the constant struggle of millions of youths for a reliable sense of control over their emotions, including their sexual urges. The achievement of that control is necessary in any life, lest a man or woman become plagued by impulsiveness. But how does one achieve a fairly sure command over one's sexual energies?

No one will be surprised by the answer to this question: that children brought up by parents who are reasonably stable and in control of themselves will have learned the same capacity from the first years of life. Such learning has to do with years of experience—day in, day out. Such learning comes from being told again and again; from criticisms voiced and understood; from encouragement; from patient, concerned, affectionate explanations; from moments of disappointment and anger, followed by times of self-satisfaction—not in the sense of smugness but of delight in having acquired a convincing control over one's own behavior.

I am breaking no new ground in the above statements, but all parents know how frightening it can be for them and for their children when such an achievement has *not* taken place by the time adolescence arrives—when a youth of 13 or 14 has *not* learned how to say no to himself or herself, has not gained a certain reliable distance from the pressure of the body's various demands. We tend to take for granted the very accomplishments that have required the longest, hardest effort, almost as if to recognize that such a cumulative effort is to be overwhelmed by the thousands and thousands of edifying and sometimes morally demanding incidents and details that, in their sum, make up a sound person's, a sound family's, life. Only when things begin to go wrong in a life are we inclined to realize how long it takes for any grown-up to become the particular person he or she is, and therefore how many chances there are for getting sidetracked psychologically.

Children who grow up in homes torn apart by fear, distrust, betrayal of one kind or another are children with higher psychological odds to face. Not that such children don't also find redemptive opportunities for themselves—ways of turning difficulties into a motivation of sorts to make sure that their parents' suffering does not take over their own lives. Anyone's developing sexuality is vulnerable, however—especially at certain critical moments—so we ought not be too surprised when the survey finds that children whose parents have had a rough time with each other are on the whole less willing or able to uphold the declared (though so often ignored) moral standards of our culture.

The issue may be also a matter of loneliness—the result of a learned difficulty in trusting other people. I'd best let a young lady (16 years old) whom my wife and I came to know in Charleston, West Virginia, during the late 1960s expand upon that explanation:

> I miss my mother when I'm with my father, and I miss my father when I'm with my mother. I *don't* miss having the two of them together, because they fought so much I was relieved when they separated. I would have wished they'd stayed together if they'd been able to be friendly in their disagreements, but they each have a temper and my brother and I heard them shout and shout, and sometimes it would get physical. My mother would scream, and we knew he'd hit her. But I never felt completely

sorry for her, or on her side, because I saw her several times tease
him and even throw things at him, and how long can you take a
whining person, daring you to do this and daring you to do this
and daring you to do this, until you say *enough*, which is what my
dad always said, and *then* she went that final step, and he'd
explode!

I've noticed that I like quiet guys, who never want to argue
about anything and who wouldn't know a temper explosion if they
saw one happening right before their eyes. I'm going out with the
strong, silent boy of our class, and he is a master at keeping us
away from arguments. Sometimes I'll catch myself—I'll see myself
being "provocative" (my dad's word) with my boyfriend, and I
quickly shut up. Other times I almost cling to him, because he
saves me, he really does, from showing the worst side of myself!
But I don't really relax with him. I hold back, I feel alone even
when we're together. I guess I've had to feel alone—it's how I
grew up.

Still, she did indeed "cling" to her friend, and ended up staying
many a night with him in his parents' summer cottage near a lake.
She worried about the sexual commitment she'd made to him; it
violated her strong religious scruples and her father's repeated
warnings that, as she had him saying it, "if you want to get
anywhere in this world, you have to work hard, and if you start
fooling around with boys when you're in high school, you'll lose
the 'drive' needed to get ahead." The daughter wasn't quite sure
what her father meant, and wondered why she couldn't both study
hard and have a boyfriend with whom she was sexually intimate.
She never felt comfortable enough, however, to ask her father to
explain himself. She certainly knew that some young people manage
to have the best of these two worlds, sexuality and academic
success, though a substantial number don't.

This particular young woman, no reader of Freud, did once
make her own estimate of her father's reasoning, and in her own
way stated a certain agreement with him:

I think my dad had a point. When I'm with Frank, I get so
immersed in him and in me with him that I don't even care what
the newspaper says, or the television; I'm just responding to him,
to us. Maybe if I was better organized, if my parents had given me
more self-assurance, then I could do both—be a leading student

and keep my friendship with Frank going full blast. But I feel so damn scared a lot of the time that our friendship will end up in trouble, so I work full-time making sure things go well between us.

The high-school psychologist said I'm afraid my friendship with Frank will end up the same way my parents' marriage ended up. He expected me to be stunned by what he said—I could tell. I was going to do what he wanted, open my eyes up wider and look as if I'd just heard thunder and the sky had been lit up by lightning and a voice from a distant planet had spoken. But I couldn't pull it off. I just said, "Yeah, I know." His face fell. He probably thought I was being sassy and ungrateful. But like my mother says, people knew lots of psychology before there ever was a subject called "psychology," and before there were guys like the one in our school who are called "psychologists."

The foregoing brings us to what may be one of the most significant psychological issues to be generated by this *Rolling Stone* survey—the data that prompt Mr. Stokes to observe that "plans for higher education are generally associated with lower sexual activity." Here the percentages are striking: Whereas 78% of the respondents who plan to finish only "some high school" are "nonvirgins," 77% of those respondents who already know they want to go to graduate school and 76% who want to complete "all of college" are "virgins"—an almost exact reversal. Moreover, those who at the time of the survey were not doing well in school were evidently more active sexually than those who were doing well in school.

In each student who has responded to this survey, there is no doubt a special set of explanations to be offered for his or her sexual activity as it relates to a level of intellectual excellence and ambition. Still, one wonders whether this questionnaire doesn't offer additional evidence that Freud's theory of sublimation, even in its rather crude and mechanistic (hydraulic, actually) imagery, isn't correct: When energy "flows" into sexuality, it is not available for the planning and studying that make those dreams become a reality. Similarly, when sexual energy is "dammed up" (as some theorists a half-century ago put it), the mind is moved to find an "outlet" for such energy to master it, deal with it, in one fashion or another.

According to psychoanalytic theory, there is a "latency age" (from 6 to 11, approximately) when children learn to set aside the promptings of instinct and impulse in favor of the rewards of a good conscience and of membership in an advanced state of "civilization." Energies get "channeled" from sensuality and aggressive assertion of this or that demand into study, athletics, chores, hobbies. And if, as Freud noted, there are consequent "discontents," then "civilization" still is the uneasy winner, and so is the individual, who has joined a particular group, both emotional and intellectual in nature, in which he or she will continue to function. Indeed, it turns out that this group is also sexual in nature, as a 19-year-old college student who definitely intends to attend "all of college" and definitely intends to attend law school makes quite clear in the following observations about himself and the Ivy League world he knows so well:

> I don't like to talk about sex; it's the one subject that I feel quite dumb about! You see? Everything has become a "subject" for me! I've lived the life of the hardworking student, the greasy grind, for so long, I've assumed this is the way everyone my age gets along. I remember all the talks I had with my parents when I was in the third grade. I'd been "horsing around" and I had a crush on a girl down the street. My parents weren't against the crush—no, they're card-carrying liberals who are all for "healthy sexual lives." They've both had psychotherapy! But they were worried sick over my poor marks, and they dragged out some IQ test that was given to me when I was in the first grade, I seem to remember, and I was way up there, bright, very bright, and so they started with that each time they got going: "Don't you realize that you'd be wasting your talents, throwing them away, if you don't start learning how to study hard and do well in school?" Then they'd recite the same thing, the *score* I got in that *test,* as if it was the proof of my divinity! If I didn't shape up and turn my mediocre C's and B-minuses into A's or at the very least B-pluses, then I was damn well renouncing my rights to royalty!
>
> Don't laugh, it's not funny. I have to laugh myself now when I'm feeling good about myself, my life. But I'll tell you, a lot of the time, when I think of those talks back then with my parents, I realize that my entire life hung in the balance—which is what they told me over and over again. Maybe it didn't, really. But how am I to know now whether I could have done it differently—not become the terrifically hard worker I started becoming in the fourth and fifth grades?

It was such a shift! I stopped being a friendly, outgoing kid, who was popular with other kids; I quit the Boy Scouts, which I'd just joined; and eventually I stopped "daydreaming," my dad called it, about Barbara, that girl I'd liked so much and sort of flirted with at the birthday parties we all went to when we were eight and nine. Instead, I began those tough, tiring tennis lessons, and I went on longer and longer bike rides, all by myself, and I studied. Oh, boy, did I study! And the more I studied, the more I realized I had to study (to get those top marks); and the more I got those A's, the more my parents smiled and bought me presents and told me I was turning out fine, just fine—and I was, I guess.

There would be twinges: when I saw Barbara, who turned into one beautiful girl, I'll tell you—when I saw her begin to date, go out with a guy I'd never liked. I was turning into a real snob by then—or a snot. I was so full of myself—honor roll every time!— that I was sure that Barbara sat home crying a lot, feeling sorry for herself, because she wasn't going out with me, she was going out with someone who's "second-rate." He's "second-rate," I kept saying to myself, Richie King, because he's lousy in school, and where will he end up, and Barbara must know she'll end up nowhere, with Richie, at the rate she's going, at the rate they're *both* going, and so why *wouldn't* she cry at home about the raw deal she's getting! Hell, I'm sure she was having a great time with Richie. He was a nice kid then, and he's fine now—he's going to the University of Massachusetts.

What's wrong with going there? Nothing! Well—in my head, with all its bullshit, *plenty* is wrong. If you don't go to Harvard, Yale, Princeton, Dartmouth, Amherst, Williams—you hear the litany! I hate hearing myself talk like this, but that's what I've become, a competitive grind who lives for his grades. Some people live for wine, or for women, or for song—to have a great, relaxing time. Some even live for all three. I live for high marks, and getting into the next place—one of the top law schools. Then there will be law review; then there will be the best firms to "crack"; and then it'll be making a partnership. By then, if I'm really lucky, I'll have found the time and energy—I'll feel relaxed enough and "on top" enough—to have found a woman who will want someone like me. (Why would she? I wonder sometimes!) When I'm married, of course, and have children, you know how it'll be. The same rat race, begun all over! Only this time I'm my dad, and my kids are me, and I'm pushing, pushing, to make sure they don't waver, not by any more than an inch here, an inch there—and in the clutch, not by even a millimeter!

No wonder I'm a virgin, and I'm almost twenty. No wonder my roommates are as sexually shy as I am. We're still kids—babes in the woods: smart about biology, but dumb about how to put our biology to work with someone else. I'm so brainwashed, though, no one could talk me out of being the way I am. I mean, I'm so tied into this way of doing things, I have no choice: After a while, as the saying goes, you are what you are! I'm not even sure I can break this habit when I become a parent. I'm a compulsive worker, probably on my way to becoming a workaholic. I guess the best hope for me is that when I finally start going out seriously with women, I'll meet someone who knows how to live with someone like me!

Of course, there is a moral side to adolescence, not necessarily grounded in intellectual and occupational ambition. Many youths who have no lofty career plans, and are not especially able in school, nevertheless have rather strong ideas about what they ought to do and ought not to do when going out with their boyfriends or girlfriends. Why else would so many youths in the survey cite alcohol as an apparently necessary precondition for a "loss of virginity"? Long before contemporary psychiatry became lodged in our nation's upper-middle-class consciousness, people of all backgrounds knew that liquor loosens inhibitions. Whence those inhibitions? To be sure, anxieties grounded in psychological growth itself—such as fear of failure—generate more than enough moments of paralysis, or spells of awkwardness and severe, self-imposed restraint. But millions of young people have been taught certain standards of behavior, certain rights and wrongs, well before they are actively dating, and trying to figure out (for themselves and with someone else) just how "far" they want to "go." The question for many is not only one of desire but of ethical choice. How far should one go, and, not insignificantly, how far would one feel "good" about having gone?

The survey does indeed tell us that those who are influenced "a large amount" or "a great deal" by religion are "far less likely" than other young people "to have had intercourse." Here we are given a hint of a powerful personal tension in many thousands of young people. The youths who have answered this questionnaire, even those high-school and private-school students who come from cosmopolitan backgrounds—the secular and agnostic ones to be found in, say, New England, the middle Atlantic states, and on the West Coast—are not generally the hedonistic narcissists evoked in many critical evaluations of our young people.

Beyond a doubt, television and the movies and all sorts of magazines push a frivolous, self-centered, manipulative, even at times weird or violent sexuality upon all of us. Beyond a doubt there is a sadly amoral aspect to certain sides of the so-called youth culture—drugs galore and rock lyrics full of nastiness or self-pity or rude egoism and lots of self-serving nihilism: Let it all hang out today, among us, and forget not only tomorrow but others, their standards, values, condition, earned moral authority. Nonetheless, if this survey deserves a hearing, deserves to be seen as a collection of valuable, suggestive hints, then so do the outspoken remarks of adolescents like the following one, who addresses someone such as myself:

> You guys, you shrinks, are full of sermons. You finger-wag others and talk your doctor sermons, but you don't even know that you're doing it, giving kids like us the big, long speech, the big, long sentence to hell. Why don't lots of people your age stop and look at themselves in the mirror and ask themselves some of the questions they throw around at us? Just look at what this country does to other countries! Just look at how a lot of people live in this country! Kids like us are "punks," or "druggies," or members of the "counterculture," or "flakes," or "sick"—but not Richard Nixon, when he twice got the American people to say yes to him; and not Henry Kissinger, who pushed us into murdering thousands of people in Asia; and not this guy who runs the country now, and his buddies.
>
> Reagan and his pals are all "clean" and "upright." They want to help train murderers in Central America—soldiers who protect the wealthy, the few families who own Salvador or Honduras or Guatemala—and they want to give tax bargains to our own multi-millionaires, and to hell with the poor guy who can't find a job, and then people say, "These damn kids, they're spoiled rotten, and they're all spaced out, and they're irresponsible." You look at those gray-flannel-suited people who run this country, "clean-cut" people, and you realize they're spaced out, too—they're high on power, not pot! They want to control everyone and they're just as vain and dangerous as any of us kids are—more so; the whole

world can end up destroyed by them. And what are you shrinks saying about *them?* Nothing! You're too busy worrying about our drug problems and our sexual hang-ups!

The point is not to be persuaded by this excursion into some of the social and political biases that do, indeed, plague us all. Here was a youth whose answers to any survey—of sexual habits or other inclinations—might well mark him as a deviant personality. His sexuality is angry and exploitative; to use a language I was trained to use, he is "polymorphous perverse"—that is, capable of almost any kind of sexual behavior. He is given to lots of hustling and self-centered opinions and nasty outbursts against, it seems, anyone and everyone. Still, there is at work in his remarks a conscience of a kind, and one that can on occasion strike tellingly at the heart of things.

Similarly, when youths such as those who participated in this survey remark on how "awful" they would feel if they had to have an abortion, how "it bothers" them, even years later, to have had one, they are revealing a side of themselves perhaps not sufficiently considered by many of us who are inclined to make critical judgments about the so-called youth culture. Youths struggling with the power of sexuality deserve to have that moral complexity in their lives acknowledged since it is often directly observable but also often to be found coming at one sideways.

Nor should the population as a whole be denied its different strengths and weaknesses, its own cultural complexity. "Only in the solid South and the mountain states does a majority disapprove of couples living together," Mr. Stokes observes. He adds that "rural teens are more conservative" than their urban or suburban counterparts. These regional differences are, of course, quite important; they tell us about the various people we are. The sexuality of America's youth is beyond any complete knowing (and maybe we should be glad for it). It splinters into millions of minds and hearts and souls, the inhabitants of millions of bodies surging with possibility—and each mind, each heart, each soul, each body amounting to one young person, with his or her stories to tell, experiences to remember, hurts to bear, hopes to maintain. This survey, like others, and like different efforts to understand the ways of humankind, requires respectful attention, and works best, perhaps, when the reader is moved to ask of himself or herself what is right— what ought be urged as desirable ethically upon oneself and upon others.

Appendix: The Questionnaire

FIRST, PLEASE ANSWER THESE FEW QUESTIONS FOR CLASSIFICATION PURPOSES ONLY ...

1. What is your AGE? _16_

2. What is your race?

¹ ☒ White

² ☐ Negro or Black

³ ☐ Oriental

⁴ ☐ Mexican American, Chicano, Mexican (Mexicano), Puerto Rican, Cuban, Central or South American, Other Spanish

⁵ ☐ Other (Specify): _____

3. How many brothers and sisters do you have? (WRITE IN)

\# OF BROTHERS: _____   \# OF SISTERS: _3_

4. Is your mother living in your home?

¹ ☒ YES   ² ☐ NO

a. What is the AGE of your mother? _39_

b. What is your parents' marital status? (CHECK ONE)

¹ ☒ Married

² ☐ Separated

³ ☐ Divorced

⁴ ☐ Widowed

5. Is your father living in your home?

1 ☑ YES   2 ☐ NO

a. What is the AGE of your father? _4 4_

6. What do you think your family's total income is? (CHECK ONE)

1 ☐ Under $6,000
2 ☐ $6,001 - $12,000
3 ☐ $12,001 - $18,000

4 ☐ $18,001 - $24,000
5 ☑ $24,001 - $30,000
6 ☐ $30,001 - $36,000

7 ☐ $36,001 - $42,000
8 ☐ $42,001 - $50,000
9 ☐ Over $50,000

7. In what CITY and STATE do you live?

CITY: _____ STATE: _Maryland_

8. In what area do you live?

1 ☐ City ➝ Do you live: 1 ☐ Inside city limits   OR   2 ☐ Outside city limits

2 ☐ Suburban area

3 ☑ Rural area

9. What kind of music do you listen to most often? (CHECK ONLY ONE)

1 ☑ Rock
2 ☐ Country

3 ☐ Disco
4 ☐ Soul

5 ☐ Jazz
6 ☐ Classical

10. How often, if ever, do you get turned on sexually by music? (CHECK ONE)

1 ☐ Never   2 ☑ Rarely   3 ☐ Sometimes   4 ☐ Often   5 ☐ Very Often

11. How much school do you plan to finish?

1 ☐ Some high school
2 ☐ All of high school
3 ☐ Some trade school or skills center
4 ☐ Some college
5 ☑ All of college (Bachelor's Degree)
6 ☐ Graduate school (Master's or Doctorate Degree)
7 ☐ Don't Know

12. Compared to other students in your school, how are your grades? (CHECK ONE)

1 ☐ Well below average   3 ☑ Average   4 ☐ Above average
2 ☐ Below average   5 ☐ Well above average

13. What is your religion?

1 ☐ Protestant   2 ☐ Catholic   3 ☐ Jewish   4 ☑ Other   5 ☐ None

a. How much does your religion affect your sexual behavior? (CHECK ONE)

1 ☐ Not at all   3 ☐ A medium amount   4 ☐ A large amount
2 ☑ A small amount   5 ☐ A great deal

14. Have you, yourself, ever used any drugs or alcohol?

1 ☑ YES   2 ☐ NO

15. Which of the following drugs, if any, have you ever used? (CHECK ALL THAT APPLY)

- 01 ☐ Marijuana
- 02 ☐ Hallucinogens (LSD, etc.)
- 03 ☐ Downers or tranquilizers
- 04 ☐ Angel dust
- 05 ☐ Uppers or stimulants
- 06 ☐ Quaaludes
- 07 ☐ Cocaine
- 08 ☐ Heroin
- 09 ☑ Alcohol
- 10 ☐ NONE

16. How often, if ever, do you smoke marijuana? (WRITE IN THE NUMBER OF TIMES)

_____ Times a day OR _____ Times a week OR _____ Times a month OR _____ Times a year

☑ NEVER

17. How often, if ever, do you go to a party? (WRITE IN THE NUMBER OF TIMES)

_____ Times a day OR _____ Times a week OR _____ Times a month OR _1_ Times a year

☐ NEVER

18. How often, if ever, do you go out on a date? (WRITE IN THE NUMBER OF TIMES)

_____ Times a day OR _____ Times a week OR _____ Times a month OR _2_ Times a year

☐ NEVER

19. Have you ever gone out on a date with a girl of a different race?

1 ☐ YES - (SKIP TO QU. 20)   2 ☑ NO - (ANSWER "a")

a. Would you date a girl of a different race?

1 ☐ YES   2 ☑ NO

20. How often, if ever, do you go out with a group of people that includes girls (e.g. to the beach, etc.)? (WRITE IN THE NUMBER OF TIMES)

_____ Times a day OR _2_ Times a week OR _____ Times a month OR _____ Times a year

☐ NEVER

21. Are you good friends with any girls with whom you are NOT romantically or sexually involved?

1 ☑ YES   2 ☐ NO

22. Have you ever had a girlfriend?

1 ☑ YES   2 ☐ NO

23. Do you have a girlfriend now?

1 ☐ YES   2 ☑ NO

24. Have you ever been in love?

1 ☑ YES - (ANSWER "a" and "b")   2 ☐ NO - (SKIP TO QU. 25)

a. How old were you the _first time_?

_11_ YEARS OLD

b. With how many girls have you been in love? _1_ GIRLS

25. Do you ever want to get married?

1 ☑ YES   2 ☐ NO

26. When can a woman become pregnant? (CHECK ONLY THE <u>ONE</u> BEST ANSWER)

1 ☐ When she has sexual intercourse (going all the way, making love) the first time

2 ☐ When she has sexual intercourse before she is 16 years old

3 ☐ When she has sexual intercourse several times during the month

4 ☐ When she does NOT have intercourse, but the boy climaxes near the opening to her vagina

☑ All of the above

27. From what source did you learn the most information about the following subjects? (CHECK ONLY <u>ONE</u> SOURCE FOR <u>EACH</u> SUBJECT)

	SCHOOL	PARENTS	SEX PARTNER	FRIENDS	BOOKS & MEDIA	CLINIC OR DOCTOR	BROTHER OR SISTER
Reproduction....................	☑ 1	☐ 2	☑ 3	☐ 4	☐ 5	☐ 6	☐ 7
Birth control...................							
Masturbation (playing with yourself sexually)............	☑ 1	☐ 2	☐ 3	☐ 4	☐ 5	☐ 6	☐ 7
Homosexuality...................	☐ 1	☐ 2	☑ 3	☐ 4	☐ 5	☐ 6	☐ 7
Sexual techniques...............							

28. If you had a question about sex, to whom would you talk? (CHECK THE <u>ONE</u> BEST ANSWER)

1 ☑ Sex partner

2 ☐ Friends

3 ☐ Brother or sister

4 ☐ Parents

5 ☐ Doctor

6 ☐ Health clinic

7 ☐ Clergy

8 ☐ Other (Specify): _____

9 ☐ Nobody, but I'd look at books and magazines

29. What are the correct methods for using condoms? (CHECK THE ONE BEST ANSWER)

1 ☐ The condom should be pulled on so that there is space at the tip
2 ☐ Condoms should not be kept in hot dry places
3 ☐ New condoms should be used each time
4 ☑ All of the above
5 ☐ Don't Know

<u>NOTE</u>: SOME TEENAGERS HAVE ENGAGED IN THE FOLLOWING ACTIVITIES AND OTHERS HAVE NOT. YOU SHOULD ANSWER THE QUESTIONS HONESTLY, BUT YOU SHOULD NOT THINK FROM THESE QUESTIONS THAT THE ACTIVITIES ARE EITHER RIGHT OR WRONG.

30. Have you ever masturbated?

1 ☐ YES - (CONTINUE)   2 ☑ NO - (SKIP TO QU. 31)

a. How old were you when you first masturbated? _____ YEARS OLD

b. How often do you normally masturbate? (WRITE IN THE NUMBER OF TIMES)

_____ Times a day <u>OR</u> _____ Times a week <u>OR</u> _____ Times a month <u>OR</u> _____ Times a year

☐ NEVER - (SKIP TO QU. 31)

c. How much do you enjoy masturbating? (CHECK ONE)

1 ☐ Not at all   3 ☐ A medium   4 ☐ A large amount
2 ☐ A small amount   amount   5 ☐ A great deal

d. How much guilt do you feel when you masturbate? (CHECK ONE)

1 ☐ NONE   2 ☐ A small amount   4 ☐ A large amount
                  3 ☐ A medium amount   5 ☐ A great deal

e. Where do you masturbate? (CHECK ALL THAT APPLY)

1 ☐ Bathroom 4 ☐ Car   7 ☐ Other (Specify): _____
2 ☐ Bedroom   5 ☐ Movies
3 ☐ School   6 ☐ Outside

31. Have you ever had a sexual fantasy?

1 ☑ YES - (ANSWER "a")   2 ☐ NO - (SKIP TO QU. 32)

a. How often do you fantasize about sexual activities, and what people do you fantasize about? (Write in under the appropriate space or check "NEVER")

	TIMES A DAY or	TIMES A WEEK or	TIMES A MONTH or	TIMES A YEAR or	NEVER
Girlfriend..............				1	☐
Strangers you see......			t		☐
Acquaintances..........					☑
Relatives..............					☑
Rock stars.............					☑
TV or movie stars......			1		☐
Make-believe people....					☑
Other (Specify): _____					☐

32. Have you ever kissed a girl?

    ¹ ☑ YES - (CONTINUE)   ² ☐ NO - (SKIP TO QU. 68)

    a. How old were you when you first kissed a girl? _13_ YEARS OLD

NOTE: SOME TEENAGERS HAVE ENGAGED IN THE FOLLOWING ACTIVITIES AND OTHERS HAVE NOT. YOU SHOULD ANSWER THE QUESTIONS HONESTLY, BUT YOU SHOULD NOT THINK FROM THESE QUESTIONS THAT THE ACTIVITIES ARE EITHER RIGHT OR WRONG.

33. Have you ever played with a girl's breasts with your hands?

    ¹ ☑ YES - (CONTINUE)   ² ☐ NO - (SKIP TO QU. 34)

    a. How old were you when you first did this? _12_ YEARS OLD

34. Have you ever played with a girl's breasts with your mouth?

    ¹ ☑ YES - (CONTINUE)   ² ☐ NO - (SKIP TO QU. 35)

    a. How old were you when you first did this? _12_ YEARS OLD

35. Have you ever played with a girl's genitals with your hands?

    ¹ ☑ YES - (CONTINUE)   ² ☐ NO - (SKIP TO QU. 36)

    a. How old were you when you first did this? _13_ YEARS OLD

    b. Have you done this with more than one girl?

    ¹ ☑ YES - (CONTINUE)   ² ☐ NO - (SKIP TO QU. 36)

    c. With how many different girls have you done this? _6_ GIRLS

36. Have you ever played with a girl's genitals with your mouth (oral sex)?

   1 ☒ YES - (CONTINUE)   2 ☐ NO - (SKIP TO QU. 37)

   a. How old were you when you first did this? __14__ YEARS OLD

   b. Have you done this with more than one girl?   1 ☒ YES - (CONTINUE)   2 ☐ NO - (SKIP TO PART "d")

   c. With how many different girls have you done this? __4__ GIRLS

   d. How much do you enjoy doing this?   (CHECK ONE)

   1 ☐ Not at all   3 ☐ A medium   4 ☐ A large amount
   2 ☐ A small amount   amount   5 ☐ A great deal

   e. How much do you think the girl enjoys having this done?   (CHECK ONE)

   1 ☐ Not at all   3 ☐ A medium   4 ☐ A large amount
   2 ☐ A small amount   amount   5 ☐ A great deal

37. Has a girl ever played with your penis with her hands?

   1 ☒ YES - (CONTINUE)   2 ☐ NO - (SKIP TO QU. 38)

   a. How old were you when she first did this? __14__ YEARS OLD

   b. Have you done this with more than one girl?

   1 ☒ YES - (CONTINUE)   2 ☐ NO - (SKIP TO QU. 38)

   c. With how many different girls have you done this? __4__ GIRLS

38. Has a girl ever played with your penis with her mouth (oral sex)?

   1 ☐ YES - (CONTINUE)   2 ☒ NO - (SKIP TO QU. 39)

a. How old were you when she first did this? _____ YEARS OLD

b. Have you done this with more than one girl?

   1 ☐ YES - (CONTINUE)   2 ☐ NO - (SKIP TO PART "d")

c. With how many different girls have you done this? _____ GIRLS

d. How much do you enjoy doing this? (CHECK ONE)

   1 ☐ Not at all   3 ☐ A medium   4 ☐ A large amount
   2 ☐ A small amount   amount   5 ☐ A great deal

e. How much do you think the girl enjoys having this done? (CHECK ONE)

   1 ☐ Not at all   3 ☐ A medium   4 ☐ A large amount
   2 ☐ A small amount   amount   5 ☐ A great deal

39. Have you ever had sexual intercourse (going all the way)?

   1 ☑ YES - (CONTINUE)   2 ☐ NO - (SKIP TO QU. 68)

a. How old were you when you <u>first</u> had sexual intercourse? _15_ YEARS OLD

b. How old was the girl when you first had intercourse? _15_ YEARS OLD

c. Where did you have intercourse the first time? (CHECK ONE)

   1 ☐ In a car   5 ☐ At someone else's house
   2 ☐ At a motel or hotel   6 ☐ Outdoors
   3 ☐ At your house   7 ☐ Other (Specify): _____
   4 ☑ At your partner's house

40. Did you or your partner use some form of birth control the first time you had intercourse?

1 ☑ YES - (CONTINUE)   2 ☐ NO
                         3 ☐ DON'T KNOW ──→ (SKIP TO QU. 41)

a. What type of contraception did you use?

1 ☐ Rhythm   6 ☐ Foam
2 ☐ Withdrawal   7 ☐ IUD
3 ☑ Condom   8 ☐ Don't Know
4 ☐ The pill
5 ☐ Diaphragm   9 ☐ Other (Specify): _____

41. What was your relationship with your partner the first time you had intercourse? (CHECK ONE)

1 ☐ Stranger (someone you had just met)
2 ☐ Friend
3 ☑ Girlfriend (going together)
4 ☐ Fiancée (planning to get married)
5 ☐ Wife
6 ☐ Other (Specify): _____

42. Before you had sexual intercourse the first time, did you talk about it with your partner?

1 ☑ YES   2 ☐ NO

a. After you had intercourse the first time, did your relationship change or did it remain the same?

1 ☐ It became weaker   2 ☑ It remained the same   3 ☐ It became stronger

b. How did you feel after you had intercourse the first time? (CHECK ONE)

☐ 1 I was sorry I had the experience
☑ 2 I had both positive and negative feelings about the experience
☐ 3 I felt glad I'd had the experience
☐ 4 I had no feelings about the experience

43. How long has it been since the last time you had sexual intercourse?

_____ days   or   _____ weeks   or   __6__ months   or   _____ years

a. Was the girl with whom you last had intercourse your girlfriend?

1 ☑ YES   2 ☐ NO

b. Do you love the girl? 1 ☑ YES   2 ☐ NO

c. Do you think you'll marry that girl? 1 ☐ YES   2 ☑ NO

d. Where did you have sexual intercourse the last time? (CHECK ONE)

☐ 1 In a car   ☐ 5 At someone else's house
☐ 2 At a motel or hotel   ☐ 6 Outdoors
☑ 3 At your house   ☐ 7 Other
☐ 4 At your partner's house   (Specify): _____

44 How long did you know that girl before the first time you had sexual intercourse with her?

_____ days   or   __6__ weeks   or   _____ months   or   _____ years

45. Do you expect to have intercourse with her again?

1 ☐ YES - (ANSWER "a")   2 ☑ NO - (ANSWER "b")

a. How long ago did that sexual relationship start?

_____ days ago or _____ weeks ago or _3_ months ago or _2_ years ago

b. How long did that sexual relationship last?

_____ days or _____ weeks or _2_ months or _____ years

46. Have you had sexual intercourse with more than one girl?

1 ☑ YES - (Answer "a")   2 ☐ NO - (GO TO QU. 47)

a. With how many different girls have you had sexual intercourse?   _8_ GIRLS

47. How often do you normally have sexual intercourse?

_____ times a day or _____ times a week or _____ times a month or _3_ times a year

48. How much do you enjoy intercourse?   (CHECK ONE)

1 ☐ Not at all   3 ☑ A medium   4 ☐ A large amount
2 ☐ A small amount   amount   5 ☐ A great deal

a. How important is it to you that your sexual partner is satisfied?   (CHECK ONE)

1 ☐ Not at all important   4 ☐ Very important
2 ☐ Slightly important   5 ☐ Extremely important
3 ☑ Moderately important

49. With which of the following have you ever had a problem? (CHECK ALL THAT APPLY)

1 ☒ Getting an erection
2 ☐ Having an orgasm
3 ☐ Coming too soon
4 ☐ NONE

50. Have you ever had an orgasm?

1 ☒ YES   2 ☐ NO ──┐
                3 ☐ DON'T KNOW ──→ (SKIP TO QU. 51)

a. Have you had an orgasm with more than one girl?

1 ☐ YES - (CONTINUE)   2 ☐ NO - (SKIP TO QU. 51)

b. With how many different girls have you had an orgasm? _____ GIRLS

51. How much do you worry about how good you are as a sex partner? (CHECK ONE)

1 ☐ Not at all   3 ☐ A medium   4 ☒ A large amount
                      amount
2 ☐ A small amount   5 ☐ A great deal

52. How often, if ever, do you smoke marijuana before sexual intercourse?

1 ☒ Never   3 ☐ Half the time   5 ☐ Always
2 ☐ Sometimes 4 ☐ Frequently

53. How often, if ever, do you drink beer, wine or liquor before sexual intercourse?

1 ☐ Never   3 ☐ Half the time   5 ☐ Always
2 ☒ Sometimes 4 ☐ Frequently

54. Which drugs, if any, make you enjoy sex more? (CHECK ALL THAT APPLY)

```
01 [ ] Marijuana                          06 [ ] Quaaludes
02 [ ] Hallucinogens (LSD, etc.)          07 [ ] Cocaine
03 [ ] Downers or tranquilizers           08 [ ] Heroin
04 [ ] Angel dust                         09 [ ] Alcohol
05 [ ] Uppers or stimulants               10 [✓] None
```

55. Which drugs, if any, make you enjoy sex less? (CHECK ALL THAT APPLY)

```
01 [ ] Marijuana                          06 [ ] Quaaludes
02 [ ] Hallucinogens (LSD, etc.)          07 [ ] Cocaine
03 [ ] Downers or tranquilizers           08 [ ] Heroin
04 [ ] Angel dust                         09 [ ] Alcohol
05 [ ] Uppers or stimulants               10 [✓] None
```

56. For how long do you normally make out before intercourse?

_15_ Minutes

57. Do you or your sexual partner normally use some kind of birth control?

```
1 [✓] YES - (CONTINUE)
2 [ ] NO  - (ANSWER "b")
3 [ ] DON'T KNOW - (SKIP TO QU. 58)
```

a. What type(s) of birth control do you or your partner normally use? (CHECK ALL THAT APPLY)

```
1 [✓] Condom        5 [ ] Foam
2 [ ] The pill      6 [ ] Diaphragm
3 [ ] Rhythm        7 [ ] Withdrawal
4 [ ] IUD           8 [ ] Other (Specify): _____
```

b. Why don't you or your partner use a type of birth control? (CHECK ALL THAT APPLY)

01 ☐ It interferes with sex
02 ☐ It's hard to use
03 ☐ It's too expensive
04 ☐ I can't get it
05 ☐ I'm afraid my parents will find out
06 ☐ I'm afraid someone else will find out
07 ☐ I'm too young to get it
08 ☐ I don't know how to use it
09 ☐ It's too embarrassing to get
10 ☐ I don't have sexual intercourse often enough to use it
11 ☐ I don't believe it is right to plan for sex
12 ☐ I believe birth control is morally wrong
13 ☐ I'm afraid of what it will do to me physically
14 ☐ Other (specify): _____

58. Have you ever made a girl pregnant?

1 ☐ YES - (ANSWER "a")   2 ☒ NO - (SKIP TO QU. 59)

a. Has a girl you made pregnant ever had an abortion?

1 ☐ YES   2 ☐ NO

59. Do you ever have more than one sexual relationship going on at the same time?

1 ☐ YES   2 ☒ NO

60. Have you ever had sexual activity with more than one person at a time (group sex)?

1 ☒ YES   2 ☐ NO

61. Have you ever had sexual intercourse with someone you didn't really know?

   1 ☑ YES   2 ☐ NO

62. Have you ever had sexual intercourse with a teacher?

   1 ☐ YES   2 ☑ NO

63. Have you ever had sexual intercourse with a prostitute?

   1 ☐ YES   2 ☑ NO

65. Does one or both of your parents know you have had sexual intercourse?

   1 ☐ YES   2 ☐ NO   3 ☑ NOT SURE

   a. To what extent do you think your parents approve of your sexual activity?

      1 ☑ Not at all

      2 ☐ A little

      3 ☐ Somewhat

      4 ☐ Completely

66. Have you ever had venereal disease (gonorrhea, syphillis, etc.)?

   1 ☐ YES   2 ☑ NO

SOME TEENAGERS HAVE ENGAGED IN THE FOLLOWING ACTIVITIES AND OTHERS HAVE NOT. YOU SHOULD ANSWER THE QUESTIONS HONESTLY, BUT YOU SHOULD NOT THINK FROM THESE QUESTIONS THAT THE ACTIVITIES ARE EITHER RIGHT OR WRONG.

68. When you were a child under 12 years old, did you ever do any of the following activities with another boy? (CHECK ALL THAT APPLY)

1. ☐ Examined each other's bodies
2. ☐ Kissed each other
3. ☐ Played with each other's genitals

a. If you checked any of the above, how old were you the first time? _____ YEARS OLD

69. Do you know anyone who is homosexual (gay)?

1. ☐ YES   2. ☒ NO   3. ☐ NOT SURE

70. Do you have any friends who are gay?

1. ☐ YES   2. ☒ NO   3. ☐ NOT SURE

71. If you found out that a male friend of yours was gay, what would you do? (CHECK ALL THAT APPLY)

1. ☐ Remain friends
2. ☐ Talk to him about it
3. ☐ Consider having a sexual experience with him
4. ☒ Try to talk him out of it
5. ☐ Stop being friends
6. ☐ Report him to the authorities
7. ☐ Other (Specify): _____

72. How often, if ever, do you fantasize about doing something sexually with another boy?

_____ times a day OR _____ times a week OR _____ times a month OR _____ times a year OR ☒ NEVER

73. Since you turned twelve, have you ever played sexually with another boy?

1 ☐ YES - (CONTINUE)   2 ☒ NO - (SKIP TO QU. 74)

   a. With how many different boys have you done the following sexual activities?

                                  (SPECIFY NUMBER OF BOYS)

      Examined each other's bodies.................. _____

      Kissed.. _____

      Played with each other's genitals............. _____

      Had oral sex.................................. _____

      Had anal sex.................................. _____

74. What do you consider yourself?

    1 ☒ Heterosexual (straight)
    2 ☐ Homosexual (gay)
    3 ☐ Bisexual (straight at times and gay at times)

75. Has a girl ever made the first sexual move on you?   1 ☒ YES   2 ☐ NO

76. Do you feel it is OK for a girl to make the first sexual move on a boy?

    1 ☒ YES   2 ☐ NO

77 Do you want to marry a virgin?   1 ☐ YES   2 ☐ NO   3 ☒ DOESN'T MATTER

78 To what extent does guilt keep you from being more sexually active than you are?

1 ☐ Not at all
2 ☐ A small amount
3 ☑ A medium amount
4 ☐ A large amount
5 ☐ A great deal

79 What activities do you think are okay for a girl to do in the following situations? (CHECK ANY THAT YOU FEEL ARE OKAY)

	MAKE OUT	TOUCH GENITALS	HAVE ORAL SEX	HAVE SEXUAL INTERCOURSE	NONE OF THESE
If a girl and boy are strangers............	1 ☑	2 ☐	3 ☐	4 ☐	5 ☐
If a girl and boy are friends or are dating....	☑	☑	☐	☐	☐
If a girl and boy are going with each other....	☑	☑	☑	☑	☐
If a girl and boy are in love..............	☑	☑	☑	☑	☐
If a girl and boy are planning to get married..	1 ☑	2 ☑	3 ☑	4 ☑	5 ☐

80. What activities do you think are okay for a boy to do in the following situations? (CHECK ANY THAT YOU FEEL ARE OKAY)

	MAKE OUT	TOUCH GENITALS	HAVE ORAL SEX	HAVE SEXUAL INTERCOURSE	NONE OF THESE
If a girl and boy are strangers............	☑	☑	☑	☑	☐
If a girl and boy are friends or are dating....	☑	☑	☑	☑	☐
If a girl and boy are going with each other....	1 ☑	2 ☑	3 ☑	4 ☑	5 ☐
If a girl and boy are in love..............	☑	☑	☑	☑	☐
If a girl and boy are planning to get married..	2 ☑	2 ☑	3 ☑	4 ☑	5 ☐

81. What activities do your parents think are okay for you to do in the following situations? (CHECK ALL THAT APPLY)

	MAKE OUT	TOUCH GENITALS	HAVE ORAL SEX	HAVE SEXUAL INTERCOURSE	NONE OF THESE
If a girl and boy are strangers.............	1 ☐	2 ☐	3 ☐	4 ☐	5 ☑
If a girl and boy are friends or are dating....	1 ☑	2 ☐	3 ☐	4 ☐	5 ☐
If a girl and boy are going with each other....	1 ☑	2 ☐	3 ☐	4 ☐	5 ☐
If a girl and boy are in love.............	1 ☑	2 ☑	3 ☐	4 ☑	5 ☐
If a girl and boy are planning to get married..	1 ☑	2 ☑	3 ☑	4 ☑	

82. What did your parents teach you about sex? (PLEASE CHECK ONLY ONE)

  1 ☐ My parents taught me that sex is healthy and normal
  2 ☐ My parents taught me that sex is not healthy and normal
  3 ☑ My parents did not teach me about sex

83. Is it hard to talk to your father about sex?   1 ☐ YES   2 ☑ NO

84. Is it hard to talk to your mother about sex?   1 ☐ YES   2 ☑ NO

85. How many of your male friends do you think have had sexual intercourse?

  1 ☐ None   2 ☑ A few   3 ☐ About half   4 ☐ Most   5 ☐ All

86. How many boys your age in the United States do you think have had sexual intercourse?

  1 ☐ None   2 ☐ A few   3 ☑ About half   4 ☐ Most   5 ☐ All

87. Is your sexual activity influenced by what your parents think?

  1 ☐ YES   2 ☑ NO

88. How much pressure do you have from your male friends to have sexual intercourse? (CHECK ONE)

1 ☑ None
2 ☐ A small amount
3 ☐ A medium amount
4 ☐ A large amount
5 ☐ A great deal

89. How much pressure do you have from your girlfriends to have sexual intercourse? (CHECK ONE)

1 ☐ None
2 ☑ A small amount
3 ☐ A medium amount
4 ☐ A large amount
5 ☐ A great deal

90. Do you think your friends would be shocked if they thought you were having sexual intercourse?

1 ☐ YES   2 ☑ NO

91. Do you think that a boy your age who has not had sexual intercourse is socially backward?

1 ☐ YES   2 ☑ NO

92. Do you think it is a good idea to live with somebody before marrying that person?

1 ☐ YES   2 ☑ NO

93. Do you think it is better if women work at home while men pursue their careers?

1 ☐ YES   2 ☑ NO

94. Do you feel women should be allowed to do anything men do whenever physically possible?

1 ☐ YES   2 ☑ NO

95. Do you think that life was more interesting in the 60's than it is now?

1 ☐ YES   2 ☑ NO

96. Do you think today's teenagers are doing more sexual things at an earlier age than teenagers ten years ago?

1 ☑ YES   2 ☐ NO

Index